Navigating the Journey

*The Essential Guide
to the Jewish Life Cycle*

Navigating the Journey

The Essential Guide to the Jewish Life Cycle

An updated and revised edition
of *Gates of Mitzvah*

EDITED BY Rabbi Peter S. Knobel, *PhD*

FOREWORD BY Rabbi Simeon J. Maslin

CENTRAL CONFERENCE OF AMERICAN RABBIS

Library of Congress Cataloging-in-Publication Data
Names: Knobel, Peter S., 1943- editor.
Title: Navigating the journey : the essential guide to the Jewish life cycle
 / edited by Rabbi Peter S. Knobel, Ph.D. ; foreword by Rabbi Simeon J.
 Maslin.
Description: Revised edition. | New York, NY : Central Conference of American
 Rabbis, CCAR Press, [2017] | An updated and revised edition of "Gates of
 Mitzvah [Shaarei Mitzvah]: a guide to the Jewish life cycle." | Includes
 bibliographical references and index.
Identifiers: LCCN 2017027446 (print) | LCCN 2017031021 (ebook) | ISBN
 9780881233025 | ISBN 9780881232936 (pbk. : alk. paper)
Subjects: LCSH: Life cycle, Human--Religious aspects—Judaism—Miscellanea. |
 Life change events—Religious aspects—Judaism—Miscellanea. | Reform
 Judaism.
Classification: LCC BM538.L54 (ebook) | LCC BM538.L54 N38 2017 (print) | DDC
 296.4/4--dc23
LC record available at https://lccn.loc.gov/2017027446

10 9 8 7 6 5 4 3 2 1

CCAR Press, 355 Lexington Avenue, New York, NY 10017
(212) 972-3636
www.ccarpress.org

Contents

Foreword: A Holy People   ix
  by Rabbi Simeon J. Maslin
Introduction   xv
Acknowledgments   xvii

1. **Birth and Childhood**   3
  Birth   5
  Entering the Covenant   8
  Naming the Child   12
  B'rit and Naming in the Case of Adoption   15

2. **Lifelong Education**   17
  Raising and Educating a Jewish Child   17
  Adult Education   23

3. **Marriage and the Jewish Home**   25
  From Engagement to Marriage   28
  The Marriage Ceremony   35
  Divorce and Remarriage   40
  Establishing a Jewish Home   42

4. **Illness, Death, and Mourning**   55
  Healing   57
  The Approach of Death   59
    From Death to Funeral   64
    The Funeral Service and Burial   69
    The Mourning Period   76

5. **What is Mitzvah?**   85
A Legacy Selection of Interpretations from Our Reform Past
The Divine Authority of the Mitzvah   91
    by Rabbi Herman E. Schaalman *z"l*
History as the Source of the Mitzvah   97
    by Rabbi David Polish *z"l*
Mitzvah without Miracles   101
    by Rabbi Roland B. Gittelsohn *z"l*
Mitzvah: The Larger Context   105
    by Rabbi Arthur J. Lelyveld *z"l*

Selections of Contemporary Voices on Mitzvah
Mitzvah and Halachah: A Dynamic Tension   113
    by Rabbi Aaron Panken, PhD
Mitzvah: It Begins with Relationship   119
    by Rabbi Dr. Rachel S. Mikva
Mitzvah and Relationship: Honoring Our Beloved's Desires   127
    by Rabbi A. Brian Stoller
The Meaning of Mitzvah for Reform Jews   135
    by Rabbi Amy Scheinerman

6. **Expanding the Thinking:**
Essays on Key Subjects from the Jewish Life Cycle   143
The Jewish Home: From the Physical to the Spiritual   145
    by Rabbi Joui M. Hessel, RJE
Tzedakah   149
    by Rabbi Neal Gold
An Introduction to Kashrut:
You Shall Not Boil a Kid in Its Mother's Milk   155
    by Rabbi Simeon J. Maslin
Jewish Value Meals   163
    by Rabbi Mary L. Zamore

A Jewish View of Sexuality 173
    by Rabbi Lisa L. Grushcow, DPhil
Table for One 179
    by Rabbi Elizabeth S. Zeller
Kiddushin: A Jewish View of Marriage 183
    by Rabbi Herbert Bronstein
The *Ketubah* 189
    by Rabbi Nancy H. Wiener, DMin
Intermarriage 195
    by Rabbi Howard L. Jaffe
Welcoming Converts 199
    by Rabbi Barry H. D. Block
Jewish Parenting through the Life Cycle 205
    by Rabbi Ariana Silverman
B'rit Milah: Covenant and Controversy 211
    by Rabbi Elyse Goldstein
Be Fruitful and Multiply: The Challenge of Infertility 219
    by Rabbi Sari Laufer
Divorce 225
    by Rabbi Lisa S. Greene
Lech L'cha, Go Forth:
Aging as an Invitation to Gaining Wisdom 231
    by Rabbi Laura Geller
Choosing Life: Making Sacred Choices as Life Ebbs 237
    by Rabbi Richard F. Address, DMin
Ethical Wills 243
    by Rabbi Lawrence W. Raphael. PhD
The Mourner's *Kaddish* 251
    by Rabbi Simeon J. Maslin
A Basic Library for the Jewish Home 255

Author Biographies 261

Foreword: A Holy People

> If you will obey Me faithfully and keep My covenant, you shall be
> My treasured possession among all the peoples. Indeed, all the
> earth is Mine, but you shall be to Me a kingdom of priests and a
> holy people.
>
> —EXODUS 19:5–6

WE, THE JEWISH PEOPLE of the twenty-first century, are the descendants of those God-intoxicated Israelites who entered into an eternal covenant that transformed a conglomeration of desert nomads into a kingdom of priests, a covenant that inspired the spawn of slaves to aspire to live as a *goy kadosh*—a holy people. The purpose of this book is to help ordinary Jews, living amid the distractions of modernity, to feel a part of this people that has for over three millennia attempted to respond to the sacred challenge of navigating the journey of life as a holy people.

A clue to our survival is found in those two little words, *goy kadosh*—a holy people.

It is, I believe, precisely because Jews have thought of themselves as heirs to the covenant at Sinai that our people has survived through centuries of triumph and tragedy, unparalleled intellectual creativity and unspeakable physical degradation, while dispersed over the face of the earth. We can find inspiration in the resilience of our people in the face of tragedy.

Rivkah Kuper was a prisoner in Auschwitz. She was one of the few survivors, and as such, she testified at the Eichmann Trial. These are her words, as transcribed in the Eichmann Trial court records:

> When we arrived on the 18th of January, 1943 . . . among the first
> things we sought were two ends of candles. Friday night we gath-
> ered together on the top tier of our block. There were about ten or

twelve girls. . . . We lit the candles and began quietly to sing Shab-bat songs. . . . We heard choked sobbing from the tiers of bunks all around us. At first we were frightened; then we understood. Jewish women who had been imprisoned months, some of them years, gathered around us, listened to the songs. Some asked us if they might also recite the blessing over the candles. . . . From then on, every Shabbat we lit the candles. We had no bread; there was nothing to eat; but somehow we managed to get the candles.

To Rivkah Kuper and her friends, the injunction "you shall be to Me a kingdom of priests and a holy people" was as real, as sanctifying in Auschwitz in 1943 as when it was first uttered thousands of years ago. They saw themselves as part of a continuum of the *goy kadosh*. How-ever, Jewish living is more than a response to hardship and tragedy. In good times as well as bad it provides a means to sanctify life. This book offers guidance to living Jewishly in the twenty-first century, for all Jews whether by birth or by choice. All are members this historic community that has inherited the responsibilities and the privileges of membership in the *goy kadosh*.

Goy kadosh, a holy people: we are that or we are nothing! By liv-ing as members of a holy people the presence of Jews inspires and catalyzes the world. Especially in North America we can be found in every social and economic stratum of society. We have made it! And yet I hear the pitiful voice of the crazed Ophelia crying, "Lord, we know what we are, but we know not what we may be." What we may be: a *goy kadosh* in the twenty-first century.

To be decent and ethical, to be even the most self-sacrificing lib-eral, demonstrating for peace and against poverty, for clean air and against assault weapons, for farm workers and against exploitation, is insufficient. It is not enough for the authentic Jew, who, according to philosopher Abraham Joshua Heschel, "has to be exalted in order to be normal."[1] There are many decent, ethical, philanthropic peo-ple in the world—Jews and non-Jews—but there are far fewer whose daily routine is shaped by the injunction to be holy.

---

1. Abraham Joshua Heschel, *The Earth Is the Lord's* (Woodstock, VT: Jewish Lights, 1995), 64.

What does it mean to be holy? The word *kadosh* and its several derivatives play a large part in Jewish tradition. At the most sacred moment of our daily and Shabbat morning services, we sing out: *Kadosh kadosh kadosh Adonai Tz'vaot*, "Holy, holy, holy is *Adonai Tz'vaot*." That prayer is known as *K'dushah*, "Holiness." And then there is the *Kiddush*, the prayer of thanks that we chant over the Shabbat and festival wine. And there is the *Kaddish*, the prayer that we recite, often through tears, as we recall our departed loved ones. But the term, derived from *kadosh*, that best indicates what it means to be a member of the *goy kadosh* is *kiddushin*. *Kiddushin*, as you will see in this book, is the word that Judaism uses to indicate marriage. We can discover in the traditional Jewish word for marriage what it means for an ordinary human being to be *kadosh*.

The Jewish concept that two people can unite in a relationship that may be designated as *kiddushin* is a negation of the view that the human being is merely an animal, that what draws two people together is animal instinct.

Judaism affirms the sacredness of the human being; it sees the other as a creature "in the image of God." In Psalms, we read that the human being was created "little lower than the angels" (Psalm 8:6). Jewish tradition places the human being somewhere between the divine and the animal, capable of participating in the holiness of God. As we read from the Torah on the afternoon of Yom Kippur, "You shall be holy, for I, the Eternal your God, am holy" (Leviticus 19:2). It is in *kiddushin* that we may best reflect that holiness.

The concept of marriage as *kiddushin* extends far beyond the name for the ceremony. As you turn the pages of this book, you will see how the traditions of Jewish living can sanctify us virtually every day of our lives. There is the potential for holiness in the home that two Jews occupy. Jewish tradition would have them build together a *mikdash m'at*—a miniature sanctuary. What makes a home into a sanctuary? There is a mezuzah at the entrance, which proclaims to all who enter that God is a partner in this home. The table is considered a *mizbei-ach m'at*—a miniature altar—which is approached not as an animal approaching the feeding trough to satisfyits hunger, but with reverence. The meal begins with a prayer, *HaMotzi*, thanking God for sustenance, and this establishes an atmosphere of serenity, communion, and sensitivity around the family table—even more so on Sabbaths and festivals, when there are candles and wine and challah, with their appropriate blessings. Through these rituals, the ordinary family table is transformed into an altar and the home into a sanctuary.

How, then, does a Jew navigate the journey of life? At every stage there are ceremonies that confirm our status as members of the holy people. When we participate in a *b'rit* ceremony, when we stand under the marital chuppah, when we affix a mezuzah to the doorpost of our home, when we participate in a Passover seder, when we read from the *M'gilah* on Purim, when we kindle the Chanukah lights—on these and so many other sacred occasions, we recite a blessing that includes the formula *asher kid'shanu b'mitzvotav*, "who has made us holy through the performance of mitzvot."

How do we retain and continually renew our status as members of a *goy kadosh*? Through the performance of mitzvot, through the sanctification of moments and acts, through a time-hallowed process that reminds us periodically that as human beings we may imitate God and that we can be holy, as God is holy.

Jewish living should sensitize us to the needs of others and prepare us to participate in acts of *tikkun olam*. Concerns about justice and the overwhelming social problems of our day are essential elements in living as members of a *goy kadosh* and remain central to Reform Judaism. And indeed, social activism and political activism continue to be essential parts of the Reform agenda. The performance of *tikkun olam* without the mitzvot of daily living is not enough. The mitzvot of daily living are what makes us Jews. Acts of *tikkun olam* are the beautiful branches, and the mitzvot of daily living are the nourishing roots.

The roots of Judaism are its mitzvot. As we perform the ritual acts of the life cycle, we are reminded that we are holy, that we are related to the people who stood at Sinai and entered into a covenant with God. This is what makes us Jews. Then, as Jews, as partners with God, we find the inspiration and the strength to attack the problems of society. As we perform a mitzvah and say the words *asher kid'shanu b'mitzvotav*, we testify, as did our ancestors, to the presence of the Ultimate in the everyday, and we affirm the fact that we were created "but little lower than the angels."

> Birth is a beginning
> And death a destination.
> And life is a journey,
> A sacred pilgrimage—
> To life everlasting.
> *(Rabbi Alvin Fine)*

—Rabbi Simeon J. Maslin

Introduction

NAVIGATING THE JOURNEY is a revision of the pioneering work
*Shaarei Mitzvah—Gates of Mitzvah: A Guide to the Jewish Life
Cycle,* edited by Rabbi Simeon J. Maslin, to whom we owe an enormous debt. That volume followed the 1972 groundbreaking work *A
Shabbat Manual.* Since then the Central Conference of American
Rabbis has created a number of volumes that seek to introduce Jews
to an observant Reform Jewish life. These original volumes have
recently been revised and updated to make Jewish practice more
accessible and to reflect the latest thinking of the Reform Movement.
This volume breaks new ground in utilizing a question-and-answer
format. It is an FAQ for understanding the Jewish life cycle. The
book is designed to be user friendly but also sufficiently comprehensive to provide a robust and attractive description of the beauty and
spirituality of experiencing each phase of life enhanced by mitzvot.
Judaism is more than a belief system. It is a way of life. Our actions
are indicative of our beliefs, and our beliefs often spring from the
experience of doing mitzvot. These volumes flesh out the meaning
of the following statement in the 1999 "A Statement of Principles of
Reform Judaism":

> We respond to God daily: through public and private prayer,
> through study and through the performance of other מִצְוֹת
> (*mitzvot*), sacred obligations—בֵּין אָדָם לַמָּקוֹם (*bein adam la
> Makom*), to God, and בֵּין אָדָם לַחֲבֵירוֹ (*bein adam la-chaveiro*), to
> other human beings.
>
> We are committed to the ongoing study of the whole array of
> מִצְוֹת (*mitzvot*) and to the fulfillment of those that address us as
> individuals and as a community. Some of these מִצְוֹת (*mitzvot*),
> sacred obligations have long been observed by Reform Jews; others, both ancient and modern, demand renewed attention as the
> result of the unique context of our own times.

Navigating the Journey: The Essential Guide to the Jewish Life

Cycle has been enriched by a series of essays that describe the many ways that Reform rabbis think about the term *mitzvah* and about the Jewish life cycle. The essays in this volume supplement the series of essays in the recently published *Mishkan Moeid: A Guide to the Jewish Seasons*. The essays from both volumes together offer diverse theological perspectives on the meaning of the term *mitzvah* by some of the best thinkers in the Reform rabbinate. The book also contains essays that complement the descriptions of the various life-cycle stages. They provide historical perspective and personal experience. The authors share not only the beauty of Jewish observance but also its conundrums and challenges. As Reform Jews we take the claims of the tradition seriously but also believe that changing circumstances cause us to rethink the best way to live out our values. While this book seeks to set out what we as Reform rabbis believe is the ideal, we also believe it is the responsibility of each individual to evaluate each of the mitzvot and determine how best to fulfill them. We recognize that there will be divergence of practice within our movement.

As a guide to Jewish observance, this volume invites the reader to engage with each section of the book as the need arises. It also beckons those who are searching for greater Jewish connections to find entry points to new observances. It is also a textbook for those who want a description of a fully observant Jewish life cycle.

Our Jewish lives are always a work in process. Our spiritual journey takes many paths. There will be twists and turns. We hope that this volume can help each Reform Jew to navigate through the journey with a little more clarity and a little more meaning. The Talmud reminds us that the path to God is found in the doing of the mitzvot. A journey begins with a single step, and an observant Jewish life begins with a single mitzvah. Where one begins the journey depends on where one finds oneself, but as *Pirkei Avot* reminds us, *mitzvah goreret mitzvah*—one mitzvah draws us toward the next mitzvah. The secret is to just begin. A life of mitzvot is the best way to fulfill the mission of the Jewish people, to be a blessing.

Acknowledgments

THIS VOLUME is the collective work of so many rabbis but it would never have come into existence without the visionary and pioneering work of Rabbi W. Gunther Plaut, who worked tireless to re-infused the concept of *mitzvah* and whose work as Chair of the Reform Practice Committee brought to life an engagement with ritual practices of Judaism. However, the real mind behind this volume is Rabbi Simeon Maslin, who succeeded Rabbi Plaut as chair of Reform Practice Committee and served as the editor of the first edition, which was published under title of *Shaarei Mitzvah—Gates of Mitzvah*. When the volume was first conceived it was considered revolutionary and controversial. Rabbi Maslin's scholarship, leadership, and political acumen were crucial in getting the volume accepted by the CCAR for publication. The current edition is the brainchild of Rabbi Hara Person, CCAR Publisher and Director of the CCAR Press, who helped recruit the authors for the many wonderful new essays, created the new format of the book using the question-and-answer model to make it more inviting and engaging, and whose editorial skills enhanced every sentence in the book. I want to thank each of the authors of the individual essays whose work added immeasurably to our understanding of the various stages of the lifecycle. The essays are both personal and scholarly and add depth and wisdom to our comprehension of the profound spiritual dimension of Jewish living.

This book would not have been possible without the work of rabbinic interns Rabbi Daniel Reiser, Andrue Kahn, and Hilly Haber, who read the previous edition and helped us update the volume to respond to the needs of a new generation of Jews and non-Jews who are seeking to create a meaningful Jewish life. I am deeply grateful for the support of the Publications Committee, chaired by Rabbi Donald Goor, and the Worship and Practice Committee, chaired by Rabbi

Joseph Skloot. The ongoing support of Rabbi Steven Fox, CCAR Chief Executive, and Rabbi Denise Eger, CCAR Past President, and Rabbi David Stern, CCAR President, make working with the CCAR a great privilege. I also want to thank the members of CCAR Press who are so wonderfully involved in every aspect of bringing this book to fruition: Ortal Bensky, Debbie Smilow, Sasha Smith, Carly Linden, Rabbi Dan Medwin, and Rabbi Beth Lieberman, as well as copyeditor Debra Corman and compositor Scott-Martin Kosofsky.

None of my work would be possible without the ongoing support of my life partner of fifty-one years, Elaine Knobel, and the love and support of my sons, Seth and Jeremy; my daughter-in-law, Alyssa; and most especially my six grandchildren, Leah, Alana, Heather, Stephen, Lily, and Oliver. Working with the CCAR to enhance Jewish life has been one of the greatest blessings of my life.

—RABBI PETER S. KNOBEL

Navigating the Journey

CHAPTER ONE

Birth and Childhood

God created the human being in [the divine] image . . . creating them male and female. God then blessed them.

—GENESIS 1:27–28

Be fruitful and multiply. A people and a host of peoples shall come from you.

—GENESIS 35:11

T HE FIRST commandment in the Torah is *p'ru ur'vu*, "Be fruitful and multiply" (Genesis 1:28). Historically, Judaism has regarded children as a blessing from God and the procreation of children as a mitzvah. Jews have seen their progeny as evidence of their love and as assurance of the continued existence of the Jewish people. Raising a Jewish family is also a way of proudly asserting one's Jewish heritage and identity in the face of current and past historical and demographic realities that threaten the vitality of Jewish communities around the world.

The Bible teaches that each birth is an event blessed by God. In Genesis we read that God says to Abraham, "I will bless her [Sarah] and, too, I will give you a son through her" (17:16). Since earliest times Jews have felt that there is an element of the sacred in each birth, that is, that procreation, no matter how a family looks or defines itself, involves far more than sexual intercourse and conception. The Bible is not vague or evasive as to the biological preconditions for birth—"The man now was intimate with his wife; she became pregnant and gave birth to Cain"—but when Eve gives Cain his name, she acknowledges, "Both I and the Eternal have made a man" (Genesis 4:1). In the biblical tradition, God is always present as the essential partner in the process of procreation.

Modern Jews, too, believe that there are spiritual dimensions to the birth of a child and that the blessing of parenthood should be shared with the entire community. Every child born of a Jewish parent is a part of the Jewish community, and the community shares in the responsibility of raising the child.[1] There are no greater communal joys than the *b'rit* and the baby naming, for every Jewish child bears the seed of continuing Jewish presence and life in the world.

It is a fundamental principle of Judaism that every child is created pure, in the divine image.[2] The first chapters of Genesis state repeatedly that the human being is fashioned "in the image of God" (1:26, 1:27, 5:1, 5:3, 9:6), implying that the child is born with the potential of growth toward ideal love, creativity, justice, and mercy. Jewish parents have the amazing power to instill in their children the values that have guided our people for generations so that they will be able to make wise and moral choices.

---

1. The Talmud is quite specific in a number of instances about the responsibility of the community for the proper raising and educating of a child. Of course, the primary responsibility rests with the child's parents, but when there are no parents or when the parents are incapable, the responsibility rests with the Jewish community. The Talmud (BT *Bava Batra* 21a) points out that there was a time when children without parents were not educated. How did the Rabbis learn that it is a mitzvah for the community to educate such children? From the verse "And you shall teach them to your children" (Deuteronomy 11:19), laying the emphasis on the word "you" (plural). In the earlier, better-known passage in Deuteronomy, the text reads "and you [singular] shall teach them" (6:7). Thus, we learn that the primary responsibility rests on the parent and the secondary responsibility on the community.

2. The doctrine is set forth explicitly in the Talmud and midrash in many places, e.g., "As God is pure, so also the soul is pure" (BT *B'rachot* 10a); "As the spirit was given to you pure, so return it pure" (BT *Shabbat* 152b). That this doctrine of innate purity is very much a part of Reform Jewish belief may be attested by the fact that the ancient Talmudic prayer thanking God for the purity of the soul ("My God, the soul that You placed within me is pure. You fashioned it; You breathed it into me; You sustain it within me; and You will one day take it from me" [BT *B'rachot* 60b]) was preserved in the old *Union Prayer Book* (page 101), in *Gates of Prayer* (e.g., page 53), and in *Mishkan T'filah* (e.g., pages 34–35), as it is in all traditional Jewish prayer books.

Judaism has developed certain traditions surrounding the birth of a child and the formative years, helping us to take note of and mark the sacred milestones and moments that punctuate everyday life.

Birth

What does Judaism say about having children?
It is a mitzvah for a married couple (heterosexual or same-sex) to recognize the sanctity of life and the sanctity of the marriage partnership by bringing children into the world. While great medical advances have increased the possibility of procreation for many couples who previously could not have children, the problem of infertility is real and painful (see "Be Fruitful and Multiply" by Rabbi Sari Laufer, page 219). In vitro fertilization and surrogacy have enabled both heterosexual and same-sex couples to have biological children. For some people, this mitzvah of parenting and creating the next generation of Jews is so important that they may choose to have or adopt children on their own, without a partner. All children, those of married parents of all genders and those of single parents, biological or adopted, are welcomed equally and with joy into the Jewish community.

There are people who, for a variety of reasons, do not become parents. Those who choose not to become parents or who are unable to do so are considered no less Jewish. For some, supporting children in the community or in their extended families, whether financially, as a teacher or volunteer mentor, or through other means, is a way to fulfill this mitzvah without having children of their own.

What is the Jewish view on adoption?
Adoption is a mitzvah equal to that of procreation.[3] All of the mitzvot and traditions that apply to biological children apply equally to adopted children. The innovative leadership of the Reform Movement

---

3. BT *Sanhedrin* 19b: "Whoever raises an orphan in his home, Scripture considers him as if he were the biological parent."

has created new and special rituals surrounding adoption as well. Ask your community's rabbi for support to frame your adoption through Jewish ritual.

Is birth control allowed in Judaism?
Reform Judaism respects the right of parents to determine how many children they should have. In considering family size, parents might reflect on the relatively small size of the worldwide Jewish population and on the Talmudic interpretation of *p'ru ur'vu* (be fruitful and multiply) as suggesting a minimum of two children. In addition, the tragic decimation of our people during the Shoah has caused some to think about a larger family to ensure Jewish survival. All of these thoughts aside, the most important consideration is how many children a couple or an individual feels able to care for and raise.

The use of birth control also supports other values important to Reform Judaism, such as women's reproductive rights and, in regard to the use of condoms as part of the practice of safe sex, the importance of caring for one's health.

What is the Jewish view on abortion?
Judaism has since ancient times permitted and even prescribed abortion in cases where the life or the physical or emotional health of the mother is in danger. Judaism affirms the right of a woman, after due regard for the sanctity of life and in accordance with the principles of Jewish morality, to determine whether she can continue the pregnancy to term. Abortion may be medically indicated in cases where genetic disease or malformation of the fetus is probable. While Judaism affirms the right of woman to determine what is best for her, it is recommended that in all such cases the couple jointly seek medical and rabbinic counseling. On a national legislative level, Reform Judaism has long and unequivocally supported women's right to choose.

What is the Jewish way to mark childbirth?

It is a mitzvah for parents to join in a prayer of gratitude for the health of the mother and the joy of new life as soon as possible after the child's birth. Science alone cannot comprehend the mystery of human birth and the wonder of parenthood. Witnessing childbirth and the miracle that is human life allows us to transcend the mundane and tap into a reality greater than ourselves. In addition to recognizing the sanctity of life, Jewish tradition provides a prayer for moments like these. The *Shehecheyanu* creates a moment and space for us to bask in the wonder and awe of childbirth—a pause in time to express our gratitude and deep appreciation for life.[4]

שֶׁהֶחֱיָנוּ
Shehecheyanu   The prayer *Shehecheyanu* is particularly appropriate:

בָּרוּךְ אַתָּה, יְיָ אֱלֹהֵינוּ, מֶלֶךְ הָעוֹלָם,
שֶׁהֶחֱיָנוּ וְקִיְּמָנוּ וְהִגִּיעָנוּ לַזְּמַן הַזֶּה.

Baruch atah, Adonai Eloheinu, Melech haolam,
shehecheyanu v'kiy'manu v'higianu laz'man hazeh.

Praise to You, Adonai our God, Sovereign of the universe, for giving us life, sustaining us, and enabling us to reach this season.

Other prayers for parents and grandparents can be found in *On the Doorposts of Your House*, pages 127–128, as well as in *L'chol Z'man v'Eit: The CCAR Life-Cycle Guide*, on pages Birth 26–29.

---

4. Procreation, in the traditional Jewish view, requires not only a man and a woman, but the presence of God as an equal creative partner. Thus, the act of procreation is sanctified and spiritualized. As the midrash teaches, "Man [does not fulfill his destiny] without woman, nor woman without man, nor the two of them together without the Divine Presence" (*B'reishit Rabbah* 8:9).

צְדָקָה
Tzedakah

It is a mitzvah to make a gift of *tzedakah* in honor of the birth of one's child. Giving *tzedakah* allows us to cultivate a practice of generosity and appreciation. Through doing so we mark a special moment in time while also thinking of those in need. A gift to the synagogue and particularly to the religious school might be particularly appropriate. In keeping with the ancient tradition of planting trees to celebrate the birth of children,[5] the purchase of trees in Israel is also a common practice. (See "*Tzedakah*" by Rabbi Neal Gold, page 149.)

Entering the Covenant

How does a child join the Jewish community?

It is a mitzvah for every Jewish child to be brought into the covenant community with prayer and appropriate ritual.

בְּרִית
B'rit

The Jewish people is a covenant (*b'rit*) community, as we read in the Torah: "'If you will obey Me faithfully and keep My covenant, you shall be My treasured possession among all the peoples. Indeed, all the world is Mine, but you shall be to Me a kingdom of priests and a holy nation.' . . . All the people answered as one, saying, 'All that the Eternal has spoken, we will do!'" (Exodus 19:5–8).

Jewish tradition is specific about the fact that both men *and* women entered into the covenant at Mount Sinai with God.[6] And so, even though the word *b'rit* has come to be associated with the circumcision of Jewish male children since the days of Abraham (Genesis 17:9–14), it should be understood that every child born into the Jewish people, male or female, is a part of the *b'rit*.

---

5. BT *Gittin* 57a: "It was the custom when a boy was born to plant a cedar tree and when a girl was born to plant a pine tree, and when they married the tree was cut down and a canopy made of the branches."

6. See Deuteronomy 29:9–14. The midrash takes the poetic parallelism of Exodus 19:3 to prove that the revelation at Sinai and the consequent covenant were participated in equally by the men and the women of Israel. "'Thus shall you say to the house of Jacob'—this refers to the women; . . . 'and declare to the children of Israel'—this refers to the men."

Why is circumcision important to Jews?

Ancient tradition prescribes the method by which a male child is brought into the covenant, as we read in the Torah: "God said to Abraham: 'As for you, you shall keep My covenant [*b'rit*]—you and

בְּרִית מִילָה

B'rit Milah

your descendants after you—in all your generations. This is My covenant that you and your descendants after you are to observe: let every male among you be circumcised'" (Genesis 17:9–10). The act of circumcision, therefore, serves as a building block for the creation of an intentional Jewish community in which the distinction between public and private spheres is blurred in recognition of a sacred and timeless act. It is a mitzvah to bring a male child into the covenant through the rite of circumcision—*b'rit milah*. There has been much discussion about *b'rit milah* in recent years. See *"B'rit Milah*: Covenant and Controversy" by Rabbi Elyse Goldstein, page 211, which suggests a completely new, alternative approach to *b'rit milah*. Where families have particular concerns, the rabbi may be a helpful resource for conversation and information.

B'rit milah is, however, more than a surgical procedure. It is a symbolic binding of one's son to the covenant community. Circumcision alone, performed as a medical procedure without the appropriate prayers, does not constitute entrance into the covenant. The *b'rit milah* service can be found in *On the Doorposts of Your House*, pages 129–132, as well as in *L'chol Z'man v'Eit: The CCAR Life-Cycle Guide*, on page Birth 12.

When is the right time to circumcise?

It is a mitzvah to circumcise a male child on the eighth day, as we read in the Torah: "In all your generations let every eight-day-old boy among you be circumcised" (Genesis 17:12). So significant is the mitzvah of circumcision on the *eighth* day that tradition requires the performance of the ceremony on that day even if it falls on Shabbat or Yom Kippur. In cases where this is not possible, the rabbi should be consulted.

While there is a strong preference that *b'rit milah* take place on the eighth day, the health of the baby is primary, and circumcision may be postponed for medical reasons. If postponed, it should be held as soon as possible consistent with the health of the child. In the case of hemophilia or any other medical contraindication, circumcision may be indefinitely postponed or contraindicated. In such cases, parents can arrange for appropriate prayers initiating their son into the covenant community. Such an uncircumcised Jewish male is considered a full member of the Jewish people and a participant in the *b'rit*.

How is *b'rit milah* celebrated?

Parents are encouraged to share the joy of the *b'rit milah* mitzvah service with family and friends.[7] This service is held most appropriately in the home but may also be held in the synagogue or in the hospital, depending on the wishes of the family and the facilities available.

Who performs the circumcision?

מוֹהֵל\מוֹהֶלֶת
Mohel/Mohelet

In keeping with the sacred nature of *b'rit milah*, parents are encouraged to consult with the rabbi about the ceremony. Whenever possible, *b'rit milah* should be performed by a *mohel/mohelet*, somone specially trained, both religiously and medically, in this procedure.[8] If a *mohel/mohelet* is not available or if the parents prefer that a doctor

---

7. The *Shulchan Aruch* prescribes a feast for circumcision, following the passage in the Talmud (BT *Shabbat* 130a): "Every precept that [Israel] accepted with joy, e.g., circumcision . . . they still observe with joy." While it is preferable to perform a *b'rit milah* in the company of friends and family, a minyan is not required.

8. The term *mohel* (ritual circumciser) is derived from *milah* (circumcision). Commenting on who is allowed to perform a circumcision, Maimonides ruled, "All are permitted to circumcise," including a woman or a non-Jew when there is no *mohel* available (*Mishneh Torah, Hilchot Milah* 2:1). Noam is an organization of certified medical professionals who are specially trained in ritual circumcision. They can be found at http://www.reformjudaism.org/mohel-search.

perform the procedure, it is preferable to select one who is Jewish and familiar with the ritual of *b'rit milah* and who will perform the surgical procedure with due regard for the sanctity of the occasion.

When neither a *mohel/mohelet* nor a Jewish doctor is available, a non-Jewish doctor may perform the circumcision with the understanding that it is being performed for religious reasons, and a rabbi or another knowledgeable Jew should be invited to recite the appropriate payers.

How are girls welcomed in to the covenant?
It is a mitzvah to bring daughters as well as sons into the *b'rit*. Reform Judaism is committed to the equality of all people, and in consonance with this principle, parents should arrange a *b'rit* service for girls either at home or in the synagogue. New rituals have emerged for bringing girls into the covenant and giving them Hebrew names. Options for *b'rit* services and naming ceremonies, often called *brit bat* or *simchat bat*, for girls can be found in *On the Doorposts of Your House*, pages 133–136, as well as in *L'chol Z'man v'Eit: The CCAR Life-Cycle Guide*, on page Birth 14.

What is the parents' role in the *b'rit*?
The responsibility for bringing a child into the *b'rit* rests upon its parents. Historically, it was the father who was required to circumcise his son or to present him to the *mohel* for circumcision. In Reform Judaism, parents share the responsibility for bringing their sons and daughters into the *b'rit*, and both mothers and fathers are involved in the ceremonies. The parents' declarations and prayers can be found in *On the Doorposts of Your House*, pages 129–136, as well as in *L'chol Z'man v'Eit: The CCAR Life-Cycle Guide*, on pages Birth 12–17.

What are other *b'rit* customs?
Several customs involving grandparents and/or honored friends have evolved over the centuries and become a part of the *b'rit* ceremony in various communities. One of these is the appointment of a *sandak* (the person who is given the honor of holding the child

during the procedure); another is the appointment of a *kvater* and a *kvaterin* (godfather and godmother) to present the child to the *mohel/mohelet*.[9] There are many ways to include close friends and relatives in the ceremony. The rabbi can assist the parents in determining how to include family members and friends in the ceremony.

Naming the Child

How, and why, does a child get a Hebrew name?

It is a mitzvah to give a child a Hebrew name.[10] The Hebrew name is given at the *b'rit* ceremony. It is also appropriate to announce the name and bless the child in the synagogue, though many choose to do so at a ceremony at home, among family and friends. Bringing

---

9. These customs and the definition of these roles varied from one Jewish community to another through the centuries. The role of *sandak* was unknown before the medieval period but became second in importance to the *mohel* in traditional communities. Usually the *sandak* holds the infant on his knees while the *mohel* performs the circumcision. The *kvater* (derived from the medieval German *Gevatter*, meaning "godfather") and the *kvaterin* (feminine form) traditionally carried the infant from the nursery to the *sandak*. This honor was often given to a childless couple, who thereby assumed a share of the responsibility for raising the child.

Another custom, which came earlier, is the chair of Elijah (*kisei shel Eliyahu*), a chair usually kept in the synagogue and taken to homes for circumcisions in order to symbolize the presence of Elijah. The source of this custom is probably the reference to Elijah in Malachi 3:1 as "the messenger of the covenant." Since Elijah was the messenger of the *b'rit*, it was only proper that he be present for the occasion. There are also many local customs regarding foods to be served at the circumcision meal. All of these are in the realm of custom and may be observed or not, as the family desires.

10. Jewish tradition ascribes special merit to those who preserve their heritage through the bestowing and retention of Hebrew names. The midrash states that one of the reasons why the Children of Israel deserved to be redeemed from Egyptian bondage was that "they did not change [i.e., Egyptianize] their names; as Reuben and Simeon they descended [Genesis 46] and as Reuben and Simeon they departed [Exodus 1]" (*Vayikra Rabbah* 32:5). The custom of bestowing both a Hebrew and a non-Hebrew name upon a person goes back to the Bible, e.g., Esther/Hadassah (Esther 2:7) and Daniel/Belteshazzar (Daniel 1:7).

the child to the synagogue to announce the name and have the child blessed usually takes place at a regular Shabbat or daily service at the earliest time after the birth of the child when parents and baby can attend, though it may happen at any time.

בֵּן, בַּת

Ben, Bat

Every aspect of the *b'rit* ritual serves to connect new life with thousands of years of tradition, forming an everlasting bond between Jewish individuals and communities through time and space. In this spirit it was customary to link the name of the child with that of the father through the connecting Hebrew words *ben* (son of) or *bat* (daughter of), for example, Yosef *ben* Daniel. Reform Jewish practice links the name of the child with both parents, for example, Yosef *ben* Rachel *v'*Daniel or Sarah *bat* Rachel v'Daniel.

How do parents choose a Hebrew or Jewish name for a child?

Different communities follow various customs as to the propriety of naming a child after a living relative or, if after a deceased relative, which one. There is no objection in Reform Judaism to naming a child after a living person.[11] Such decisions should be left to the parents; controversy over the choice of names should not be allowed to mar the joy of the naming.

For a more complete discussion of the naming of Jewish children from ancient to modern times, see B. Kaganoff, *A Dictionary of Jewish Names and Their History* (Northvale, NJ: Jason Aronson, 1996). Lists of Jewish names can be found in *The Comprehensive Dictionary of English and Hebrew First Names* by Alfred Kolatch (New York: Jonathan David, 2004); *The Complete Book of Hebrew Baby Names* by S. Shir Sidi (New York: HarperOne, 1989); and *Milon Even-Shoshan* by Avraham Even-Shoshan (Jerusalem, 2003), vol. 6.

11. Among Jews of Middle European and Eastern European origin (i.e., Ashkenazim), it is considered proper to name children after deceased relatives. However, among Jews of the Mediterranean or Eastern countries, (i.e., Sephardic or Mizrachi Jews), it is common to name children after living grandparents. And so parents should not be deterred from naming a child after a loved one, living or deceased, because it is "against Jewish custom." We are heir to many different customs in the area of naming.

However, a name should be chosen with sensitivity and with the realization that the child will generally have to carry it through life.[12] Parents should realize that the choice of a name is often symbolic of one's aspirations for the child, whether by naming the child after a particularly beloved or praiseworthy person or by the choice of a name with a particular meaning. In some families there are Yiddish rather than Hebrew names that are meaningful and connected to a beloved relative. In such cases parents may wish to give the child a Yiddish name rather than a Hebrew name. The parents may want to consult the rabbi to help them choose a Hebrew/Jewish name.

How else is the birth of a new baby celebrated?

קִדּוּשׁ
Kiddush

עֹנֶג שַׁבָּת
Oneg Shabbat

One way for parents to share their joy on the occasion of the naming of a child is to host a *Kiddush* or an *Oneg Shabbat* for the congregation following the service and naming ceremony.[13]

---

12. Children are sometimes given names that are in inappropriate or even embarrassing in adulthood. And while Jewish tradition has always ascribed special merit to those who strengthened the Jewish heritage by bestowing and carrying Jewish names (see note 10, p. 12), it must be mentioned that as far back as the Bible, some Jewish parents gave children "non-Jewish" names, i.e., names typical of the country in which they lived. Moses is an Egyptian name; many of the rabbis of the Mishnah had Greek and Roman names; Saadyah and Maimonides bore names typical of their Arab environment. The Talmud admits ruefully that "the majority of Jews in the Diaspora have names similar to their heathen neighbors" (BT *Gittin* 11b). Though we cannot accept the biblical idea that "like his name, so he is" (I Samuel 25:25) as a general rule, surely the name that a person carries through life is of importance and should be chosen thoughtfully. "Every person has three names: the one given by his father and mother, the one that others call him, and the one he acquires for himself" (*Kohelet Rabbah* 7:1).

13. It is a custom of long standing to prepare a *s'udat mitzvah* (a mitzvah feast) to celebrate joyous occasions such as the birth of a child, a circumcision, and so on. The traditional literature refers to many such opportunities to share one's joy with the community, e.g., *s'udat bar mitzvah* (a feast in honor of a bar mitzvah), *s'udat chatanim* (a feast in honor of bride and groom), *s'udat mazal tov* (lit. "a good luck feast," given in honor of the birth of a daughter after her naming). The earliest such feast in honor of a child in Jewish tradition can be found in Genesis 21:8: "On Isaac's weaning day, Abraham held a great feast."

פִּדְיוֹן הַבֵּן
Pidyon Haben

The ritual of *pidyon haben* (redemption of the first-born son)[14] is generally not observed in Reform congregations. However, the birth of the first child, boy or girl, in a family is a unique event that deserves special celebration. The Reform Movement has created a ceremony called *kiddush peter rechem* (sanctification of the firstborn) to celebrate the profound joy of having a first child. The ceremony can be found in *L'chol Z'man v'Eit: The CCAR Life-Cycle Guide*, on pages Birth 40–43.

B'rit and Naming in the Case of Adoption

What rituals are followed in the case of adoption?

An adopted son should be named and entered into the *b'rit* as soon as the initial legal procedures for adoption have been completed.[15] If a male child is not an infant, the rabbi and a doctor should be consulted about the circumcision. If the adopted son or daughter was born of non-Jewish or undetermined parents, the rabbi should also be consulted so that the child can be formally welcomed into the Jewish people and the Jewish community. This may involve taking the child to the mikveh, which is a joyous, symbolic covenantal act.

---

14. *Pidyon haben* is based on Exodus 13:2 and 13:11–15, where Israel is commanded to redeem all male issue who "breach the womb," i.e., who are firstborn to the mother. These firstborn sons are "redeemed" from the priesthood through a ritual in which a *kohein* (descendant of Aaron the priest) is given five shekels. Firstborn sons of priests or Levites are exempt from this ritual, which derives from the ancient custom of dedicating firstborn sons to the priesthood. Since Reform does not recognize a hereditary priesthood and does not believe that firstborn sons should be differentiated in any way from daughters or other sons, this ceremony is generally considered incongruous for Reform Jews.
15. According to most current statutes on adoption in the United States and Canada, adoptive parents have the right to circumcise their child as soon as the initial order of temporary custody has been issued by the court. It is not necessary to wait for the order of permanent custody, which is generally issued six months later. In all such cases, one should consult with legal authorities before proceeding.

CHAPTER TWO

Lifelong Education

Take to heart these instructions with which I charge you this day.
Teach them to your children.

—DEUTERONOMY 6:6–7

Raising and Educating a Jewish Child

What is a parent's responsibility in raising a Jewish child?

תַּלְמוּד תּוֹרָה
Talmud Torah

The mitzvah of *talmud Torah*, that is, ongoing Jewish learning, is a lifelong pursuit. The words of the daily morning service in the prayer book teach us:

> These are the things that are limitless, of which a person enjoys the fruit of the world, while the principal remains in the world-to-come. They are: honoring one's father and mother, engaging in deeds of compassion, arriving early for study, morning and evening, dealing graciously with guests, visiting the sick, providing for the wedding couple, accompanying the dead for burial, being devoted in prayer, and making peace among people. But the study of Torah [*talmud Torah*] encompasses them all. (BT *Shabbat* 127a)

All these behaviors are important parts of living a Jewish life steeped in the practice of mitzvot.

It is a parent's responsibility to teach one's child the traditions and beliefs of Judaism, as it says in the Torah: "Take to heart these instructions with which I charge you this day. Teach them to your children. Recite them when you stay at home and when you are away" (Deuteronomy 6:6–7). Parents are a child's most important role models. Even parents who feel they don't know much about Judaism or who weren't brought up Jewish themselves can fulfill the mitzvah of *talmud Torah* by learning as they teach. When a parent approaches Judaism with a sense of joy, the child learns that Judaism is both something positive and important.

What is the role of the community in raising Jewish children?

In the raising of a Jewish child, responsibility is shared by the family and the Jewish community. The family and the community can partner together to create a culture of learning and love for Judaism in which a child can be immersed and thrive. Working together, parents and the community can provide children with both formal and informal learning experiences that will help build and bolster young Jewish identities and practices. It is important to find or help create a Jewish community that is an appropriate fit for the values of each individual family. It is also therefore important to support the community and its institutions so that it can fulfill its role in providing education, worship, opportunities for *tikkun olam* (social justice), and life-cycle mitzvot for its members.

How can a parent create a Jewish home?

The best way for parents to strengthen the connection between Jewish practice and regular ritual is to live and celebrate their Judaism at home[1] as well as in the synagogue. In this way parents become role models for their children and impress upon them their own commitment to Judaism and the Jewish people. This commitment involves active membership in a congregation, prayer, discussion of topics of Jewish concern, *tzedakah,* the purchase of Jewish books and periodicals, participation in acts of *tikkun olam,* enrollment in synagogue adult classes, and other means of involvement in the life of the Jewish community (see "Establishing a Jewish Home," page 42).

---

1. There are scores of deeply meaningful and beautiful home ceremonies that are a part of the life of the observant Reform Jew. Most of these revolve around the holy days of Judaism. It is strongly recommended that parents keep copies of *On the Doorposts of Your House, Gates of Shabbat, Mishkan Moeid: A Guide to the Jewish Seasons,* and other books on the festivals in their homes for ready reference (for a list of suggestions, see "A Basic Library for the Jewish Home," page 255).

How can a parent serve as a Jewish role model for the child?

צְדָקָה
Tzedakah

Tzedakah literally means "righteous giving." It is understood to be a basic obligation, in contrast to the English word "charity," which is more optional. The giving of *tzedakah* is one of the foundations of a Jewish life—all people are expected to help those less fortunate. Parents can model this behavior for children, incorporating the giving of *tzedakah* into regular family ritual in a myriad of creative ways. Children learn not only by seeing but by doing. Many families use birthday celebrations as means to do *tzedekah*—for example, by limiting the number of gifts a child receives and having the participants in the celebration take part in activities that benefit others but are also enjoyable to children, such as baking cookies for a local soup kitchen. The possibilities are endless, and the lessons learned can be applied throughout one's life.

Why is going to synagogue important in a child's Jewish education?

Congregational prayer is central to Jewish life. Sharing congregational prayer with one's children is an important part of a positive familial spiritual experience. Parents can help to ensure that their congregation provides a proper and inspiring environment for Jewish worship and education and they can immerse children in the life of the congregation. Whenever possible, parents and children should participate in worship together. In this way, parents and children can create a joint experience that enhances the meaning and function of prayer in their lives. Most congregations offer family or children's services. Attending services together can be a vehicle for encouraging families to begin creating their own rituals to be used at home.

What is Jewish religious education, and why does it matter?

There are a number of settings in which Jewish education occurs, some formal and some informal. Jewish summer camps, early childhood programs, congregational religious schools, and day schools all offer significant opportunities for learning. Ideally, each of these provides children with an environment that cultivates a deep love for Jewish tradition and knowledge in a nurturing setting surrounded by Jewish peers and role models. Through providing children with an opportunity to learn about and experiment with prayer, Hebrew, and Jewish history and values, religious education can serve as the cornerstone for a strong Jewish identity. Many congregations mark the beginning of religious education through a ceremony on Simchat Torah or some other time, often called consecration, designed to impress children with the joy and importance of entrance into their Jewish education.

At a time when children have a myriad of supplementary and after-school activities, it is crucial for parents to emphasize their own commitment to the importance of religious education. Supplementary religious education can sometimes be challenge. After a long day of school and on weekends, children have many competing activities and concerns. Parents who themselves participate in adult or family Jewish studies, worship, and activities can help their children see Jewish education as a positive and important mitzvah. Religious education can be a family activity, one that both strengthens Jewish identity and deepens the connections among family members.

How can I help support education within my community?
So important is the place of learning within Jewish tradition that just as it is a mitzvah to teach the beliefs and traditions of Judaism to one's own children, it is equally a mitzvah to teach Judaism to the children of the community. Illustrating the importance of this mitzvah, the Talmud teaches, "Teaching Torah to the child of another is the same as giving the child life" (BT *Sanhedrin* 19b).

What is the role of Hebrew in raising a Jewish child?
Hebrew is called *l'shon hakodesh*.[2] Its revival in Israel as a modern spoken language is a great miracle unprecedented in Jewish history.

---

2. Hebrew is referred to in Jewish tradition as *l'shon hakodesh*—the holy language. The Talmud goes so far as to promise the blessings of "the world-to-come" to those who speak Hebrew (JT *Shabbat* 1:3).

Most of our basic literary and legal texts were originally written in Hebrew, and we are fortunate to live at a time when so many of them are available in translation. But the ability to access the Hebrew directly possesses a certain magic and connects us to the totality of Jewish history and the worldwide Jewish community. Hebrew is a language of depth and beauty, a language that renders consonants, vowels, and punctuation infinitely meaningful, a language that articulates the soul of the Jewish people. It is a mitzvah to learn and teach the Hebrew language. It is the key to a deeper understanding of the Torah and the other classical sources of Judaism.

What is bar or bat mitzvah?

עֲלִיָּה
Aliyah

It is a mitzvah to be called to the reading of the Torah and to recite the appropriate blessings.[3] This is called an *aliyah* (lit. "going up") and takes place for the first time when the child reaches the age of thirteen and thus becomes a bar mitzvah or a bat mitzvah.[4] An *aliyah* may also be used to mark a special occasion or to honor a member of the community.

בַּר\בַּת מִצְוָה
Bar/Bat Mitzvah

קִדּוּשׁ
Kiddush

סְעֻדַּת מִצְוָה
S'udat Mitzvah

The bar/bat mitzvah ceremony is a meaningful and traditional way to mark the beginning of puberty, the accomplishment of a degree of Hebrew and prayer proficiency, and the enter-

---

3. The Torah blessings can be found in the Reform prayer book *Mishkan T'filah*, page 368, in Hebrew, English, and transliteration.

4. The meaning of *bar mitzvah* is "one who is responsible for the performance of mitzvot." The Mishnah refers to a thirteen-year-old as responsible for the fulfillment of mitzvot (*Avot* 5:21); elsewhere the Mishnah specifies that a thirteen-year-old is responsible for his own oaths (*Nidah* 5:6). Rabbi Asher ben Yechiel (the most authoritative Jewish legal authority of the thirteenth and fourteenth centuries) in his responsa established the thirteenth birthday as a basic part of Judaism by asserting, "It is a law given to Moses at Sinai that a male must take responsibility for his transgressions [*bar onshin*] at the age of thirteen and a girl at twelve." Since Reform Judaism believes in the value of equality between the sexes, in Reform congregations, both boys and girls become bar or bat mitzvah at age thirteen. Those who observe the tradition of *t'fillin* (phylacteries; see Deuteronomy 6:8) begin at age thirteen also.

ing of a new phase in a young person's relationship to his or her Jewish identity as an emerging adult. The worship service emphasizes the sanctity of the occasion and introduces the new and unique responsibilities the bar/bat mitzvah will be able to take on. By placing emphasis on the customary *Kiddush* and the sharing of a festive meal (*s'udat mitzvah*),[5] parents preserve the beauty and meaning of the ritual. The party following the worship service and *Kiddush* can be an opportunity for not only further celebration but also a meaningful act of *tzedakah* in honor of the occasion. At the same time, an act of *tzedakah* connected to the occasion is an important way to recall our responsibilities to neighbors and fellow human beings.

While the goal of Hebrew language study extends beyond becoming bar/bat mitzvah, this ceremony generally includes recitation of

דְּבַר תּוֹרָה
D'var Torah

prayers, the reading of passages from the Torah and haftarah, and the delivery of a *d'var Torah* (a commentary on the Torah portion). However, congregations generally customize the requirements based on the ability of each individual student and adjust the requirements as necessary for those with special needs. While a milestone in the life of a young Jewish person, becoming a bar/bat mitzvah is really only the beginning of a meaningful Jewish education. When a child has reached a certain intellectual maturity, students are prepared for a higher level of study. By encouraging their child to continue Jewish education through *Kabbalat Torah* (confirmation) and through high school, parents can help their children understand that the richness and vastness of the Jewish heritage can best be experienced through the same sophisticated lens that will inform their secular education.

---

5. It is a custom of long standing to prepare a *s'udat mitzvah* (a mitzvah feast) to celebrate joyous occasions such as the birth of a child, a circumcision, and so on. The traditional literature refers to many such opportunities to share one's joy with the community, e.g., *s'udat bar mitzvah* (a feast in honor of a bar mitzvah), *s'udat chatanim* (a feast in honor of bride and groom), *s'udat mazal tov* (lit. "a good luck feast," given in honor of the birth of a daughter after her naming). The earliest such feast in honor of a child in Jewish tradition can be found in Genesis 21:8: "On Isaac's weaning day, Abraham held a great feast."

What is confirmation?

The mitzvah of confirmation, or *Kabbalat Torah* as it's sometimes known, is to be confirmed in the Jewish religion as a member of the Jewish people. Originally, the ceremony of confirmation was established by the Reform Movement as a means of educating young women equally with young men and keeping students involved in the process of Jewish education beyond the age of thirteen. Confirmation typically took place on Shavuot, which commemorates the receiving of the Torah on Sinai. In fact, in some synagogues confirmation replaced bar and bat mitzvah for some time. In many synagogues today, the confirmation class guides young adults in their transition from religious school students to active leaders within their respective Jewish communities. In recent years confirmation is being renamed as *Kabbalat Torah* (receiving Torah) in some communities, signifying that as our ancestors stood at Sinai and affirmed their place in the covenant community, so do these young adults affirm their place as members of the Jewish community.

The age for *Kabbalat Torah* varies in different congregations, from the end of tenth grade to the end of high school, but at whatever age it is held, it should leave participants with the tools and passion to pursue ongoing Jewish education. Its purpose is to encourage the intellectual and spiritual growth of young people, to strengthen the bonds between them and the Israelites who received the Torah at Sinai (Exodus 19:3–8 and Deuteronomy 29:9–14), and to stimulate their love for God and the Jewish people.

Adult Education

What kind of Jewish study opportunities are available for adults?

תַּלְמוּד תּוֹרָה
Talmud Torah

Every Jew, no matter his or her age, can engage in *talmud Torah*, Jewish education. Whether or not one acquired a Jewish education as a child, everyone should have access to the knowledge and wisdom his or her tradition teaches. For those who are not Jewish but are raising Jewish children, engaging in Jewish education can be valuable as well.

What options are available for adults who did not have a bar/bat mitzvah or confirmation as children?

בַּר\בַּת מִצְוָה
Bar/Bat Mitzvah
It is always possible to celebrate the joyous mitzvot of bar/bat mitzvah and confirmation, no matter your age. Adults who have not celebrated their own bar/bat mitzvah or confirmation but who are interested in strengthening their Jewish knowledge and experiencing these traditions should seek out opportunities for further study within their communities. Many synagogues offer classes for adults that lead to becoming bar/bat mitzvah or being confirmed. Embarking on this kind of study as an adult can be deeply meaningful and fulfilling.

Why is the impact on the family when the parents embark on Jewish learning?

The essential mitzvot of *talmud Torah* for children and for adults may be observed most powerfully when they are interlinked, for example, when parents bring their children to religious school and then attend adult classes or lectures, when parents and children attend a Shabbat service, program, or weekend retreat together, or when the family sets aside a regular hour for Jewish study together in the home. In the same way that parents can be models of Jewish living for their children, raising children can bring new meaning and understanding to Jewish rituals and values for parents. A commitment to learning about and experiencing rituals and texts with family fosters a connection to Judaism and ensures that both parents and children will not let their Jewish practices and identities stagnate.

CHAPTER THREE
Marriage and the Jewish Home

So it is that a man will leave his father and mother and cling to his wife, and they become one flesh.[1]

—GENESIS 2:24

Unless the Eternal builds the house, its builders labor in vain.

—PSALM 127:1

Let me be a seal upon your heart,
A seal upon your arm.
For love is strong as death. . . .
Vast floods cannot quench love,
Nor rivers drown it.

—SONG OF SONGS 8:6–7

I am my beloved's
And my beloved is mine.

—SONG OF SONGS 6:3

Jonathan's soul became bound up with the soul of David;
Jonathan loved David as himself.

—I SAMUEL 18:1

The traditional Hebrew word for marriage is *kiddushin*. It is derived from *kadosh*, "holy," and this describes quite accurately the Jewish attitude toward marriage (see *"Kiddushin*: A Jewish View of Marriage" by Rabbi Herbert Bronstein, page 183). The Bible describes

---

1. The Torah did not contemplate same-sex marriage, which would have been beyond the understanding of the biblical imagination. Today Reform Judaism considers all marriages, same sex or opposite sex, to be worthy of sanctification and equal in sanctification. This verse from Torah can be understood more broadly to mean that when people become adults they will leave the parental home and find a life partner.

marriage as the natural state intended by God. The Torah teaches, "So it is that a man will leave his father and mother and cling to his wife, and they become one flesh" (Genesis 2:24), or as we might read this today, when people become adults they leave their parents' home and find a life partner of their own. And the Rabbis went further: "He who is without a wife dwells without blessings, life, joy, help, good, and peace."[2]

Judaism strongly promotes marriage as the ideal relationship but recognizes that this idea can be challenging, or difficult to achieve. A Rabbinic parable tells of a confrontation between a skeptical Roman matron and Rabbi Yosei ben Chalafta (second century):[3]

> The woman asked the rabbi, "In how many days did God create the world?"
> "In six days," he answered.
> "Then what has God been doing since then?" she asked.
> "God sits and makes marriages," he answered, "assigning this person to that person, and this person to that person."

The story goes on to describe how the matron, unimpressed by the image of God as a cosmic matchmaker, married off her slaves, two by two, claiming that she could do the same as Rabbi Yosei's God. But the next day there was pandemonium in the Roman villa, bruised bodies, complaints and protests, until finally the matron relented. She summoned Rabbi Yosei and admitted, "There is no god like your God."

The story implies that finding an appropriate life's companion is no easy matter and that to do it well might even require divine wisdom.

The world has changed in many ways, and with those changes have come different Jewish understandings of both the role of marriage and the definition of marriage. In older times, marriage helped foster a stable society, provided economic benefits, and aided in the creation of a next generation. However, in the modern world,

---

2. *Midrash T'hillim* 59.
3. *B'reishit Rabbah* 68:4.

Judaism understands that marriage is not the right choice for everyone and that single people lead fulfilling and productive lives, including parenting, something the Rabbis of old would not have understood. Similarly, they could not have imagined or anticipated the way in which people meet, date, and make choices about sexual intimacy, all of which contemporary Judaism understands the choices about whether or not, and when, to enter into marriage. So too, the Bible did not anticipate same-sex marriage, a concept foreign to its worldview that reflects a certain place and time in history. Today same-sex marriage is seen by Reform Judaism as the complete equivalent to heterosexual marriage—both are equally sanctified; both are *kiddushin*. The values that apply to heterosexual marriage apply equally to same-sex marriage.

The degree of holiness that Judaism ascribes to marriage is attested by the tradition that God can be present in the marriage partnership: "When two partners are worthy, the Divine Presence abides with them."[4] The idea that the bond of marriage is sacred and eternal, a reflection of the *b'rit* between God and the people Israel, goes back to the Bible, particularly to the prophecies of Jeremiah (2:2), Ezekiel (16:6–8), and Hosea (2:2–22). And in the Middle Ages the mystic poets of Safed embellished the Shabbat liturgy with the image of joyous conjugal union as a symbol of the *b'rit* between God and Israel.[5]

It is in this tradition of sacred covenant that two people who love

---

4. BT *Sotah* 17a. This passage continues: "But when they are not worthy, fire consumes them." The contrasting of the presence of God in a good marriage with the presence of fire in a bad marriage is derived by the Rabbis from the Hebrew words *ish* (man) and *ishah* (woman). Common to both words are ש-א, which spells אֵשׁ (*eish*)—fire. But when a י is added to ש-א, changing it to אִישׁ (*ish*), "man," and when a ה is added to ש-י-א, changing it to אִשָּׁה (*ishah*), "woman," then we have the completed man and woman. It is not coincidental, the Rabbis implied, that these essential letters י and ה together spell יָהּ (*Yah*), i.e., the name of God. And so, they taught, when God is present in the marriage, then it is truly *kiddushin*—holiness (*Pirkei D'Rabbi Eliezer* 12).

5. See the prayer *L'cha Dodi*, composed in the sixteenth century by Solomon HaLevi Alkabetz, in *Mishkan T'filah*, pages 138–139.

each other are inspired to build together the *mikdash m'at*—the miniature sanctuary—that the Jewish home should be, a place of serenity sanctified daily by the performance of mitzvot. In such an atmosphere a couple can raise children capable of absorbing the traditions of Judaism so that Israel may survive eternally as a "kingdom of priests and a holy nation" (Exodus 19:6). Consequently, of all the joyous occasions of Judaism, one of the heartiest "*Mazal tov's!*" is reserved for the wedding.

Even with all this emphasis on marriage as the ideal, today's Jewish community acknowledges that marriage is not always an option or the desired choice for everyone. Moreover, Judaism has always recognized the possibility and reality of divorce. All contemporary Jewish communities contain a rich diversity of people, with both single and married individuals, those divorced and widowed, participating in and helping to enrich the community.

From Engagement to Marriage

What is the Jewish view of marriage?

קִדּוּשִׁין

Kiddushin

It is a mitzvah for any couple, gay or straight, to marry[6] and to live together as spouses in a manner worthy of the traditional Hebrew designation for marriage, *kiddushin*—set apart for each other in a sanctified relationship.[7] In Juda-

---

6. While there is no specific law in the Bible directing people to marry, it is clearly implied in Genesis 2:24 and in all the corollary laws regulating aspects of marriage. Maimonides, in *Sefer HaMitzvot*, lists marriage as one of the 248 positive commandments, deriving it from Deuteronomy 24:1, "When a man takes a wife and marries her... " (lit., "takes her").

7. The Talmudic tractate that contains the laws of marriage is called *Kiddushin*, from *kadosh*—sacred or holy. The root meaning of *kadosh* in Hebrew is "set apart," i.e., forbidden to anyone else. Thus the implication of *kiddushin* is that of a special relationship, in which the two partners have a unique bond like no other.

8. The marriage of two people in Judaism should be a reflection of the allegorical marriage between God and Israel as described by the prophet Hosea (2:21–22): "I will betroth you unto Me forever; I will betroth you unto Me in righteousness and justice, in loving-kindness and compassion. And I will betroth you unto Me in faithfulness, and you shall know the Eternal."

ism, the decision to marry implies a willingness to enter wholeheartedly into a sacred covenant with another person.[8]

How does Judaism view intermarriage?

There was a time when a Jew marrying another Jew was understood as the only way to ensure that the sacred heritage of Judaism would be transmitted to the next generation. This was, in many ways, a survival technique.[9] Today, however, we live in an open society in which it is natural that people will meet and fall in love with those from different backgrounds. Therefore marriage between Jews and non-Jews has become quite common.

A significant number of Reform rabbis and cantors do officiate at weddings where one partner is Jewish and the other is not, often with certain requirements. However, it is up to the individual rabbi or cantor to decide according to his or her conscience. If a rabbi or

---

9. There are many biblical passages forbidding marriage between Jews and non-Jews (historically seen as idolaters), e.g., "You shall not intermarry with them [i.e., the Canaanite nations]: do not give your daughters to their sons or take their daughters for your sons" (Deuteronomy 7:3; see also Exodus 34:16; Joshua 23:12; Ezra 9:1–2, 10:10–11; and Nehemiah 10:31). Maimonides includes the prohibition against intermarriage among the 365 negative commandments in *Sefer HaMitzvot*, basing himself on Deuteronomy 7:3 and on the following statement in the Talmud: "The prohibition against marrying their daughters is a biblical ordinance" (BT *Avodah Zarah* 36b; see also BT *Sanhedrin* 81b). From time to time rabbinic authorities discussed whether or not the prohibition against intermarriage with heathens should apply to intermarriage with Christians or Muslims, but the question was usually a moot one in that the predominant Christian and Muslim authorities forbade intermarriage with Jews. The American Reform rabbinate made its first statement on this subject at its 1909 convention: "Mixed marriages are contrary to the tradition of the Jewish religion and should therefore be discouraged." This position was reiterated by the CCAR in 1947 and 1973. However, intermarriage is now understood as a reality of modern Jewish life. The focus today has shifted to warmly welcoming interfaith families into the Jewish community. In 1979 the UAHC (now URJ) adopted a resolution on outreach following the initiative of its president, Rabbi Alexander M. Schindler. Rabbi Eric Yoffie, who succeeded Schindler, continued to stress outreach and welcome. Rabbi Rick Jacobs, who followed Rabbi Yoffie, introduced the concept of "audacious hospitality," emphasizing an approach of welcome and inclusion.

cantor declines to officiate, it should not be taken as a rejection or judgment, rather simply as that rabbi's or cantor's understanding of his or her role as a marriage officiant.

When a rabbi or cantor does work with an intermarrying couple, the non-Jewish partner may be invited to consider conversion to Judaism, but that is a choice that should be made without pressure and from a true desire to join the Jewish people rather than out of wanting to please a spouse or in-laws. Some rabbis or cantors may require that the couple take a basic Judaism class together to make sure they have a good sense of the building blocks of Jewish life. With conversion or without, couples have the power to envision a beautiful family life for themselves that reflects their respective values and heritages.

Today many Jewish children are being raised in homes where one parent is Jewish and one is not. Reform synagogues typically have many intermarried families who have chosen to raise their children as Jews, as well members who are Jews-by-choice. Rabbis within the Reform Movement welcome non-Jewish partners wholeheartedly into their congregations and acknowledge the great gift these partners are giving the Jewish community in choosing to raise Jewish children. Many Reform synagogues have special educational opportunities for non-Jewish parents. While non-Jewish partners may not be able to engage in every ritual practice conducted at the synagogue, the emphasis is on welcome and inclusion. Many Reform synagogues have non-Jewish partners of Jews in leadership roles within the community, and their commitment is deeply appreciated.

Couples from different religious backgrounds will be faced with the challenge of determining how to accommodate the needs of each partner. Decisions about the wedding ceremony, child-rearing, and the religious observance of the home should be carefully discussed with a competent counselor to ensure that each partner fully understands the expectations and needs of the other. The Jewish partner has the responsibility to assess the role that Judaism will play in his or her life and to decide how those decisions will affect Jewish continuity. For more on Reform views on intermarriage, see "Intermarriage" by Rabbi Howard Jaffe, page 195.

Are there any other concerns about whom Jews should or shouldn't marry?

Since biblical times the laws of consanguinity (blood relationship) and affinity have prohibited marriages between certain relatives. These laws derive from the Torah and were extended in the Talmud.[10] Reform Judaism retains these prohibitions,[11] as does civil law generally.

When is the right time to meet with a rabbi or cantor to discuss a wedding?

Creating and planning a wedding ceremony is a beautiful and rich process that can reflect on and channel a couple's love for one another and the vision they share for their life together. A couple might want to consult *Beyond Breaking the Glass: A Spiritual Guide to Your Jewish Wedding*, Revised Edition, by Rabbi Nancy H. Wiener (New York: CCAR Press, 2012) as part of their preparation. A rabbi or cantor who knows the couple well can help advise them in shaping the ceremony. Further, many rabbis offer pre-marriage counseling for couples to support them in the creation of a partnership and home guided by Jewish values and traditions. The better the rabbi or cantor knows the couple, the more meaningful and personal the wedding ceremony will be.

---

10. BT *Y'vamot* 21a, derived from Leviticus 18:6–18. Since civil law and Jewish tradition are not identical in this area, if there is a concern it would be wise to consult one's rabbi.

11. For a table of prohibited marriages by degrees of consanguinity, see *Rabbi's Manual*, ed. Rabbi David Polish (New York: CCAR Press, 1988), pages 234–235. For a discussion of the interaction of civil law and ritual marriage practice, see *L'chol Z'man v'Eit: The CCAR Life Cycle Guide*, ed. Rabbi Donald Goor (New York: CCAR Press, 2015), "Halakhic Notes," pages 23–24. See also the related discussion in *Reform Responsa for the Twenty-First Century*, ed. Rabbi Mark Washofsky (New York: CCAR Press, 2010), vol. 1, no. 5757.1, pages 347–356.

The content of the premarital consultations will vary with each rabbi and couple, but the couple should take advantage of the rabbi's experience and consult not only about the details of the wedding ceremony, but about the meaning of a Jewish home, Jewish attitudes toward sex and parenthood, the place of the couple in the congregation, and whatever else might concern them as they approach their new status in life. Some rabbis or cantors may suggest that couples meet with professional counselors to more deeply explore their relationship.

Does a Jewish wedding require a civil license?
Civil law requires a marriage license in order to marry.[12] It is illegal for a rabbi or cantor to marry a couple in a religious ceremony without also filling out a civil license.

What else should we be thinking about?
The fundamental Jewish principle of the sanctity of life suggests that it is a mitzvah for a couple to be tested for genetic diseases before marriage.[13] In those rare cases where both partners are found

---

12. When officiating at a marriage ceremony, the rabbi acts with both religious and civil authority. Since civil law requires the registration of all marriages and authorizes the rabbi to act as an officer of the state for that purpose, the rabbi may not officiate at a marriage without a civil license, nor may the rabbi fail to register the marriage with the proper state agency. The principle of *Dina d'malchuta dina* ("The law of the government is the law," i.e., it is binding on Jews; see BT *Gittin* 10b) applies here; since the civil law requires the licensing and registration of marriages, the rabbi is forbidden to officiate unless the couple complies with these civil requirements. To do otherwise is considered to be perpetrating a fraud.
13. Recent medical research has identified certain genetic diseases, some of them fatal, of which Jews are carriers in disproportionate numbers to the general population. These include but are not limited to Tay-Sachs disease, Canavan disease, familial dysautonomia, and Niemann-Pick disease. A 1975 resolution of the CCAR calls upon all rabbis "to urge those couples seeking their officiating at marriage ceremonies to undergo screening for Tay-Sachs and other genetic diseases which afflict Jews to a significant degree." This need for screening before planning a pregnancy is recommended for all couples, regardless of the religious or ethnic background of each partner. However, since both members of the couple need to

to be carriers, they can seek out the best medical advice in advance of beginning to plan a family.

Are there any special rituals that take place *before* the wedding?

Aufruf

עֹנֶג שַׁבָּת

Oneg Shabbat

קִדּוּשׁ

Kiddush

Couples who are about to marry are often blessed in the synagogue. The timing and the ceremony may take different forms, depending on the practices of the congregation. The historical ceremony is often referred to as an *aufruf*, or *Shabbat chatan*, where the couple may be called to the Torah or to the bimah for a blessing.

On the Shabbat when the couple receives a blessing, the families of the couple may wish to sponsor the *Oneg Shabbat* or *Kiddush* in their honor.

What is the Jewish view on sexuality within a marriage?
Judaism acknowledges the importance of sexuality in marriage and how it can enhance this sacred relationship. It is a mitzvah for a couple to take pleasure in sex[14] and to thereby enrich and strengthen

---

be carriers in order to have a child with the disease, only one member of the couple initially needs to undergo genetic testing. If that person tests negative, there is no need for the other person to be tested.

14. It would be wrong to state unequivocally that all Jewish authorities prescribed joyful, enthusiastic, and regular sexual intercourse in marriage. But considering the puritanical voices through history that have suggested the opposite attitude toward sex in marriage, it is noteworthy how many Jewish authorities have understood sexuality to be a gift from God to be accepted with gratitude and joy. This attitude of joy in marital sex can be found in many Talmudic passages, notably *N'darim* 20b, *Nidah* 31a–b, *Y'vamot* 34b, and *Sanhedrin* 85b. The fact that the Talmud in several instances allows a woman to use a contraceptive (*moch*; see, e.g., *Y'vamot* 12b, 100a; *K'tubot* 39a; *Nidah* 45a) indicates that intercourse was allowed for the sake of conjugal pleasure. For a fuller discussion, see Rabbi Marc Katz, "The *Kavanah* of the Bedroom: Sex and Intention in Jewish Law," in *The Sacred Encounter: Jewish Perspectives on Sexuality*, ed. Rabbi Lisa J. Grushcow (New York: CCAR Press, 2014), pages 111–120; and Rabbi Eugene B. Borowitz, "Reading the Tradition on Marital Sexuality," in ibid., pages 355–371.

Three rabbinic texts touching on aspects of conjugal relations are worthy of

their marriage. A more complete understanding of the Jewish perspectives on sexuality can be found in the *The Sacred Encounter: Jewish Perspectives on Sexuality*, edited by Rabbi Lisa J. Grushcow. (New York: CCAR Press, 2014).

What is the Jewish view on equality within a marriage?

כְּתֻבָּה
Ketubah

Although the Bible and later Rabbinic literature attempted to protect married women, especially through the device of the *ketubah* (marriage contract; see "The Ketubah" by Rabbi Nancy H. Wiener, page 189), it is clear that Judaism, which developed in a patriarchal society, historically positioned the husband as the dominant figure in marriage, while the wife was often subject to her husband's authority and as such was subject to many indignities.[15] In the Reform Jewish view however, *kiddushin* establishes a bond of mutuality between a man and a woman. They are equal partners in the home, consecrated to one another unconditionally. Therefore, any aspect of a marriage or the preparations for a marriage that suggests the dominance or the diminution of one or the other partner should be recognized as such and prevented. The concept of equal partnership applies both to heterosexual and same-sex partners.

---

note (see also "A Jewish View of Sexuality" by Rabbi Lisa Grushcow, page 173):

a. JT *Kiddushin* 4:12: "A person will be held accountable to God for refusing to enjoy those pleasures that are permitted to him."

b. *Igeret HaKodesh* (attributed to Nachmanides, thirteenth century): "Intercourse is a holy and pure thing when done in an appropriate way, in an appropriate time, and with appropriate intention. We believe that God created all things in accordance with His wisdom.... If our sexual organs are a disgrace, how could it happen that God created something shameful or ugly?"

c. *P'sikta Rabbati* 17b: "The Torah teaches gentle manners; the bridegroom should not enter the marriage chamber until the bride gives him permission."

15. It is important to note that the progressive Jewish stance on gender equality has evolved substantially over time. Though "the [historic] Rabbis seem to have loved their wives . . . [and] the position of the wife was one of much influence and importance" (C. G. Montefiore and H. Loewe, *A Rabbinic Anthology* [New York: Cambridge University Press, 2012] page 507), a modern, feminist understanding of gender roles advocates for full equality between sexes. The Reform approach to ritual and liturgy reflects this evolution in progressive thinking.

Are there any dates when a Jewish wedding cannot be held?
Jewish tradition has set aside certain days and periods during which weddings may not be held, primarily Sabbaths and major festivals.[16] Many rabbis would also consider Tishah B'Av, Yom HaShoah,[17] and certain mourning periods (see "The Mourning Period," page 76) as times not suitable for the joy of a marriage ceremony.[18]

Because of these and other prohibitions and the variations of practice among rabbis, it is extremely important to choose the date of the wedding in consultation with the officiating rabbi or cantor.

How does a death in the family affect the wedding?
If the death of a close relative of the couple (particularly a parent, brother, or sister) occurs shortly before the scheduled marriage, the

---

16. The phrase "major festival" refers to all those holy days called *mikra-ei kodesh*—holy convocations—in Leviticus 23:2ff.: Shabbat (23:3); the first day of Pesach (23:7); the last day of Pesach (23:8); Shavuot (23:21); Rosh HaShanah (23:24); Yom Kippur (23:27); the first day of Sukkot (23:35); Sh'mini Atzeret (Simchat Torah; 23:36).

17. Tishah B'Av (lit. "the ninth [day] of [the Hebrew month] Av") is the traditional day of fasting and mourning in commemoration of the destruction of the two Temples in ancient Jerusalem as well as subsequent tragedies in Jewish history. Yom HaShoah is Holocaust Remembrance Day, the twenty-seventh of Nisan, commemorating the destruction of European Jewry by the Nazis before and during World War II.

18. Some rabbis will also refrain from officiating at marriages on several other days when tradition prescribes that no wedding take place: the intermediate days of Pesach and Sukkot, the days of the counting of the Omer, and the three-week period preceding Tishah B'Av. The counting of the Omer begins on the second evening of Pesach and continues for forty-nine days through the day before Shavuot. Orthodox and traditional rabbis will not officiate at weddings during most of this period, which since the days of the Roman persecution has been considered a time of mourning. (There are several exceptional days during this period when weddings may be held, even by traditional rabbis: Lag BaOmer, Rosh Chodesh, and the last three days of the counting.)

The three-week period before Tishah B'Av is traditionally referred to as *Bein HaM'tzarim* (*in extremis*; see Lamentations 1:3), i.e, the period between the day when the walls of Jerusalem were breached by the Babylonians (the seventeenth of Tammuz) and Tishah B'Av. The more traditional Jewish communities observe certain mourning customs during this entire period, including the abstention from weddings.

couple may think about postponing the ceremony. This is something to discuss candidly with the officiating rabbi or cantor.

The Marriage Ceremony

Where can a Jewish wedding be held?

קִדּוּשִׁין
Kiddushin

קִדוּשָׁה
K'dushah

Historically, the most appropriate place for a Jewish marriage ceremony is in one of the sanctuaries of Judaism, the synagogue or the home.[19] The marriage ceremony, which is known as *kiddushin*—sanctification—should take place in an atmosphere of *k'dushah* (holiness). Many couples choose to return to the old custom of holding marriage ceremonies under the open sky.[20] Restaurants, hotels, and catering halls can also be appropriate venues for weddings today. Whatever location is chosen, the guiding principle is that the wedding be held in an atmosphere of *k'dushah*.

What are the different parts of a Jewish wedding?

חֻפָּה
Chuppah

כְּתֻבָּה
Ketubah

The essential features of a Jewish marriage ceremony are the declarations made to each other by the couple, the sharing of wine, the exchange of rings, and the recital of traditional blessings.[21]

19. Jewish tradition refers to both the home and the synagogue as *mikdash m'at*, "miniature sanctuary" (see page xi).

20. The *Shulchan Aruch* prescribes that the marriage ceremony take place in the open air whenever possible (*Even HaEizer* 61:1).

21. At Reform wedding ceremonies the rabbi or cantor will generally sing or recite the *Sheva B'rachot* (the traditional Seven Blessings, which are first noted in BT *K'tubot* 7b–8a). These *b'rachot* are as follows: (a) for wine, (b) for Creation, (c) for the creation of humankind, (d) for the creation of the human capacity for reproduction, (e) for the future joy of Zion and her children, (f) for the joy of groom and bride, and (g) for love, kinship, peace, friendship, and the joyous sounds of grooms and brides at feast in redeemed Jerusalem. (See "*Kiddushin*: Jewish View of Marriage" by Rabbi Herbert Bronstein, page 183.) In Talmudic times the marriage ceremony was divided into two distinct parts, often held a year apart (probably deriving from biblical custom; see Deuteronomy 20:7). The first part was called *eirusin*, or betrothal, and the second part was called *nisuin*,

Generally, the marriage ceremony will also include some or all of the following:[22] a marriage canopy (chuppah),[23] escorts for each partner (bridesmaids and ushers),[24] the reading of a *ketubah*, and the breaking of a glass.[25]

---

or marriage. During the Middle Ages these two ceremonies were combined, as they are in the Orthodox ceremony today, the only vestiges of their former separateness being the recitation of two introductory *b'rachot*—the first for wine and the second for the laws concerning whom one may or may not betroth—over the first of two goblets of wine.

22. Several features of the marriage arrangement between Rebekah and Isaac in Genesis 24 provided the basis for later Jewish marriage customs, such as the necessity of the bride's consent (vv. 57–58) and the veil (v. 65) (see the brief essay "On Marriage" following the story of Rebekah's betrothal, in W. Gunther Plaut, ed., *The Torah: A Modern Commentary*, (New York: Reform Jewish Publishing, an imprint of CCAR Press, 2005, 2006, 2015), page 165). In Central and Eastern Europe it was (and among some still is) customary for the groom and the officiant to go to the place where the bride and her attendants were waiting and to cover her face with a veil. This was called *bedeken* in certain communities, and it was accompanied by the groom or others saying to the bride, "O sister, may you grow into thousands of myriads . . ." (Genesis 24:60).

23. The chuppah, or marriage canopy, usually it consists of a piece of material, possibly a tallit, suspended on four poles above the heads of the couple during the ceremony. (In some communities a tallit is draped over the shoulders of bride and groom.) The chuppah symbolizes the marriage chamber in which the couple share conjugal privacy. According to the Talmud, the bride is considered married from the moment that she steps under the chuppah (BT *K'tubot* 48a–b; see especially *Tosafot* commentary, bottom 48a; see also Maimonides, *Mishneh Torah, Hilchot Ishut* 4:2).

24. In the Bible and the Talmud there is mention of the presence of the best friends of the bride and the groom at the wedding ceremony, but the custom of bridesmaids and groomsmen, or attendants, to escort the groom and the bride to the chuppah, is relatively modern. See the description in Wiener, *Beyond Breaking the Glass*, page 30–33.

25. The breaking of the glass probably derives from ancient psycho-sexual symbolism. It is a feature of most Jewish weddings and is given a variety of interpretations, e.g., that it represents the destruction of the Temple and the tragedies of Jewish history and thus links the new couple to the Jewish people, whether in sadness or in joy (this is the interpretation found in most traditional sources, derived from Psalm 137:6); that it represents our fragmented society, where so many are in need, and suggests that the couple can find meaning and fulfillment by making theirs a marriage that helps work toward the betterment of the world;

How can the wedding ceremony be personalized?

There are a number of ways of personalizing the ceremony. The couple might want to include material particularly meaningful to them, like poetry, a piece of literature, or a special song, or to involve a particular family member or friend or a unique or specially chosen *ketubah* (see below). The couple should discuss all their ideas about the ceremony with the officiant during the premarital meetings so that there is a clear understanding of what will and will not be included and what the officiant requires as part of the ceremony.

Certain features of a wedding, such as the procession, the attendants, the degree of formality, and so on, are matters of custom and etiquette that vary from family to family and from community to community.

For an excellent discussion of the ceremony and ways one might customize it, see Rabbi Nancy H. Wiener, *Beyond Breaking the Glass* (New York: CCAR Press, 2012).

Do rings get exchanged during the wedding ceremony?

Since the Reform wedding ceremony is one of equality between partners, regardless of gender, the vows should be recited by both parties. Tradition prescribes that the couples recite the following words as they place the ring on their beloved's finger: *Harei at m'kudeshet li b'tabaat zo k'dat Mosheh v'Yisrael*—"Behold, you are consecrated to me by this ring according to the tradition of Moses and Israel" (to a woman) or *Harei atah m'kudash li b'tabaat zo k'dat Mosheh v'Yisrael* (to a man). Several other options of vows are also available. (For additional options, see Wiener, *Beyond Breaking the Glass*, page 47–53). The ring or rings used may be plain or ornate.[26]

---

that it represents the fragility of the marriage bond and, therefore, the need for love and understanding if the marriage is to survive and flourish. (For a detailed study of this subject, see J. Z. Lauterbach's essay "The Ceremony of Breaking a Glass at Weddings," *HUC Annual*, 1925, pages 351–380; and Wiener, *Beyond Breaking the Glass*, page 56–59.)

26. The traditional declaration by the groom is derived from BT *Kiddushin* 5b–6a. According to tradition, the wedding ring must be smooth and of clearly

What is a *ketubah*?

כְּתֻבָּה
Ketubah

The *ketubah* is a Jewish marriage document that is signed by the officiant and the couple and witnessed, generally before the ceremony. It attests that a Jewish wedding has taken place.[27]

Jewish weddings historically require a *ketubah*. At one time these wedding contracts were legal documents, written in Aramaic,[28] that specified the groom's obligation to support and maintain the bride and the financial settlement to the bride in the event of a divorce or the death of the groom. It was, in its time, quite revolutionary in that it served to protect women in the case of death or abandonment by a spouse. In a historical setting in which women had few rights, the *ketubah* did much to secure their economic welfare. Today the *ketubah* has become less of a legal document and more of a values statement, generally written in Hebrew and English. These contemporary documents omit the finances and legalisms and focus instead on the shared spiritual ideals and aspirations of a couple. Creating a *ketubah* is also a very meaningful way for the couple to sketch out their vision for the marriage together. Many couples choose to purchase a beautifully decorated *ketubah* to hang on their wall as a reminder of their sacred vows to each other.

---

determinable value, since it is with the ring that the groom "acquires" the bride, i.e., for value received. Since Reform Judaism does not consider the presentation of the ring to be an act through which the groom acquires the bride, it does not matter to some rabbis or cantors what the ring is made of, whether or not it is engraved, or whether or not it has stones. This is a conversation to have with one's rabbi or cantor.

27. The witnesses at a Jewish wedding should be Jewish adults and not related by blood to either member of the wedding couple (*Shulchan Aruch, Even HaEizer* 42:5). While the tradition requires male witnesses, in a Reform ceremony both men and women may serve in this capacity.

28. Aramaic was the *lingua franca* of the North Semitic peoples for most of the period from the fourth pre-Christian century to the sixth or seventh century of our era. It is a language closely related to Hebrew and was used as the vernacular and in legal documents by most Jews during that period. Much of the Babylonian Talmud is written in Aramaic.

What kind of music can be used in the wedding?

קְדוּשָׁה
K'dushah

As with all other aspects of a Jewish wedding, a sense of *k'dushah* as defined by the couple should govern the choice of music for the ceremony. Jewish wedding music is readily available and should be selected in consultation with the rabbi, cantor, or music director of the congregation.

What is the role of *tzedakah* in a Jewish wedding?

צְדָקָה
Tzedakah

It is a custom to make a gift of *tzedakah* in honor of one's marriage or in honor of the marriage of one's children.[29] Making the choice of where to give can be a productive process for the couple in exploring and clarifying their shared values.

Divorce and Remarriage

What is the Jewish view of divorce?

Judaism has allowed divorce since earliest times,[30] often on quite liberal grounds. However, because the sanctity of home and family are central principles of Judaism, divorce in the Jewish community was relatively rare and until recent times and was historically considered a necessary misfortune.[31]

Today divorce is as common in the Jewish community as it is in society as a whole. Couples who are experiencing difficulty in their relationship may seek the input of rabbis, who will generally recommend professional counseling along with rabbinic support. A frank reappraisal of the strengths and weaknesses of a marriage under professional guidance can sometimes bring together alienated people and reestablish a marriage on more solid, possibly more

---

29. See "*Tzedakah*" by Rabbi Neal Gold, page 149.

30. The earliest laws of divorce in Judaism can be found in the Torah (Deuteronomy 24:1–4) and in the Talmudic tractate on divorce, *Gittin*. See "Divorce" by Rabbi Lisa Greene, page 225.

31. The Talmudic tractate on divorce, after ninety folios covering all its legal ramifications, concludes with the following words: "If a man divorces his first wife, even the altar sheds tears" (BT *Gittin* 90b).

sacred, foundations. But Jewish tradition acknowledges that divorce is sometimes the best solution, enabling each member of the couple to go on to live a more fulfilling and satisfying life.

What is a *get*?

גֵּט

Get

While historically Judaism has required the obtaining of a religious divorce decree (a *get*) before a divorced person may remarry,[32] Reform rabbis will generally accept a civil divorce as sufficient. The decision as to whether it is advisable to obtain a *get* before remarriage should be made in consultation with your rabbi. Lawyers involved in a divorce should be advised to familiarize themselves with the procedures related to obtaining a *get* in order to counsel their clients more fully.

After receiving a civil divorce, the couple or individuals might consider whether a religious ritual might be appropriate to mark their new status. Many couples and rabbis choose to use *Shtar P'reidah*, a document of separation available through CCAR. In addition, there are many contemporary rituals that have been created to help couples transition out of a marriage. See also Rabbi Mark Washofsky, "Getting Our *Get* Back: On Restoring the Ritual of Divorce in American Reform Judaism," in Grushcow, *The Sacred Encounter*, page 407.

What is the Jewish view on remarriage?

Judaism, with its emphasis on love and companionship, has historically been supportive of remarriage after divorce or death of a

---

32. In traditional Judaism a person who has only a civil but not a religious divorce (*get*) is not considered divorced. Subsequent remarriage by such a person and the legitimacy of the children of such a remarriage will be questioned wherever traditional law is binding (as, for example, in Israel).

The traditional process for acquiring a *get* is complex and requires the convening of a rabbinical court (*beit din*) and the services of a scribe (*sofer*). A *get* is usually issued by a rabbinical court only after a civil divorce has been granted. Because a traditional *get* involves the husband agreeing to grant his wife a divorce and is thus inherently not egalitarian in nature, Reform rabbis do not typically require one. However, the CCAR provides a contemporary, egalitarian *get*, called "A Document of Separation and Release," which serves as a symbolic Jewish way to acknowledge the end of a marriage.

spouse. While someone who has been divorced or widowed is encouraged to date and enter a new relationship that could possibly lead to marriage, it is important to go through a meaningful period of emotional growth or mourning and not rush too quickly into a new relationship. Once a remarriage is being planned, it is appropriate to consider a role for the children (if any) at the wedding, while also taking into account their potentially complicated feelings about the marriage.

Establishing a Jewish Home

What is the significance of the home in Judaism?

מִקְדָּשׁ מְעַט
Mikdash M'at

The home has a special status in Jewish tradition. The home is referred to as a *mkdash m'at*—a miniature sanctuary (Ezekiel 11:16). It is the Jewish home, along with the synagogue, that has preserved the traditions and values of Judaism through centuries of dispersion.[33] It is a mitzvah to create a home that is worthy of such a lofty designation.

Each person, whether single or married, has the opportunity and responsibility to define what exactly will be the character of their sacred space.

What are some of the practices and values that transform a home into a sacred place?

The possibilities are almost endless and may include home rituals, intentional eating practices, ritual objects, or unique customs created by the members of the household themselves. Determining the exact role that Judaism will play in their personal or family life can be an exciting spiritual experience and strengthen the sense of holiness (*k'dushah*).

---

33. "How fair are your tents, O Jacob; your dwellings, O Israel" (Numbers 24:5). This poetic parallelism suggests that the houses of study (synagogues) and the homes of the Jewish people are twin sources of strength.

What are some of the rituals that strengthen the Jewish character of a home?

בְּרָכוֹת
B'rachot

קִדּוּשׁ
Kiddush

זְמִירוֹת
Z'mirot

הַבְדָּלָה
Havdalah

סֵדֶר
Seder

סֻכָּה
Sukkah

In Judaism, the combination of home-centered rituals and ceremonies with those that are synagogue-centered mutually strengthen Jewish life. *B'rachot* (blessings) over food, Shabbat and festival candles, *Kiddush* and *z'mirot* (table songs), *Havdalah*, the Passover seder, Chanukah lights, building a sukkah—these are but a few of the mitzvot that add to the sanctity of the Jewish home and family

Prayers and services for these home ceremonies can be found in *On the Doorposts of Your House, Mishkan T'filah: A Reform Siddur, Mishkhan Moeid: A Guide to the Jewish Seasons, Gates of Shabbat,* and many other books that may be suggested by the rabbi. (See "A Basic Library for the Jewish Home," page 255.)

What does Judaism say about prayer in the home?

It is a mitzvah to set aside a time for daily prayer. In communities where there are daily services in the synagogue, joining the community for prayer is an important way to fulfill the mitzvah, but finding a creative way to bring prayer into the home is equally important. This mitzvah may seem at odds with the modern world, but creating a personal prayer practice can have a profound impact on one's personal and family life.[34] Daily services can be found in *On the Doorposts of Your House* and *Mishkan T'filah: A Reform Siddur.* One may add to these such personal prayers as the heart and circumstances might prompt.

---

34. While the synagogue replaced the ancient Temple as the primary locus of Jewish worship, the Jewish home is considered a "miniature sanctuary" (a reference to a vision of decentralized worship in Ezekiel 11:16), and Judaism teaches that God is as much in the home, the marketplace, and the school as in the synagogue. Rabbi Mendel of Kotzk taught, "Where is God? Wherever you let God in" (quoted in *Mishkan HaNefesh for Yom Kippur,* page 105).

The moments after rising in the morning and before retiring at night are particularly appropriate times for private or family prayer.[35] Judaism teaches that one of prayers to be recited before retiring and upon rising is the *Sh'ma*. Beginning and ending the day with prayer can add an important spiritual dimension to one's life.

It is also possible for family members to create rituals together that speak to the individual styles and needs of their household. This can be a very meaningful way for families to frame reflective and daily conversations and moments through a Jewish lens. (See the CCAR *Good Night/Good Morning* App for families with young children.)

What is the significance of a mezuzah?

מְזוּזָה
Mezuzah

שְׁמַע יִשְׂרָאֵל
Sh'ma Yisrael

A mezuzah is one of the physical markings that transform a home into a *mikdash m'at*. It is a mitzvah to affix a mezuzah to the doorpost of a Jewish home.[36] The mezuzah is a small parchment scroll, usually inserted into a tubular case, upon which is written the *Sh'ma* and two passages from the Torah (Deuteronomy 6:4–9 and 11:13–21) that speak of the love due to God and God's teachings. Some follow the tradition of affixing a mezuzah not only to the main-entry doorpost, but also to the doorposts of each major room in the house. The mezuzah is not a good luck charm.[37]

---

35. "Recite them when you stay at home and when you are away, when you lie down and when you get up" (Deuteronomy 6:7).

36. Maimonides includes the mezuzah among the 248 positive commandments in his *Sefer HaMitzvot*, deriving it from "Inscribe them on the doorposts of your house and your gates" (Deuteronomy 6:9). The word *mezuzah* means "doorpost." "This ancient symbol speaks to us of our need to live by the words of Adonai. We affix the mezuzah to the doorposts . . . with the hope that it will always remind us of our duties to one another as members of the Household of Israel" (*On the Doorposts of Your House*, ed. Chaim Stern [New York: CCAR Press, 2010], page 158).

37. Maimonides, *Mishneh Torah, Hilchot Mezuzah* 5:4, where it says that those who consider the mezuzah a charm to ward off evil are in error. The real purpose of the mezuzah is to make us aware, upon entering or leaving our home, of the unity of God and our moral obligations as believers in God.

It is, rather, a symbolic acknowledgment of the Jewish character of the home and that God is a partner in the home: "Unless the Eternal builds the house, its builders labor in vain" (Psalm 127:1).

What is the ritual for the dedication of a new home?

חֲנֻכַּת הַבַּיִת
Chanukat HaBayit

The ceremony of home dedication is called *chanukat habayit*. Its most important feature is the act of affixing the mezuzah to the entry door. The mezuzah should be fastened to the upper part of the right doorpost (as one enters) in a diagonal position (the top part inward)[38] so that it may be seen easily on entering or leaving the home. One may affix the mezuzah privately or invite friends and family for a *chanukat habayit* ceremony. The following blessing is recited as the mezuzah is attached:

בָּרוּךְ אַתָּה, יְיָ אֱלֹהֵינוּ, מֶלֶךְ הָעוֹלָם,
אֲשֶׁר קִדְּשָׁנוּ בְּמִצְוֹתָיו וְצִוָּנוּ לִקְבֹּעַ מְזוּזָה.

Baruch atah, Adonai Eloheinu, Melech haolam,
asher kid'shanu b'mitzvotav v'tzivanu likbo-a m'zuzah.

Praise to You, Adonai our God, Sovereign of the universe, who hallows us with mitzvot, commanding us to affix the mezuzah.

A complete service for the dedication of a home can be found in *On the Doorposts of Your House*, pages 155–159.

---

38. Rabbi Jacob ben Moses Moellin (fourteenth century, Mainz; known as the Maharil), at the conclusion of his collection of laws related to the mezuzah, gives the following reason for the slanting position of the mezuzah: Rashi (the great eleventh-century commentator) and his grandson, Rabbeinu Tam, came to opposite conclusions as to the proper placement of the mezuzah. Rashi stated that it should be attached to the doorpost in a horizontal position, and Rabbeinu Tam stated that it should be vertical. Maharil ruled that we should not contravene either of these great authorities and therefore that we should compromise, affixing the mezuzah on the diagonal. In keeping with the spirit of this tradition, the mezuzah may also serve as a symbol of compromise, i.e., that those who live in a house where a mezuzah is affixed to the doorpost are willing to compromise for the sake of *sh'lom bayit*—family harmony.

What are some of the elements that make a home Jewish?

תַּלְמוּד תּוֹרָה
Talmud Torah

Talmud Torah (see pages 17 and 146–147) is one of the most important mitzvot. Therefore it is particularly appropriate to include ways for the home to be an important venue for Jewish study. We are taught to "meditate on it [the Torah] day and night" (Joshua 1:8 and Psalm 1:2), that we should "teach it diligently" to our children, and that we should discuss it in our homes (Deuteronomy 6:7). (See "A Basic Library for the Jewish Home," page 255.) Through the ongoing study of Torah and its principles, families can better allow Jewish values to permeate their daily lives. This might mean developing a personal study practice, going to the local synagogue's Torah study class or another adult education class, reading weekly Jewish study blogs or Torah interpretations online, or reading Torah stories at bedtime to children.

תִּיקּוּן עוֹלָם
Tikkun Olam

Ongoing engagement with Jewish ideas also impacts on the family's *tikkun olam* practices, the ways in which they participate in making the world a better place. This might be reflected in the family's giving habits, as well as volunteering and participating in community activities that involve helping others.

צְדָקָה
Tzedakah

Shabbat and festival candlesticks, a *Kiddush* cup, a seder plate, and a *tzedakah* box are among the items that will be needed for the celebration of Shabbat and the festivals. Just as you can set aside moments for ritual and study, try to also set aside regular times for putting money into the *tzedakah* box. The final moments before kindling the Shabbat or festival candles is a good opportunity for the mitzvah of *tzedakah*.

חֲנוּכִּיָּה
Chanukiyah

The presence of Jewish ritual objects in the home is also an important part of establishing a Jewish home. These objects include a *Kiddush* cup, Shabbat candlesticks, a *chanukiyah* (Chanukah menorah), a seder plate, and mezuzot on the front door and interior doorways. Additional objects would include things like a special platter and knife for challah, a challah cover, a matzah plate for Passover, a matzah cover, dreidels for Chanukah, a festive plate for apples and honey at Rosh HaShanah, and Jewish art to hang on the wall. A visit to a Judaica store or website will show the wide range of Jewish objects that are available for the home. Jewish books, including reference books, prayer books, books about Jewish art, Jewish fiction and poetry, and cookbooks, as well as Jewish children's books, also offer rich ways to enhance a Jewish home.

Is there more than one way to keep kosher?

כַּשְׁרוּת
Kashrut

Many Reform Jews observe certain traditional dietary disciplines as a part of their attempt to establish a Jewish home and lifestyle. For some, adhering to a traditional interpretation of keeping kosher will enhance the sanctity of the home and be observed as a mitzvah; for some, a degree of kashrut (e.g., the avoidance of pork products and/ or shellfish) may be meaningful; for some, creating a form of ethical kashrut may be the way to find meaning in intentional choices about eating; and still others may find nothing of value in kashrut (see "Jewish Value Meals" by Rabbi Mary L. Zamore, page 163; see also *The Sacred Table: Creating a Jewish Food Ethic*, edited by Rabbi Mary L. Zamore). Since eating is among the most basic aspects of a person's life, making Jewish choices about eating is an opportunity to express Jewish identity and values.

What are the blessings related to eating?

הַמּוֹצִיא
HaMotzi

Gathering with family or friends for meals can be an opportunity to make the dinner table a sacred table. It is a mitzvah to treat daily family mealtime as a sacred event. One way to mark the beginning of this time is with the recitation of the prayer known as *HaMotzi*:

בָּרוּךְ אַתָּה, יְיָ אֱלֹהֵינוּ, מֶלֶךְ הָעוֹלָם,
הַמּוֹצִיא לֶחֶם מִן הָאָרֶץ.

Baruch atah, Adonai Eloheinu, Melech haolam,
hamotzi lechem min haaretz.

Our praise to You, Adonai our God, Sovereign
of the universe, who brings forth bread from the earth.

HaMotzi is the blessing for meals that involve bread. Different foods
require other blessings. The full range of food blessings can be found
in *On the Doorposts of Your House*, pages 21–22, and in *Birkon Mikdash M'at: NFTY's Bencher*, pages 22–23 (also available as an app).

בִּרְכַּת הַמָּזוֹן
Birkat HaMazon

Traditionally the meal concludes with a
prayer of thanks, *Birkat HaMazon*,[39] which can
be found in *On the Doorposts of Your House*,
pages 23–40; *Mishkan T'filah: A Reform Siddur*, pages 606–609; and
Birkon Mikdash M'at: NFTY's Bencher, pages 24–44 (also available
as an app). The recitation of the *Birkat HaMazon* not only marks the
conclusion of a meal, but helps to cultivate a culture of gratitude and
appreciation within the home. Daily meals as well as Shabbat and
festival meals are opportunities to include the blessing of thanksgiving and gratitude.

What is holy about a meal at home?

מִקְדָּשׁ מְעַט
Mikdash M'at

The ideal Jewish home is a *mikdash m'at*—a miniature sanctuary (see page 42), and the table can

---

39. "When you have eaten your fill, give thanks to the Eternal your God" (Deuteronomy 8:10). This passage, which indicates that mealtime should be much
more than an occasion to fill one's stomach, is contrasted with the Genesis
passage that cites, as an example of Esau's wicked contempt for his birthright,
the crude manner in which he ate: "Jacob . . . gave Esau bread and lentil stew.
He ate, drank, got up, and left,. Thus did Esau disdain his birthright" (Genesis
25:34). The implication is that if he were the true spiritual heir of Abraham and
Isaac, he would have taken the time to thank God for his food rather than leave
abruptly as soon as his stomach was full.

become a *mizbei-ach*—an altar.[40] Mealtime is an excellent opportunity for family members to check in with one another and discuss matters that transcend the trivial. Ideally, a daily family dinner hour that transforms the table into an altar will strengthen both a family's bonds and its Jewish identity. In reality, the pace of life today often makes a daily family dinner difficult. Therefore, making the weekly observance of Shabbat dinner a high priority can be an opportunity to gather together and reconnect in a meaningful way.

What are the ritual elements of the Shabbat meal?
Since the Jewish home is a miniature sanctuary during the ordinary days of the week, how much more so on Shabbat and festivals. It is a mitzvah for the family to gather together and consecrate the Shabbat and festival table with candles, *Kiddush* wine, and challah and to recite the appropriate blessings.[41] Imagine a prolonged Shabbat and festival dinner that would include *z'mirot* (table songs), study and discussion (the Torah portion of the week is particularly appropriate), and *Birkat HaMazon*. What a beautiful moment in time for you and your family to relish each other's company and Jewish tradition. Songs and services can be found in *Gates of Shabbat*, *On the Doorposts of Your House*, and *Mishkan T'filah: A Reform Siddur*.

לְהַדְלִיק נֵר
Lighting Candles

It is a mitzvah to light Shabbat candles to mark the beginning of Shabbat. Some will follow the practice of lighting candles eighteen minutes

---

40. In Rabbinic writings, the family table is often compared to the altar of the Temple. It is for this reason that the custom arose to sprinkle salt on the bread or challah after *HaMotzi*, as we read in Leviticus 2:13, "You shall season your every offering with salt." Also in keeping with the analogy of the table to the altar is the tradition of utilizing mealtimes for study: "If three have eaten at a table and have spoken no words of Torah, it is as if they had partaken of sacrifices to dead idols" (*Pirkei Avot* 3:4).

41. Maimonides includes the recitation of the Sabbath *Kiddush* at the family table as one of the 248 positive commandments (*Sefer HaMitzvot*). He derives it from "Remember the Sabbath day to keep it holy" (Exodus 20:8). "To keep it holy" in Hebrew is *l'kad'sho*. "This is the commandment of *Kiddush*," according to Maimonides.

before sunset. Many will choose to light candles when the family gathers for Shabbat dinner.[42]

A special loaf of braided bread called challah is used on Shabbat, as well as on festivals. *HaMotzi*, the blessing thanking God for bringing forth bread from the earth, is recited over it. On Shabbat the custom is to use two loaves, because the Torah teaches that a double portion of manna was given to our ancestors during their wanderings through the desert on the day preceding Shabbat, since manna did not fall on Shabbat itself. Challah gets its name from the fact that when the bread is a made, a small piece of dough is removed and burned, reminiscent of the dough offering described in the Torah that is known as *challah*.

חַלָּה
Challah

Kiddush is the blessing said over wine or grape juice that sanctifies Shabbat as holy time. The blessing has two parts. First is the blessing of the wine, thanking God for bringing forth the fruit of the vine. This is followed by the blessing of sanctification, a reminder that Shabbat is a memorial to both Creation and the Exodus from Egypt. These two references correspond to the reason for the existence of Shabbat, given in the two versions of the Ten Commandments in Exodus (20:8–11) and Deuteronomy (5:12–15). The words of the Shabbat evening *Kiddush* can be found in *On the Doorposts of Your House*, pages 61–62; *Mishkan T'filah: A Reform Siddur*, pages 122–123; and *Birkon Mikdash M'at: NFTY's Bencher*, pages 5–7 (also available as an app).

קִדּוּשׁ
Kiddush

---

42. It is a custom to light at least two candles, one to represent the commandment from the Torah to remember Shabbat (Exodus 20:8) and on the commandment to keep or observe Shabbat (Deuteronomy 5:12).

What other traditions are observed at the Shabbat meal?

Jewish ritual also prescribes a moment for parents to pause and express their appreciation for their children. It is a custom for parents to bless their children at the Shabbat table each week.[43] Families may establish their own ritual of blessing or use the traditional words:

FOR A BOY:

יְשִׂמְךָ אֱלֹהִים כְּאֶפְרַיִם וְכִמְנַשֶּׁה.

Y'simcha Elohim k'Efrayim v'chiM'nasheh.

May God inspire you to live like Ephraim and Menasseh.

FOR A GIRL:

יְשִׂמֵךְ אֱלֹהִים כְּשָׂרָה, כְּרִבְקָה, כְּרָחֵל, וּכְלֵאָה.

Y'simeich Elohim k'Sarah, k'Rivkah, k'Rachel uch'Leah.

May God inspire you to live like Sarah, Rebekah, Rachel and Leah.

FOR BOTH BOYS AND GIRLS:

יְבָרֶכְךָ יְיָ וְיִשְׁמְרֶךָ.
יָאֵר יְיָ פָּנָיו אֵלֶיךָ וִיחֻנֶּךָּ.
יִשָּׂא יְיָ פָּנָיו אֵלֶיךָ
וְיָשֵׂם לְךָ שָׁלוֹם.

Y'varech'cha Adonai v'yishm'recha.
Ya-eir Adonai panav eilecha vichuneka.
Yisa Adonai panav eilecha
v'yaseim l'cha shalom.

May God bless you and keep you.

May God's light shine upon you,
and may God be gracious to you.

May you feel God's Presence within you always,
and may you find peace.

---

43. The custom of blessing children goes back to the very origins of Judaism; see the blessing of Jacob and Esau by Isaac (Genesis 27) and the blessing of the twelve sons and two grandsons by Jacob (Genesis 48–49).

It is a mitzvah to welcome guests to the table, especially for the celebration of Shabbat, the Passover seder, and festivals. One should pay particular attention to strangers and others who do not have families of their own. This mitvah of inviting in guests is called *hachnasat or'chim*, and Jewish tradition includes it among those that merit eternal reward.[44]

הַכְנָסַת אוֹרְחִים
Hachnasat Orchim

What are times, other than Shabbat, Seder and festivals, for celebration?

In our busy schedules, it is often difficult to pause for a moment and appreciate the activity and beauty that surround us. The recitation of a blessing not only serves to mark a special occasion, but also encourages us to take note of natural wonders and life-cycle events we too often overlook. Joyous family occasions, such as birthdays, anniversaries, the birth of children and grandchildren, marriages, and academic and career achievements are all opportunities to mark with prayers of gratitude. Several suggested prayers can be found in *On the Doorposts of You House*, pages 123–169, or one may offer a personal prayer.

---

44. The Talmud (BT *Shabbat* 127a), elaborating on the Mishnah (*Pei-ah* 1:1), lists *hachnasat or'chim* among those mitzvot for which "a person is rewarded in this world and in the world-to-come." One does not have to believe in physical reward and punishment to accept the idea that the performance of *hachnasat or'chim* (and the other humanitarian mitzvot on this list; see pages 17 and 146–147) is eternally rewarding.

In the same Talmudic passage, Rabbi Judah went even further in praise of *hachnasat or'chim*, teaching that "welcoming guests is of greater merit even than welcoming the presence of God." Today, considering the great number of fragmented families and single adults in our society (see "Table for One" by Rabbi Elizabeth S. Wood, page 179) and the particular difficulty that such people have in observing home-centered mitzvot, it is of the greatest importance to include them in *chavurot* (congregational subgroups that meet to study Judaism and/or celebrate Shabbat and festivals) and to invite them into the family circle.

The traditional prayer for all occasions of joy is as follows:

בָּרוּךְ אַתָּה, יְיָ אֱלֹהֵינוּ, מֶלֶךְ הָעוֹלָם,
שֶׁהֶחֱיָנוּ וְקִיְּמָנוּ וְהִגִּיעָנוּ לַזְּמַן הַזֶּה.

Baruch atah, Adonai Eloheinu, Melech haolam,
shehecheyanu v'kiy'manu v'higianu laz'man hazeh.

Praise to You, Adonai our God Sovereign of the universe,
for giving us life, sustaining us, and enabling us to reach
this season.

What are other ways to express Jewish values and identity?
Joining and participating in a Jewish community is one way to
express our ties to other Jews and the Jewish people. Congregational
life provides wonderful opportunities to delve into Jewish learning,
communal ritual, large-scale social justice initiatives, and worship.
It is a mitzvah for each Jew and each Jewish family to be part of a
Jewish community, whether by joining a synagogue or being part of
a *chavurah* (study or prayer group) or minyan of some sort, and to
make use of its facilities for prayer, Jewish education, and communal
activities.[45]

---

45. There are many statements in Rabbinic literature about the centrality of the
synagogue. Among these are: "Whosoever has a fixed place for his prayer has the
God of Abraham as his helper"; "A person's prayer is heard only in the synagogue";
and "When a person leaves the synagogue, he should not walk hastily . . . but when
he goes to the synagogue, it is a mitzvah to rush" (BT *B'rachot* 6a–b). The synagogue as we know it is, of course, a postbiblical institution, and as such there could
be no biblical mitzvah to join or attend a synagogue, but the Rabbis used several
biblical verses as *ex post facto* underpinnings for the centrality of the synagogue;
for example: "What is the meaning of the verse 'But as for me, let my prayer come
to You, O Adonai, in an acceptable time' [Psalm 69:14]? When is 'an acceptable
time'? When the congregation is praying" (BT *B'rachot* 8a). And, of course, there
is the famous dictum of Hillel: "Do not separate yourself from the congregation"
(*Pirkei Avot* 2:5).

What is the connection between the synagogue and the Jewish home?

It is the synagogue that, in partnership with the home, has historically preserved the Jewish people, providing it with a center for prayer (*beit t'filah*), for study (*beit midrash*), and for assembly (*beit k'neset* or *beit am*). While prayer and study in the home are mitzvot of great importance, the synagogue serves as the communal center for these activities. Through attendance, initiative, and support from congregants, the synagogue helps to foster community and increase the diversity and vibrancy of one's participation in Jewish life. Judaism's emphasis on a minyan (quorum) for certain prayers is a reminder of the role community can play in one's life.

בֵּית תְּפִלָּה
Beit T'filah

בֵּית מִדְרָשׁ
Beit Midrash

בֵּית כְּנֶסֶת
Beit K'neset

בֵּית עָם
Beit Am

Within Reform synagogues, there is complete equality between all people regardless of where they fall on the spectrum of gender and sexuality. There is no religious function limited by gender or sexual orientation. So too, Reform synagogues are welcoming to those members of Jewish families who are not themselves Jewish.

CHAPTER FOUR

Illness, Death, and Mourning

Though I walk through the valley
of the shadow of death,
I shall fear no evil,
for You are with me.

—PSALM 23:4

They are like grass that renews itself;
in the morning it flourishes anew;
in the evening it withers and dries up. . . .
Teach us to count our days rightly,
that we may obtain a wise heart.

—PSALM 90:5–6, 12

Naked I came from my mother's womb,
and naked shall I return there.
The Eternal gave and the Eternal has taken away;
blessed be the name of the Eternal.

—JOB 1:21

"Judaism teaches us to understand death as part of the divine pattern of the universe. . . . Mortality is the tax we pay for the privilege of love, thought and creative work."[1] Thus, Judaism has developed numerous mitzvot and customs relating to death and mourning, to help the mourners cope with their loss and their grief. Jewish tradition encourages a realistic acceptance of the inevitability of death and teaches the sacredness of grief, sympathy, and memory.

The mitzvot related to death and mourning are governed by four principles. The first concerns the process of grieving. Jewish tradition established the various periods of mourning in order to

---

1. Joshua Loth Liebman, as quoted in *Gates of Prayer: The New Union Prayerbook* (New York: CCAR Press, 1975), p. 625.

allow and encourage the expression of grief. But these periods were also meant to provide limits to mourning. The grieving process is complex, and while everyone mourns differently, the traditional mourning periods are meant to prevent the bereaved from indulging in elaborate, painful, and lengthy periods of mourning that would interfere with the ability to live a full life. With the Jewish emphasis on life, the tradition teaches, "We must not mourn for the dead excessively."[2]

The second principle is the recognition of the reality of death.[3] Tradition prescribes certain conduct at the bedside of a dying person, in the preparation of the body for burial, at the funeral, and in the house of mourning. These rituals are designed to help mourners accept their loss and express their grief, so that the pain might be eased gradually and the mourners adjust to life without their loved one.

A third principle is respect for the dead (*k'vod hameit*). Since biblical times, Judaism has established the principle that every dead person, even the basest criminal, must be accorded the honor of proper burial (Deuteronomy 21:22–23). The body, which is the house of the soul, is to be treated with dignity. Historically, if there was no family, the mitzvah was incumbent upon the Jewish community, every member of which was expected to assist at the burial of the dead[4] and the comforting of mourners.

---

2. *Shulchan Aruch, Yoreh Dei-ah* 394. The Talmud imposes clear limits on the various periods of grief (see note 41, p. 77) and suggests that God says to those who choose to mourn excessively, "You should not be more compassionate to the dead than I am" (BT *Mo-eid Katan* 27b).

3. Jewish tradition prescribes a multitude of acts, from the bedside vigil to shoveling earth into the grave, that are meant to help us accept the reality of death. Modern psychotherapists confirm the wisdom of such funeral and mourning procedures, emphasizing "the deeper psychological and spiritual wisdom inherent in mourning observances, and [in] Jewish teachings about life after death" (S. P. Raphael, "Grief and Bereavement," in Dayle A. Friedman, ed., *Jewish Pastoral Care* [Woodstock, VT: Jewish Lights, 2005], page 401).

4. "Where there is no one to attend to the burial of a corpse, it is called a *meit mitzvah* [a dead person whose burial is a commandment], that is to say, a corpse whose burial is obligatory upon every person" (Maimonides, *Sefer HaMitzvot*,

And the fourth principle is equality in death: "the small and great are there alike, and the servant is free of his master" (Job 3:19). Time and again in the traditional texts of Judaism we see evidence of the sensitivity of the Rabbis toward the poor, but nowhere is this more marked than in the meticulously spelled out funeral procedures, where we find a deep compassion for the mourners as well as an understanding of their vulnerability.[5]

It is the spirit of these time-hallowed principles that underlie the mitzvot and customs of death and mourning in Judaism.

Healing

What is the Jewish view of healing?

Healing does not necessarily mean a cure. Healing has both physical and spiritual components. Modern medicine may often provide a cure for serious illness or at least mitigate the effects of the disease or injury. However, spiritual support is an important component of dealing with many conditions. Healing can often be effected when no cure or only amelioration is possible. Healing often comes when

---

Positive #231). Maimonides derives this mitzvah from Deuteronomy 21:23, "You shall surely bury him."

5. Commenting on the Mishnaic rule that food should not be brought to a house of mourning on trays or salvers or in fancy baskets, but rather in plain baskets, the Talmud says:

> Formerly they would bring food to the house of mourning, the rich in silver and gold baskets and the poor in baskets of willow twigs, and the poor felt shamed. They therefore instituted that all should bring food in baskets of willow twigs, out of deference to the poor. . . .
>
> Formerly they would bring out the rich for burial on stately beds and the poor on plain biers, and the poor felt shamed. They therefore instituted that all should be brought out on plain biers, out of deference to the poor. . . .
>
> Formerly the expense of burying the dead was a greater blow to the family than the death itself, so that the dead person's kin would abandon him. Finally, Rabban Gamliel came forward and, disregarding his own dignity, gave orders that he [himself] be buried in plain linen garments. Thereafter the people followed his example and all were buried in linen garments." (BT *Mo-eid Katan* 27a–b)

people learn to find meaning in life in spite of physical or mental limitation. It has become the practice in many synagogues today to recite the prayer for healing at services. Many congregations also offer support groups as well as special worship services to help individuals and their families cope with acute or chronic conditions. One's rabbi can often be a resource to help individuals and their families find appropriate support to deal with specific conditions.

What is the role of prayer in healing?

מִי שֶׁבֵּרַךְ

Mi Shebeirach

The *Mi Shebeirach* prayer is commonly recited in the prayer service today, inviting all present to share the names of those in need of healing. While Judaism prescribes prayer by and for the sick, it never prescribes prayer as a substitute for competent medical treatment. Prayer directs one's heart to God, who is ultimately the source of healing, as we read: "My cure comes from God, the Creator of physicians."[6]

The collection *Mishkan R'fuah: Where Healing Resides* offers healing readings, meditations, and prayers to use for a wide range of circumstances.

How can gratitude be expressed after recovery?

It is a mitzvah to offer a prayer of thanks, either privately or in the synagogue, when one recovers from a serious illness or injury. The following is the traditional prayer, known as *Birkat HaGomeil*, to be recited upon recovering:

בָּרוּךְ אַתָּה, יְיָ אֱלֹהֵינוּ, מֶלֶךְ הָעוֹלָם,
שֶׁגְּמָלַנִי כָּל־טוֹב.

Baruch atah, Adonai Eloheinu, Melech haolam,
sheg'malani kol tov.
Blessed are You, Adonai our God, Sovereign of the universe,
who has bestowed every goodness upon me.

---

6. Testament of Job 38:11. Also in the Apocrypha we read: "Cultivate the physician as you need him, for him too has God ordained" (Ben Sira 38:1).

Other prayers that may be recited in illness or on recovery can be found in *On the Doorposts of Your House*, pages 170–176, and in *Mishkan R'fuah: Where Healing Resides*.

Many people express their gratitude through an act of *tzedakah*, for example, a donation to the synagogue, the hospital, or an organization dedicated to the particular disease or condition from which the person has recovered.

Why do some change the name of a critically ill person?
The custom of changing the name of a critically ill person or of adding an extra name is rooted in the old belief that it will confuse the angel of death and ward off death. Many Reform rabbis discourage the practice because of its superstitious origins. In some cases though, it may help a patient or family to face the reality of the situation and to offer hope and healing. The rabbi can help families to determine what is best in their particular circumstances.

The Approach of Death

**What does Judaism teach us about our obligations
to the seriously ill and dying?**
It is a mitzvah to visit the seriously ill and dying, when possible, and to offer prayers on their behalf in private or in the synagogue. (See *Bikur Cholim* below.)

Appropriate prayers can be found in *On the Doorposts of Your House*, pages 176–177: *Mishkan R'fuah: Where Healing Resides*; and in Psalms (especially Psalms 6, 23, 88, 121, and 130). In most synagogues, prayers for healing are offered as part of the service. In some congregations, a list of those for whom the congregation has been asked to pray is read aloud, while in others, those present may be asked to call out names or think about those for whom they are praying. One should inform and consult with the rabbi in cases of serious illness.

What is the way to respond to a friend or family member's illness?

בִּיקוּר חוֹלִים

Bikur Cholim

Jewish tradition places great emphasis on the importance of the mitzvah of visiting the sick.

Bikur cholim—the visiting of the sick—is considered such an important obligation that Jewish tradition even suggests that the person who performs this mitzvah will achieve eternal reward.[7] The object of *bikur cholim* is to relieve the isolation of the sick, to cheer them, to be of service, and to give them hope.[8] For some, *bikur cholim* can seem difficult, daunting, or frightening, but the tradition strongly encourages individuals to perform this important mitzvah. A simple visit is a basic aspect of *bikur cholim*. When someone is seriously ill or in great pain, a short visit is preferable. To help both the visitor and the ill person, Jewish tradition recommends behaviors to make a visit more comfortable. If it is possible and appropriate, visitors should remove their coats and sit by the person's bedside rather than remain standing. Sometimes a simple touch says more than an entire conversation. In some instances the offering of a prayer is desired and appropriate. Some congregations have special training sessions for members of the congregation who want to perform the mitzvah of *bikur cholim* on behalf of their congregation.

When a person is dying, the mitzvah of *bikur cholim* can have special significance. The presence of relatives and friends ensure that the dying person is surrounded by loving presences and will not die alone. If appropriate, those present might hold or touch the hand of the dying person to remind the person that he or she is loved. It is important to remember that conversations around the deathbed should focus on the dying person and that there is some evidence that the dying can often hear but not respond. In keeping with the idea that each person is created in the image of God, the dying person should be treated with respect. Keeping the lights low,

---

7. The Talmud (BT *Shabbat* 127a), elaborating on the Mishnah (*Pei-ah* 1:1), lists *bikur cholim* as one of the ten basic mitzvot for which "a person is rewarded in this world and in the world-to-come." See also note 20, p. 69.

8. "A person who visits the sick helps them to recover" (BT *N'darim* 40a).

preventing loud noises, and maintaining a warm temperature are all helpful actions in the room of a person near death. Those present often find that these last moments are powerfully positive experiences for which they remain grateful the rest of their lives.

What are the Jewish end-of-life rituals?

It is a mitzvah for a critically ill person to recite the *Vidui*, an end-of-life confessional prayer. The *Vidui* can also be said by others on behalf of someone else if the person is not well enough to be able to recite it. A critically ill person or those present may also choose to recite the *Sh'ma*.[9] There are also newly created Jewish rituals meant to meet the needs of those facing end-of-life conversations and decision-making. Readings and prayers for these moments, as well as for the critically ill, and multiple versions of the *Vidui* can be found in *On the Doorposts of Your House*, page 178, and in *Mishkan R'fuah: Where Healing Resides*, pages 66–76.

What does Judaism teach about euthanasia?

Judaism teaches that respect for life and the preservation of life is an important mitzvah. When a person is dying, the individual and in many cases family members may have to make difficult and crucial decisions about whether to cease treatment or take other steps that allow the terminally ill person to die. Judaism forbids euthanasia in the sense of actively hastening a death. With the advent of modern medicine and the ability to artificially prolong the process of dying, the decision-making has become far more complex.[10] Many of the

---

9. The Talmud teaches, "If one falls sick and his life is in danger, he is told, "Make confession,' for all who are sentenced to death make confession" (BT *Shabbat* 32a). The traditional prayer of confession, *Vidui*, implies that the death of a person will serve as an atonement for the person's sins (BT *Sanhedrin* 43b).

10. Judaism forbids the taking of life except in self-defense and in the case where one person is pursuing another to kill him. The "pursuer" is considered a murderer and may be killed. (This principle is also applied to a fetus whose birth might result in the death of the mother. Such a fetus is considered a "pursuer" and may be aborted; see "Birth," page 6.)

The act of killing a sick person for whatever reason is absolutely forbidden. According to the *Shulchan Aruch*, even when a person is dying, he may not be disturbed in any way that might hasten his death (*Yoreh Dei-ah* 339).

classic texts of Judaism assert with equal authority that despite the prohibition against euthanasia, neither should one hinder the departure of the soul (i.e., passive euthanasia). People should be allowed to die without having their lives unnecessarily prolonged and suffering needlessly. "Heroic measures" to keep a person alive through artificial systems of life support are therefore discouraged.[11]

These are complex medical and ethical issues. It is therefore important for everyone to have advance directives to ensure that should a person no longer be able to make medical decisions, others will know the person's wishes in regard to medical intervention. Since the laws differ from state to state, it is important to have the documents appropriate to the specific location. When critical decisions need to be made, the rabbi can often help the patient or family with what are difficult and emotionally charged decisions.

What does Judaism teach about organ donation?

פִּקּוּחַ נֶפֶשׁ
Pikuach Nefesh

The most important mitzvah in Judaism is the saving of human life. According to Jewish tradition, *pikuach nefesh*—the saving of life—takes precedence over everything.[12] Therefore, Judaism approves the

---

11. While Jewish tradition forbids any overt act to hasten death, most authorities agree that nothing need be done to keep a dying person alive artificially. The classic story is that of Rabbi Judah HaNasi, who was being kept alive by the unceasing prayers of his colleagues (BT *K'tubot* 104a). A servant, recognizing that the case was hopeless and that Rabbi Judah was in great pain, diverted the rabbis' attention so that they stopped praying, and Rabbi Judah died peacefully.

In *Sefer Chasidim* (thirteenth century) it says, "If a person is sick and in pain and dying and asks another person to kill him mercifully, this request must not be fulfilled, nor may the person take his own life. *Still, you may not put salt on his tongue to keep him alive longer*" (page 10, #315–318). Putting salt on the tongue was believed to be a method of prolonging life.

For Reform responses to these concerns, see, for instance, "Hospital Patient beyond Recovery," in *American Reform Responsa*, ed. Walter Jacob (New York: CCAR Press, 1983), pages 257–260; "Living Will," in *New American Reform Responsa*, ed. Walter Jacob (New York: CCAR Press, 1989), pages 254–259; and Responsum 5763.3, "Hastening the Death of a Potential Organ Donor," in CCAR Responsa Online (https://ccarnet.org/responsa/nyp-no-5763-3/).

12. *Pikuach nefesh* — the saving of a life — is the most urgent mitzvah in

donation of the organs in order to save a life or to heal a deficiency. In many states people can indicate on their driver's license that they wish to be an organ donor. One should also inform one's physician and family of one's desire to be an organ donor.

What is the function of an ethical will?

צַוָּאָה
Tzavaah
A person's legacy is more than the material resources they bequeath their relatives. Each person has a sacred narrative (an *aggadah*) and important values that they hope will continue to inspire their relatives, friends, and their community. Therefore it is a custom to prepare an ethical will, a *tzavaah*, for the moral edification of the family and friends.[13] An ethical will is an important document that allows individuals to think about and write down what has been most important in their life and then to pass it on to the next generation.

Judaism. "Nothing must take precedence over saving a life" (BT *Yoma* 82a). There is a general principle in traditional Judaism (based on BT *Sanhedrin* 47b) that the body of the dead may not be used for the benefit of the living. But even most modern Orthodox authorities agree that the prohibitions on deriving benefit from the dead may be set aside in cases of *pikuach nefesh* and that organ transplants are permitted even in cases where the recipient is not in imminent danger of death. See responsa of Rabbi I. Y. Unterman, *Shevet MiYehudah*, pages 313ff.; "Bank of Human Organs," in *Contemporary American Reform Responsa*, ed. Walter Jacob (New York: CCAR Press, 1987), pages 128–132; and Responsum 5763.2, "Live Liver Transplant," in CCAR Responsa Online (https://ccarnet.org/responsa/nyp-no-5763-2/]).

13. There are many examples of ethical wills in Rabbinic literature. The Talmud quotes Rabbi Judah HaNasi's final moral instructions to his sons. It is a classic example of an ethical will: "When Rabbi was about to die, he said, 'I require the presence of my sons.' When his sons entered, he instructed them: take care that you show due respect to your mother. The light shall continue to burn in its usual place, the table shall be laid in its usual place, and my bed shall be spread in its usual place'" (BT *K'tubot* 103a). The custom of leaving or speaking an ethical will for one's children actually goes back to the Bible (see Genesis 49, especially verse 33; 50:24–25; and Deuteronomy 33). The medieval ethical wills of Maimonides, Nachmanides, and Rabbi Judah HaChasid are particularly noteworthy, as are the more recent wills of the Vilna Gaon and Rabbi Moses Sofer; see also "Ethical Wills" by Rabbi Lawrence W. Raphael, page 243.

It is important to prepare such a will (as one would prepare a legal will) when one is in good health and strength. (For examples of notable ethical wills, see "Ethical Wills" by Rabbi Lawrence W. Raphael, page 243.) An ethical will is a spiritual document, but it is no substitute for preparing appropriate legal documents for the distribution of material assets. While it can be difficult at any stage of life to contemplate one's own death, it is a mitzvah to ensure that relatives and friends will have legal guidance in the distribution of one's worldly possessions. In preparation of these documents, one will want to consider acts of *tzedakah* as part of the estate plan.

From Death to Funeral

What is the Jewish response upon hearing about a death?

In response to the news of the death of a member of one's immediate family (i.e., children, parents, spouses, and siblings), it is a mitzvah to recite the following prayer:

בָּרוּךְ אַתָּה, יְיָ אֱלֹהֵינוּ, מֶלֶךְ הָעוֹלָם,
דַּיַּן הָאֱמֶת.

Baruch atah, Adonai Eloheinu, Melech haolam,
Dayan ha-emet.

Praise to You, Adonai our God, Sovereign of
the universe, the righteous Judge.[14]

This traditional prayer is called *Tziduk HaDin*[15]—the justification of

צִדּוּק הַדִּין
Tziduk HaDin

the decree—and is an affirmation of one's faith in God and of the acceptance of the inevitability of death, even in a moment of grievous loss.

---

14. This prayer in shortened form—*Baruch Dayan ha-emet*—is prescribed in the Mishnah (*B'rachot* 9:2) on the occasion of "hearing bad news." Later authorities, especially the *Shulchan Aruch* (*Yoreh Dei-ah* 339), prescribed the prayer in its fuller form to be recited by the family as soon as death occurs.

15. The term *Tziduk HaDin* as a justification of the divine decree of death is first used in the Talmud in a passage describing how Rabbi Chananya ben Teradion (second century), his wife, and his daughter were sentenced to death by the Romans. "As the three of them went out [from the Roman tribunal], they declared

What are the first steps upon learning of a death in the family?

Among the first steps in preparing for the funeral and seeking advice and comfort, a family member should inform their rabbi. The rabbi can be very helpful in both practical and emotional ways.

What is involved with preparing for a funeral?

While it is normal for people to avoid thinking about their own death, one should purchase burial plots and make known one's wishes about funeral and burial *before* the time of need, because it will help to alleviate some of the anguish and confusion for the family surrounding death when the time comes. In many communities, congregations have specific funeral plans that can inform the individual or family about what is considered most appropriate, because even the most simple funerals can often be expensive. Some individuals, long before their death and while still in good health, choose to prepay their funeral expenses, in order to spare the survivors any financial burden. However, it is not appropriate to make specific funeral arrangements (i.e., time or date) for a dying person until death has actually occurred.

The purpose of the funeral is to memorialize the deceased and to comfort the mourners. In cases where the deceased leaves unusual instructions (e.g., that there be no funeral or that something other than a conventional religious service be held), the sensitivities of the survivors should be taken into consideration. In such case or where the deceased leaves instructions contrary to the Jewish tradition, the rabbi should be consulted.

---

their submission to righteous judgment [i.e., God's will]." The passage proceeds to describe how each of the three quoted verses from the Bible (Deuteronomy 32:4 and Jeremiah 32:19) thereupon became part of the Jewish burial service. "Rabba said: 'How great were these righteous ones in that the three scriptural passages expressing submission to divine justice [i.e., *Tziduk HaDin*] readily occurred to them just at the appropriate time for the declaration of such submission'" (BT *Avodah Zarah* 18a).

Does Judaism permit autopsies and donating one's body to science?

Autopsies are permitted[16] but are often discouraged. However, if there is a specific reason—for example, to help family members or for the clear purpose of increasing medical knowledge that cannot be gained in another way—an autopsy may be appropriate. Of course, in the case that an autopsy is required by law, there is no objection. If the deceased has left instructions prohibiting an autopsy, these instructions should be honored except where there is the danger of epidemic or where civil law requires it.

While Jewish tradition forbids the donating of one's entire body to science, Reform Judaism permits this practice provided that the scientific institution to which the body is donated is known to treat the body with respect and that, when the study is completed, the remains are buried or cremated.[17]

---

16. Respect for the dead and reverence for the human body are major principles of Jewish law; consequently autopsies were strictly for bidden by the early Rabbis. However, when the principle of *pikuach nefesh* (see note 12) comes into conflict with the reverence due a dead body, *pikuach nefesh* takes precedence. Thus, we find that most Orthodox authorities after the eighteenth century permit autopsies in cases where there is a clear benefit to the health of others to be derived from the autopsy. Particularly interesting in this regard is the agreement reached in 1944 between the Chief Rabbi of Palestine and the Chief Rabbi of Jerusalem and Dr. Chaim Yassky of the Hadassah Hospital "permitting autopsies in the following cases: (1) when the civil law demanded it in cases of crime and accidental death; (2) to establish the cause of death when it was doubtful; (3) in order to save lives; and (4) in cases of hereditary disease" (*Encyclopaedia Judaica*, vol. 3, col. 932). See "Autopsy," in *American Reform Responsa* (New York: CCAR Press, 1925), pages 130–134 and "Autopsy for Future Knowledge," in *Contemporary American Reform Responsa*, ed. Walter Jacob (New York: CCAR Press, 1987), pages 140–142.

17. For a complete discussion of the matter of donating one's body to science from both the traditional and Reform points of view, see the following responsa by Solomon B. Freehof: "Donating a Body to Science" in *Reform Responsa* (Cincinnati, OH: Hebrew Union College Press, 1960), pages 130–131; "Remain of Bodies Donated to Science" in *Modern Reform Responsa* (Cincinnati, OH: Hebrew Union College Press, 1971), pages 278–280; and "Bequeathing Parts of the Body" in *Contemporary Reform Responsa* (Cincinnati, OH: Hebrew Union College Press, 1974), pages 216–223.

Does the entire family have to be informed about a death?

It is a mitzvah to notify all members of the family at the time of a death. This applies even to cases where certain members of the family are estranged, in the hopes that the period of family mourning might promote reconciliation.

How is a body prepared for burial?

טָהֳרָה
Tohorah

חֶבְרָה קַדִּישָׁא
Chevrah Kadisha

תַּכְרִיכִים
Tachrichim

טַלִּית
Tallit

The human body is always to be treated with respect both during life and after death. In Judaism the human being is both body and soul, each to be equally valued and respected. This Jewish value undergirds many of the rituals around preparing the body for burial.

There are many beautiful traditions connected with *tohorah*, the cleansing and preparation of the body for burial. Though often family members do not make arrangements for this mitzvah today, many who do have come to appreciate the significance of *tohorah*. *Tohorah* can be arranged by a funeral director or the local *chevrah kadisha* (Jewish communal burial society). In some communities, the congregation may have or participate in a specific *chevrah kadisha*; in these cases the deceased is prepared for burial by members of their own community. Being part of a *chevrah kadisha* and participating in the sacred task of preparing the deceased for burial is often a very powerful and meaningful spiritual experience.

The dead may be buried in ordinary clothing or in shrouds. *Tachrichim* (traditional linen burial shrouds) may be used but are not required. However, if *tohorah* is performed, *tachrichim* are often required by the *chevrah kadisha*. It is a beautiful custom for one to be buried with his or her tallit (prayer shawl) or with a pouch of earth from the Land of Israel.

Since Judaism prescribes that the body should be returned to the dust from which it came, embalming is discouraged except when required by law or circumstances.

Should the coffin be open or closed for the funeral?

The body, after having been prepared for burial, should be put into the coffin and the coffin closed. Out of respect for the dead, Jewish tradition is opposed to the public viewing of the deceased in an open coffin. The family may view the body privately before the funeral service if they wish, but the coffin should be permanently sealed before the service begins.[18]

The custom of pre-funeral visitation in the chapel is not in keeping with Jewish tradition and is discouraged.

What is rending the garment, and why do we do it?

קְרִיעָה
K'riah

K'riah, the rending of one's garment or the symbolic cutting of a black ribbon, is a sign of mourning.[19] It represents the rend in mourners' lives and hearts caused by the death of their loved one. By wearing the ribbon or the torn garment, people let others know that they are mourners and thus enable them to perform the mitzvah of *nichum aveilim* (comforting the mourner).

What are the obligations of friends and relatives to the mourners before the funeral?

It is a mitzvah to help the bereaved through the many difficult details of funeral arrangements. Recognizing the emotional vulnerability of mourners in these most painful hours of grief, the time between death and burial, relatives and close friends should offer whatever help they can, but this is not a time for ordinary condolence calls.

---

18. It is understood that before the coffin is closed a member of the family or their representative will have established the identity of the body.

19. The Talmud (BT *Mo-eid Katan* 24a) and the *Shulchan Aruch* (*Yoreh Dei-ah* 340:1) require the rending of one's clothes (actually the symbolic rending of the upper part of one's outer garment) on the death of one's parent, wife, child, or sibling. The custom is an ancient one and is often mentioned in the Bible (e.g., Genesis 37:34, when Jacob heard about the alleged death of Joseph). For the Reform Jew, the cutting or tearing of a garment or ribbon might be an appropriate symbolic act of grief, as a reminder of loss, and as a means of informing others of one's recent tragedy.

The Funeral Service and Burial

What are some the considerations about the burial of the dead?

It is a mitzvah to bury the dead with all due respect. The Rabbis taught that there are ten mitzvot for which a person would enjoy eternal reward;[20] among these is tending to the dead (see page 67).

The mitzvah of burying the dead is the responsibility of a person's children or spouse, or in the case of a child, the parents.[21] In cases where there are no children or spouse, it is the responsibility of the nearest relative. Where there is no family, the mitzvah should be assumed by the entire Jewish community.[22]

When does a burial happen?

Funeral services and burial should not be delayed needlessly. Tradition teaches that we should bury within a day after death.[23] Today

---

20. The Talmud (BT *Shabbat* 127a), elaborating on the *Mishnah* (*Pei-ah* 1:1), lists *halvayat hameit* (accompanying the dead; see pages 17 and 146–147) as one of the ten mitzvot for which "a person is rewarded in this world and in the world-to-come."

21. Chapter 23 of Genesis is the first reference to burial in the Bible. In it we read of the great concern of the patriarch Abraham for a proper burial place for his wife, Sarah, and how he, as the principal mourner, took care of this sacred task himself. The fact that Isaac, Sarah's only son, is not mentioned in Genesis 23 as being involved in the burial gave rise to several Rabbinic legends explaining his absence.

22. "Where there is no one to attend to the burial of a corpse, it is called a *meit mitzvah* [a dead person whose burial is a commandment], that is to say, a corpse whose burial is obligatory upon every person" (Maimonides, *Sefer HaMitzvot*, Positive #231). Maimonides derives this mitzvah from Deuteronomy 21:23, "You must bury him."

23. Maimonides, basing himself on the commandment to bury the corpse of an executed criminal on the day of death (Deuteronomy 21:23), extends this to all Jews: "Every Israelite must be buried on the day of his death" (*Sefer HaMitzvot*, Positive #231). Such haste, though, was recognized in the *Shulchan Aruch* as not always possible or advisable: "One may leave the body overnight if it is for the honor of the dead, e.g., to procure a coffin and shrouds or to await the arrival of relatives. . . . The Torah forbade any delay in burial only when such delay would indicate contempt for the dead, but we may delay for the honor of the dead" (*Shulchan Aruch, Yoreh Dei-ah* 357).

the principle is to conduct the funeral and burial as soon as is practical, taking into account the necessity of family members to travel from out of town. Generally, this means within two days of death. The rabbi should be informed as soon as death occurs and should be consulted about the time of the service.

May a funeral take place on Shabbat or a festival?
Funeral services are not held on Shabbat or major festivals.[24] The rabbi can help determine whether burial on the second day of a festival is appropriate for a specific situation.[25]

What guidelines does Judaism offer regarding funeral arrangements?
Simplicity and dignity are the governing principles for Jewish funeral arrangements. A funeral should never become an occasion for a display of wealth.[26] It is preferable to use a simple wooden coffin, but whatever the specific details, the principle of simplicity should be honored. The same principle applies to the use of flowers.

What is an appropriate way to memorialize someone?

צְדָקָה
Tzedakah

It is a mitzvah to express sympathy by making a gift of *tzedakah* in memory of the deceased. Many families include a request to send contributions to charity (e.g., "in lieu of flowers") in the obituary notice. Many people

---

24. The phrase "major festival" refers to all those holy days called *mikra-ei kodesh*—holy convocations—in Leviticus 23:2ff.: Shabbat (23:3); the first day of Pesach (23:7); the last day of Pesach (23:8); Shavuot (23:21); Rosh HaShanah (23:24); Yom Kippur (23:27); the first day of Sukkot (23:35); Sh'mini Atzeret (Simchat Torah) (23:36).

25. Most Orthodox and Conservative Jews (outside of Israel) observe a second day for all the festivals (see note 24, above) listed in Leviticus 23 except Shabbat and Yom Kippur. Since certain members of the family and the Jewish community might observe the second day, it would be best to consult with the rabbi. However, even among traditional Jews, burial on the second day of a festival is allowed in some cases.

26. See note 5, p. 57.

arrange for gifts (*tzedakah*) in their memory in their estate planning so that their values will be perpetuated after their death.

May people other than the rabbi and/or cantor participate in the funeral service?

The rabbi can aid the family in determining who is appropriate to participate in the funeral. It is important to consult the rabbi before an invitation is extended.

Must a funeral include a eulogy?

הֶסְפֵּד
Hespeid

While a eulogy (*hespeid*) is not required, it is appropriate in most cases to reflect on a person's life and values as a way of preserving their legacy and memory.[27] In all cases the eulogy should be sensitive to the realities of the deceased person's life. There are no restrictions in Reform Jewish practice as to the days on which eulogies may be given.[28]

Is it important to attend a funeral?

הַלְוָיַת הַמֵּת
Halvayat HaMeit

It is a mitzvah for all who are able to do so to attend a funeral service. This mitzvah is referred to as *halvayat hameit*, "accompanying the dead."[29] Going not only to the service but also to the cemetery for burial is integral to this mitzvah for those who are able to do so. However, sometimes the family requests privacy for the interment, and in those cases the family's wish should be respected.

---

27. Funeral orations or eulogies go back to antiquity in Judaism (see II Samuel 1:17–27, 3:33–34). In Talmudic times they were commonplace: "From the funeral eulogy pronounced over a man we know whether eternal life is his or not" (BT *Shabbat* 153a).

28. Traditionally eulogies were not offered and the funeral service itself was abridged if burial took place on a Friday, the eve of a festival, or a day when there was no mourning (i.e., a semi-holy day like Rosh Chodesh, Purim, or Chanukah).

29. The Talmud (BT *Shabbat* 127a), elaborating on the Mishnah (*Pei-ah* 1:1), lists *halvayat hameit* (accompanying the dead; see pages 17 and 146–147) as one of the ten mitzvot for which "a person is rewarded in this world and in the world-to-come."

Where can a funeral take place?
The proper places for funeral services are the home of the deceased, the graveside, a funeral home, a cemetery chapel, or the synagogue.

Is burial the only appropriate practice in Judaism?
Burial is the most widely practiced method of disposition of the body among Jews and is, in fact, the method preferred by tradition.[30] However, it is clear that other methods (e.g., interment in caves) were practiced among Jews in ancient times. And so, while both cremation and entombment in mausoleums are acceptable in Reform Judaism, burial is the normative Jewish practice.

The Jewish dead should, if possible, be interred in Jewish cemeteries or in the Jewish sections of community cemeteries or mausoleums. In cases of cremation, the ashes should be buried in a Jewish cemetery if permitted or on one's private property (if permitted by law) or placed in the niche of a Jewish mausoleum.[31] In general the scattering of ashes is discouraged, because it is important for most people to have a locus for mourning and to have a marker that memorializes the deceased.

**Can non-Jewish family members be buried in
Jewish cemeteries or mausoleums?**
Reform Judaism permits non-Jewish members of Jewish families to be interred in Jewish cemeteries or mausoleums where that is per-

---

30. Burial is one of the most ancient traditions in Judaism. "Dust you are and to dust you shall return" (Genesis 3:19); the Bible refers to burial in several instances, beginning with the burial of Sarah by Abraham (Genesis 23). However, burial as described in the Bible and the Mishnah often seems to refer to interment in caves and rock niches (see Isaiah 22:16 and *Mishnah Bava Batra* 6:8). Most post-Mishnaic authorities indicate earth burial as the proper Jewish mode of interment, and this became the norm, as described in *Shulchan Aruch, Yoreh Dei-ah* 362.
31. For a more complete discussion of the question of the proper disposal of cremation ashes, see "Scattering the Ashes of the Dead" and "A Tombstone for Scattered Ashes," in *Questions and Reform Jewish Answers: New American Reform Responsa*, ed. Walter Jacob (New York: CCAR Press, 1992), pages 306–309; and "Burial of Ashes in a Mausoleum," in *Contemporary American Reform Responsa*, ed. Walter Jacob (New York: CCAR Press, 1987), pages 306–309.

mitted by the cemetery, provided that non-Jewish services are not recited and non-Jewish symbols are not displayed.[32] In some cases Jewish cemeteries have special sections for intermarried families. Every cemetery has its own rules and policies.

May burial vaults be used?
While Jewish tradition has in the past mandated burial without a burial vault, it is now often common practice, because of cemetery regulations or in some cases state law, to use a burial vault. For those who are required to use a vault but want direct burial in the ground, there are bottomless vaults that provide direct contact with the earth.

Is it appropriate for children to attend funerals?
Children should not be excluded from attendance at family funerals. Children should be recognized as mourners, and their need to mourn should not be overlooked. In special cases, the rabbi can help the family to determine if a child's presence is appropriate. Children's questions about death, the funeral, and burial should be answered honestly, and they should be helped in every way to accept the reality of death.

Is *Kaddish* recited at graveside, and is a minyan required?

קַדִּישׁ
Kaddish

מִנְיָן
Minyan

Kaddish is a prayer of mourning that is generally recited for the dead for the first time at the burial. While desirable, Reform Judaism does not require the presence of a minyan[33] for the recitation of *Kaddish*[34] at the graveside. This *Kaddish* should be recited by the

---

32. See K. Kohler, "Burial of Non-Jewish Wives in Jewish Cemetaries" in *CCAR Yearbook*, vol. 24 (1914), page 154.

33. According to tradition, a quorum of ten Jewish men—a minyan—is required for the recitation of certain prayers, among them *Kaddish*. A minyan is not required in Reform Judaism, but it is certainly desirable in that it emphasizes the importance of community. Women are, of course, counted equally in a Reform minyan.

34. The mitzvah of *Kaddish* is described on page 80 and in "The Mourner's *Kaddish*" by Rabbi Simeon Maslin, page 251.

children, spouse, siblings, and parents of the deceased. Relatives and friends normally join the mourners in the *Kaddish*. If the deceased was not survived by any of the above, the *Kaddish* should be recited by the closest relative or friend present or by the rabbi.

What is the tradition about filling in the grave at a Jewish funeral?
Jewish tradition prescribes that the family of the deceased remain at the graveside for the lowering of the coffin and the refilling of the grave. The custom is to fill in three shovelfuls of earth, which represent intention to fill the whole grave. In cases where the family chooses not to remain through the completion of the burial, a representative of the family may want to remain until the coffin is covered with earth. One of the more powerful customs is that those present assist in completely filling the grave. Participation in the burial in these ways is a mitzvah and is understood to be a way to care for a loved one even after death. Individuals who are physically or spiritual unable are exempt from this mitzvah.

May pregnant women attend funerals?
There are many folk superstitions about prohibiting pregnant women from attending funerals or going to cemeteries. These are only superstitions and do not represent Jewish law. It is understandable that our ancestors would have had concerns about bad luck and wanting to prevent anything from going wrong with a pregnancy. It should be up to the woman herself to decide what is right for her, and she should certainly not be prohibited from participating in the mitzvot around death and funerals.

Are there those for whom a funeral should not be conducted?
It is a mitzvah to conduct a regular funeral service for all Jews, regardless of the style of their lives or the manner of their death.[35] All

---

35. The primary consideration here is suicide. Tradition forbade the burial of suicides in Jewish cemeteries and the performance of mourning rites for them. The governing Talmudic text is as follows: "If one destroys himself consciously, we

should be treated with the respect due every member of the Jewish community and should be buried in the Jewish cemetery in the midst of their families.

Is it appropriate to conduct funerals for infants, stillbirths, or fetuses?

While tradition taught that funeral and mourning customs should not be observed for the stillborn child or for an infant who does not live for thirty days, in our day these losses are much rarer and therefore perhaps even more poignant than in ancient times. Today Judaism recognizes that ceremonies, prayers, and mourning customs can help a family deal with this tragic loss. Indeed, many new rituals and prayers have been created for families facing the loss of an infant or a pregnancy. For an infant who survives birth, a simple funeral and burial are appropriate. In the case of abortion, miscarriage, or stillbirth, consulting with a rabbi for the appropriate rituals can be very helpful. If other family members or community members are informed of the death, recognition of the profound loss can provide comfort. Both parents are to be considered mourners and require comfort. At the same time, it is important to respect the privacy of the parents and take their lead on how to mark their loss. Readings and prayers for these difficult losses can be found in *On the Doorposts of Your House*, pages 180–181, and in *Mishkan R'fuah: Where Healing Resides*, pages 49–51.

How is a funeral conducted when a body is donated to science or in the case where there is no body?

A regular funeral service is conducted for those whose bodies have been donated to science and for those whose bodies have been lost or cannot be recovered or identified.[36] When there is no body pres-

---

do not involve ourselves with his funeral . . . and we do not say a eulogy for him" (Massechet *S'machot* 2:1). Today even Orthodox Jews find ways to interpret the law more liberally. In Reform Judaism there should be no distinction between suicides and others.

36. "Mourning rites are not withheld in any respect from one who fell into the sea or was carried away by a stream or killed by a wild beast" (Massechet *S'machot* 2:12).

ent, the service is often described as a memorial service. When the body is irreparably lost or unidentified, the service is held and the period of mourning begins as soon as it becomes clear that there is no hope of recovering the body.[37]

The Mourning Period

Are there different periods of mourning?

It is a mitzvah to mourn for one's dead.[38] Grief, however, is a very personal emotion; it cannot be legislated. The Talmud, even as it established the laws of mourning, recognized that there is a difference between formal rites of mourning and private grief, "for grief is borne in the heart alone."[39]

Jewish tradition prescribes several periods of mourning, differing in intensity and obligation, following the death of a loved one. These are *aveilut*, *aninut*, shivah, *sh'loshim*, and the first year.

אֲבֵלוּת   *Aveilut* is the term applied generally to the entire
Aveilut   mourning period.

---

37. The question of mourning for a person who has disappeared is related to the problem of the *agunah* (a woman whose husband has disappeared and who, according to tradition, is forbidden to remarry because of the chance that he might be alive; see note 15, page 34). According to Reform Judaism, if the civil authorities declare that a person is dead, mourning rites are observed, and the widow is free to remarry.

38. There is no specific law in the Torah about mourning for one's dead. Maimonides, however, does include it as a positive commandment, deriving it from the law of the *kohein* who must defile himself for his immediate relatives (Leviticus 21:2–3). "On this commandment is based the duty of mourning; i.e., the obligation incumbent upon every Israelite man to mourn after the loss of relatives, who are six in number" (i.e., mother, father, son, daughter, brother, and sister; mourning by and for husband and wife is a Rabbinic extension; *Sefer HaMitzvot*, Positive #37). The many complex laws in the Talmud regulating aspects of mourning make it clear that the early Rabbis considered mourning for those enumerated above as a mitzvah.

39. *Mishnah Sanhedrin* 6:6.

Aninut is the period between death and burial. During this period

אֲנִינוּת
Aninut

the mourner is involved in making funeral arrangements and is free from all ritual, professional, and social obligations except the observance of the Sabbath (if it occurs).[40]

Shivah is the seven days of mourning following the funeral. Mourn-

שִׁבְעָה
Shivah

ers are encouraged to remain at home during these days (except on Shabbat or festivals, when it is appropriate for them to join the congregation in prayer), to refrain from their ordinary pursuits and occupations, and to participate in daily services in the home. (Home services for shivah can be found in *Doorposts of the House*, pages 131–208, and in *Mishkhan T'filah for the House of Mourning*). The first three days of the shivah period are considered the most intense,[41] and while in most Reform congregations the first three days are considered the minimum mourning period, mourners are encouraged to observe the full seven days.

Sh'loshim is the thirty-day period (including shivah) when normal life

שְׁלֹשִׁים
Sh'loshim

gradually resumes and the mourners return to their daily activities while yet observing certain aspects of mourning. During this period it is customary for

---

40. "One whose dead relative lies before him [i.e., has not yet been buried] is exempt from the recital of the *Sh'ma* ... and from all the mitzvot in the Torah. ... On the Sabbath, however, he may recline and eat meat and drink wine ... and he is subject to all the mitzvot in the Torah" (BT *B'rachot* 17b–18a).

41. The Talmud takes a text from the prophet Jeremiah as the basis for its regulation regarding periods of intense mourning. "'Do not weep for the dead or bemoan him' [Jeremiah 22:10]; 'Do not weep for the dead' means excessively [i.e., do not weep excessively]; 'or bemoan him' means beyond measure [i.e., do not bemoan him beyond measure]. How is this understood? Three days for weeping and seven for lamenting and thirty to refrain from cutting one's hair and wearing pressed clothes [i.e., thirty days during which one should not have to worry about one's personal appearance]. Thereafter, the Holy One, blessed be God, says, 'You should not be more compassionate toward the departed than I'" (BT *Mo-eid Katan* 27b).

the mourner to avoid joyful social events and entertainment. This is the traditionally prescribed period of mourning for relatives other than parents.

The First Year   The first year is the period during which a mourner recites *Kaddish* for a parent (see page 81).

What happens when Shabbat or holidays occur during the mourning period?

Formal mourning (i.e., the observance of shivah) is suspended for the observance of Shabbat and festivals, at which times the mourners are encouraged to attend synagogue services and observe the customs of the day.

חוֹל הַמּוֹעֵד   Tradition prescribes the complete termination of shivah when a
Chol HaMo-eid   festival intervenes, but while Reform Jewish practice adheres to the suspension of formal mourning for the holy day itself, the family may decide to resume shivah after a festival, particularly when the festival falls within a day or two of the death. If death occurs during the intermediate days (*chol hamo-eid*) of a festival (i.e., Chol HaMo-eid Pesach or Sukkot), the rabbi can help the family determine the appropriate parameters of the mourning period.[42]

What is the tradition about the first meal after returning from the cemetery?

סְעֻדַּת הַבְרָאָה   It is a mitzvah for friends to prepare the first
S'udat Havraah   meal eaten by the mourners upon returning from the cemetery in order to spare the mourners the need of preparing food at the height of their grief. This meal of consolation (traditionally known as *s'udat havraah*)[43] is integral to

---

42. According to tradition, if burial occurs before a festival, the festival cancels the shivah, i.e., the mourner is relieved of the necessity to follow the customs of shivah (see page 78). If, on the other hand, burial occurs during the intermediate days of Passover or Sukkot, tradition prescribes the observance of the full shivah period after the festival (BT *Mo-eid Katan* 19a; *Shulchan Aruch, Yoreh Dei-ah* 399).
43. See BT *Mo-eid Katan* 27a and note 5, p. 57 above.

the mourning process; it can be a time for family and close friends to come together to lend their strength to the bereaved. There is a tradition in which non-mourners serve the meal to the mourners and refrain from eating until all the mourners have been served. During shivah, many people send or bring food or baked goods. Those who attend will often partake of these refreshments. The mourners, however, are under no obligation to provide refreshments to those who come to perform the mitzvah of *nichum aveilim*, which is central to the healing process following a loss.

How should mourners be comforted?

נְחוּם אֲבֵלִים
Nichum Aveilim

צְדָקָה
Tzedakah

It is a mitzvah to go to a house of mourning to comfort the mourners and to join them in prayer; this is the mitzvah of *nichum aveilim* (comforting the mourners). When performing the mitzvah of *nichum aveilim*, one may want to speak about the deceased in a manner that is comforting to the mourner. The days of shivah are consecrated to the memory of the deceased, and it is therefore a mitzvah to speak about them to the mourners and to do acts of *tzedakah* in their memory.[44]

Are there other customs about a shivah service?

דְּבַר תּוֹרָה
D'var Torah

It is appropriate to include a *d'var Torah* (a brief Torah lesson) in shivah services.[45] Sharing thoughts related to a Jewish text or values is a fitting way to memorialize a loved one.

---

44. Tradition pictures God as setting the example in the comforting of mourners (see note 41, p. 77). The Talmud teaches that "God in all God's glory went to console Isaac when his father, Abraham, died" (BT *Sotah* 14a). There are several instances of consolation in the Bible. Possibly the most instructive is the story of Job's comforters: "They sat down upon the ground with him seven days and seven nights, but none of them spoke a word to him, for they saw how great was his suffering" (Job 2:13). The Rabbis took this verse to teach that one should not speak to a mourner until he is ready, as the Talmud says: "Silence is meritorious in a house of mourning" (BT *B'rachot* 6b).
45. The custom of including a Torah lesson in the service in a house of mourning

What is the significance of the shivah candle?

It is customary to light a seven-day candle on returning from the cemetery as a memorial to the deceased, symbolic of the light brought by the deceased to the mourners during life.[46] (A brief service can be found in *On the Doorposts of Your House*, page 193.) This candle should be put in a conspicuous place so that it may be seen, especially during shivah services. The candle may be lit by one of the mourners. As it is lit, the family says:

נֵר־לְרַגְלִי דְבָרֶךָ, וְאוֹר לִנְתִיבָתִי.
בְּאוֹרְךָ נִרְאֶה אוֹר.

Ner l'ragli d'varecha v'or lin'tivati.
B'or'cha nireh or.

Your word, O God, is a lamp to my feet, a light to my path. By Your light shall we see light. (Psalms 119:105, 36:10)

For how long are mourners obligated to recite *Kaddish* for the deceased?

It is a mitzvah for mourners, both men and women, to recite the

קַדִּישׁ
Kaddish

יָאר־צֵיִט
Yahrzeit

Kaddish prayer in memory of the dead at daily services during shivah at home and thereafter in the synagogue.[47] If they do not attend daily services in the synagogue, mourners should recite *Kaddish* with their families or

probably developed from the notion that mitzvot done in the name of the deceased would help their souls to rise to paradise. *Talmud Torah*—learning Torah—is considered the equal of all other mitzvot combined (*Mishnah Pei-ah* 1:1), and the Talmud teaches that "all sins are forgiven the person who studies Torah" (BT *B'rachot* 5a). Just as tradition taught that the faithful recitation of the *Kaddish* (*Mishnah Eduyot* 2:10; also see "The Mourner's *Kaddish*" by Rabbi Simeon Maslin, page 251) would help the soul to ascend, the performance of the mitzvah of *talmud Torah* in the name of the deceased and in his or her home would surely help. Reform Judaism does not teach that mitzvot help dead souls to rise, but it does encourage Torah study as a mitzvah and a fitting way to honor the dead.

46. The custom of lighting a candle in memory of the dead is related to the biblical verse "The spirit of a person is the light of the Eternal" (Proverbs 20:27).

47. See "The Mourner's *Kaddish* by Rabbi Simeon Maslin, page 251.

privately.[48] In addition to *Kaddish*, one or more of the following appropriate psalms may be added to one's public or private prayers during the week of shivah and on the *yahrzeit*: Psalms 15, 16, 23, 49, 90, and 121.

It is a mitzvah to recite *Kaddish* for parents for a year[49] and for other members of the family for a month. As the memory of loved ones inspires the performance of such mitzvot as prayer, charity, and study, the dead are immortalized in the lives of those who remember them. While some will want to find a daily minyan to recite *Kaddish*, others will fulfill this mitzvah by attending a weekly Shabbat service to say *Kaddish*. Since Reform Judaism not does not require a minyan for saying *Kaddish*, the mourner who is not attending regular daily worship may desire to pause during the day to think about his or her parent and recite *Kaddish* privately. The text for the *Kaddish* can be found in *Mishkan T'filah: A Reform Siddur*, page 598, and in *On the Doorposts of Your House*, page 206.

The mitzvah of *Kaddish* is incumbent on the mourners themselves. Though there is an old custom of paying someone else to attend services and recite *Kaddish* in his or her place, that is not understood to be an appropriate or respectful way to fulfill this mitzvah.

It is a mitzvah to observe the *yahrzeit* (the anniversary of the day of death) each year with the recitation of *Kaddish* and attendance at synagogue services.[50] It is customary to light a twenty-four-

---

48. While Reform Judaism does not require the presence of a minyan for the recitation of *Kaddish* or any other prayer, it is appropriate that a minyan of both men and women be assembled whenever possible.

49. There is no basis in Reform Judaism for the custom of reciting *Kaddish* for eleven months only (see "The Mourner's *Kaddish*" by Rabbi Simeon Maslin, page 251), a that idea is based on outdated superstition.

50. The term *yahrzeit* means literally "year's time," i.e., anniversary. The custom of *yahrzeit* is not mentioned in the Talmud or the medieval codes by that name. We find the word for the first time in the writings of a prominent fourteenth-century German Talmudist, Rabbi Jacob ben Moses Moellin (Maharil; see note 38, p. 45). In Talmudic times people followed the custom of a private fast day (*taanit yachid*) on the anniversary of the death of a parent (BT *Sh'vuot* 20a). The custom of burning a memorial lamp during the *yahrzeit* day originated in the Middle Ages and probably derives from the Christian custom of votive candles. By the

hour candle on the eve of the *yahrzeit* date. A family may choose to observe either the Hebrew or the secular date of death. A home *yahrzeit* service can be found in *On the Doorposts of Your House*, pages 208–209.

Yahrzeit is a day that can be consecrated each year to the memory of the dead. It is sometimes accompanied by renewed feeling of grief and longing, and while it is not an occasion for formal mourning, it is often a rather emotional time. One way to deal with the emotions that can arise at *yahrzeit* is for the family to choose to the perform mitzvot (e.g., *tzedakah* and study) in honor of the deceased.

What is *Yizkor*, and how is it observed?

יִזְכּוֹר
Yizkor

Yizkor is a special set of prayers related to memory in honor of our loved ones who have died. It is a mitzvah to recite *Yizkor*, which is incorporated into the liturgy of our festival services (Yom Kippur, Sh'mini Atzeret–Simchat Torah, the seventh day of Pesach, and Shavuot), during which we recall the names of our loved ones.[51] Accompanying the recitation of *Yizkor* with the mitzvah of appropriate *tzedakah* in memory of the deceased can enhance the meaning of the occasion.

---

nineteenth century it was a solid enough Jewish custom to be prescribed by Rabbi Solomon Ganzfried in his *Kitzur Shulchan Aruch*. (The Ganzfried passage on *yahrzeit* also makes explicit mention of the traditional belief that *Kaddish* and other mitzvot help the soul to ascend to higher spheres; see note 45, p. 79, and the essay on Kaddish on p. 251.) The term *yahrzeit*, though Yiddish, is listed in the authoritative Israeli Hebrew dictionary *HaMilon HeChadash* (Jerusalem: Even-Shoshan, 1969) because of its common usage.

51. *Yizkor* (lit. "May God remember") is the popular name of the special prayer prescribed in the liturgy for recitation on certain holy days, especially Yom Kippur, in memory of the dead. The custom of *hazkarat n'shamot* (calling to mind the memory of the dead) is an ancient one, but the *Yizkor* prayer as recited in Ashkenazic congregations probably dates from after the Crusades. The Sephardic memorial prayer is known as *Hashkabah*. *Yizkor* is recited in all Reform congregations on Yom Kippur and the last day of Pesach and in many congregations on Shavuot and Sh'mini Atzeret–Simchat Torah also (see *Mishkan T'filah: A Reform Siddur*, pages 574–583).

Are there other customs surrounding shivah and mourning?

There are many mourning practices and abstinences that have had wide currency among Jews through the centuries, some of which are not generally observed by Reform Jews today. The rabbi can help mourners determine which are most appropriate for them and their families.

What is the minimum period a person should wait until remarrying after the death of spouse?

Judaism, with its emphasis on a life of love and partnership, encourages remarriage when a person has found a suitable spouse, but the choice to remarry, and the timing of remarriage, is a personal decision (see page 41).

When and how does a marker or tombstone for the deceased get set up?

מַצֵּבָה

Matzeivah

It is a mitzvah to set up a tombstone or memorial marker—a *matzeivah*—in memory of the dead.[52] The same principles of simplicity and dignity that govern the choice of coffins (see page 70) should govern the choice of tombstones.

Tombstone dedications or unveilings are not required by Jewish tradition. However, it has become a common and praiseworthy practice for a family to go to the cemetery together at some time after the monument or marker is set in place for a consecration service. This service may be held after *sh'loshim* (see page 77) or on or before the date of the first *yahrzeit*. Common practice is to do it approximately eleven months after the funeral. The dedication

---

52. The custom of erecting a monument (*matzeivah*) over a grave is an ancient one (see Genesis 35:20 and II Samuel 18:18), but it did not become normative in Judaism until the Middle Ages. A great thirteenth-century Spanish authority, Rabbi Solomon Adret, prescribed the use of a *matzeivah* as a way of honoring the dead. But much earlier tradition disagrees; "Rabbi Simeon ben Gamliel taught: 'We need not erect monuments for the righteous; their accomplishments are their memorials'" (*B'reishit Rabbah* 82:11).

service may be read by members of the family. A suggested service for "Consecration of a Memorial" can be found in *On the Doorposts of Your House*, pages 198–205.

When is the right time to visit the graves of deceased relatives?

כְּבוֹד הַמֵּת

K'vod HaMeit

It is customary to visit the graves of loved ones before the High Holy Days. This is part of the mitzvah of *kavod hameit,* honoring the dead. It is, however, inappropriate to visit graves on Sabbaths or festivals. Some people will visit at other times, for example, on a *yahrzeit* or on another occasion when the person is especially missed, such as their birthday or anniversary.

What is the best way to pay tribute to the values of the deceased?

The mitzvah of *tzedakah* in their name may be used as an appropriate way to honor their memory. Depending on its means, the family may establish such a lasting memorial in the form of a significant act of *tzedakah*.

CHAPTER FIVE

What Is a Mitzvah?

This section approaches the question "What is a mitzvah?" from multiple perspectives. Each of the first four essays on mitzvah that follow was written by a rabbi and past leader of the Reform Movement for whom mitzvah was a way of life. Although none of these four great rabbinic leaders are still with us today, but all of their legacies live on in writings such as these.

In introducing them, however, it is necessary to explain that Jewish tradition makes a distinction between *mitzvot bein adam La-Makom*—commandments between a person and God—and *mitzvot bein adam lachaveiro*—commandments between one person and another. The former category includes all those mitzvot related to the observance of Sabbaths, festivals, and the life cycle, that is, the *ritual* aspects of Judaism; the latter includes such mitzvot as "You shall love your neighbor as yourself," "You shall not oppress the stranger," "The wages of an employee may not remain unpaid overnight," that is, *ethics*.

Jewish tradition does not identify one mitzvah or one group of mitzvot as more important than another. The devout Jew observes both ethical and ritual mitzvot. In fact, it is often difficult to distinguish between the two. For example, what mitzvah could be more elaborately ritualistic than the Passover seder, with its myriad details? But the purpose of the seder is to teach a supreme ethical principle: that God created us to be free. Is the observance of Passover, then, a ritual or an ethical mitzvah?

The purpose of this book is to help Jews make *Jewish* decisions, to give their lives *Jewish* depth and character; as such it deals primarily, though not exclusively, with ritual mitzvot. But given that the laws of ethical conduct are basic to Judaism—or, as Rabbi Akiva said

of "Love your neighbor," it is a *k'lal gadol,* a "supreme principle"—
Rabbi Arthur J. Lelyveld (*z"l*) was invited to write the essay "Mitzvah: The Larger Context." That "larger context," for Rabbi Lelyveld
(*z"l*), is "action in the world in behalf of human rights, justice, and
peace." To publish a book on the mitzvot of Judaism without some
reference to its ethics would be unthinkable.

The essays of Rabbis Roland B. Gittelsohn (*z"l*), David Polish (*z"l*),
and Herman E. Schaalman (*z"l*) are concerned primarily with the
source of the mitzvot. Each of them urgently prescribes the performance of mitzvot as a means of enriching one's personal and family
life and contributing to the perpetuation of Judaism, but each comes
to that urgency from a different place. Each suggests that a mitzvah—
commandment—must derive from a *m'tzaveh*—commander (or, one
who commands)—but each defines that *m'tzaveh* differently.

Rabbi Schaalman hears the voice of the commanding God as the
m'tzaveh behind each mitzvah; "it all depends on whether I am
ready to live my life in relationship to God, in response to God, in my
acceptance of God's being Commander and of me as God's covenant
partner." Rabbi Polish apprehends the mitzvot through the history
and shared experience of the Jewish people: "When we perform one
of the many life-acts known as mitzvot . . . what was only a moment
in Jewish history becomes eternal in Jewish life."

Rabbi Gittelsohn's essay is shorter than the others and is
actually a naturalist commentary on the Schaalman and Polish essays and should be read along with them. Gittelsohn too, posits a
m'tzaveh as the source of mitzvot and speaks of historic encounters
between this *m'tzaveh* and the Jewish people, but he defines the
m'tzaveh as "the Spiritual Energy, Essence, Core, or Thrust of the
universe, not a discrete Supernatural Being."

Rabbis Gittelsohn, Lelyveld, and Schaalman wrote their essays for
the earlier edition of this book; Rabbi Polish's essay is a reworking of
the introductory essays that he wrote along with Rabbi Frederic A.
Doppelt (*z"l*) for *A Guide for Reform Jews* (New York, 1957). The inclusion of the Polish essay serves as a tribute, not only to the authors
of that pioneering attempt to bring Reform Jews to lives consecrated

by mitzvot, but to all those rabbis who have written guides for their congregations or for wider Jewish audiences. Many of these works were consulted in the preparation of this volume; we are grateful to all those colleagues who worked so diligently that "you shall remember to observe all My commandments and to be holy to your God" (Numbers 15:40).

While the four essayists come to mitzvot from different directions, all would agree that a Jewish life devoid of mitzvot is a pale shadow of what it might be and that mitzvot "represent the difference between talking or philosophizing about Judaism and *living it*" (Gittelsohn). Some readers will prefer one approach; some will prefer another. Such diversity of views is not new in Judaism. "For three years there was a dispute between the schools of Shammai and of Hillel. Then a heavenly voice proclaimed: *Both are the words of the living God!*" (JT *B'rachot* 1:7).

THESE FIRST FOUR ESSAYS are followed by four additional essays by contemporary rabbinic leaders who serve the Reform Movement today. They offer new ideas about mitzvah and how we might engage with the concept of mitzvot in the contemporary world.

Rabbi Aaron Panken's essay is based on a distinction between mitzvah and halachah that he learned from Professor Michael Chernick. The mitzvah is "eternal, inflexible, and unchanging," and halachah is the working out of how the mitzvah is to be observed. The mitzvah as stated in the Torah does not necessarily explain how it is to be observed. Its precise observance is developed by the rabbis through discussion and debate. This is an ongoing process that can alter the way a mitzvah is observed as time and circumstances change. Rabbi Panken uses the mitzvah of procreation as an example to demonstrate the nature of the halachic process, beginning with the Talmudic Sages and continuing to our own time. The observance of mitzvot is an act of personal faith that allows us to partake in the eternal and live meaningful Jewish lives.

Rabbi Dr. Rachel S. Mikva connects mitzvot not to authority but to relationships. She retranslates *mitzvah* as "attachment, companionship, joining together" based on an Aramaic root that is identical to the Hebrew root *m-tz-h*. By performing mitzvot, we engage with both the narrative of the Jewish people and in our individual narratives. She offers three powerful stories about individuals who learn the meaning of mitzvot by understanding their lives as covenant relationships.

Rabbi A. Brian Stoller also begins with the concept of relationship. He analogizes the mitzvot to the obligations that come from our human relationships. We know what our beloved wants us to do, and as long as it does not violate a core personal principle, we choose to do it. It is the same with our relationship with God. Obligation and autonomy are perfectly compatible. He offers the examples of three core Jewish concepts—*t'filah* (prayer), *kashrut* (dietary practice), and *kiddushin* (marriage)—as demonstrations of how mitzvot work.

Rabbi Amy Scheinerman sees mitzvot as the paving stones on the Jewish path through life. She offers a critique of the legal paradigm that has dominated Judaism and turns to the legal scholar Robert Cover, who sees law as the "universe of meanings, values, and rules, embedded in stories." She then offers three stories to illustrate how the new paradigm might work. At the end she turns to the concept of relationships to family, friends, God, and the Jewish community and suggests that rather than "commandment," we understand mitzvah as "that which enhances and enriches our important relationships."

All eight of these perspectives on mitzvah form a rich dialogue about a complex idea. Mitzvah is a challenging but core Jewish concept that can bring deep meaning to our personal and communal lives. As you make your way through these eight explorations from our recent past and present, perhaps one will spark a meaningful connection.

*A Legacy Selection
of Interpretations
from Our Reform Past*

WHAT IS A MITZVAH *89*

RABBI HERMAN E. SCHAALMAN *z"l*

The Divine Authority of the Mitzvah

WHY SHOULD I perform mitzvot? What does it mean to say, "A commandment, a mitzvah, has been given to me"? Who commands? Who has the authority to summon me to do or not to do a given thing, sometimes even at a given time?

Some would say, "This is our tradition, the Jewish way." And while, obviously, some are satisfied thus to accept this tradition and, more or less unquestioningly, to insert themselves into its chain, others will ask, "Who started this tradition? Who first accepted the mitzvot? How did it all begin?"

Some might answer these questions by explaining that mitzvot are the peculiar way by which the Jewish people created and expressed its specific, unique style of life. In this view the mitzvot are the customs, the laws, the directives, which Jews have formulated from the beginning in much the same way that similar religious folkways appear in other cultures and among other groups. According to this view, the authority of the "commandment" resides in the *people*. As long as I am a member of my people, as long as I identify as a Jew, the "commandments" of my people apply to me and are the most obvious and effective demonstration of my belonging, of my identity as a Jew.

Were the Jews a people like any other people, then this would be a sufficient, a good answer. What is puzzling, though, is that these "customs" and "folkways" are called mitzvot, commandments. The Hebrew vocabulary is rich in terms that could have said it in other ways. There are terms such as *minhag*, "custom," or *derech eretz*, "the way things are done," and others. Why would the Jewish people have chosen the term *mitzvah*?

The word, as well as the history of our people as stated in the

Torah, points to a different answer. A mitzvah—commandment—comes from a *m'tzaveh*, a commander. In our case, indisputably, that Commander was God, first by way of Moses and then by way of prophets and rabbis, the spiritual descendants of Moses.

Of course, this answer immediately raises a host of other questions. What do we mean by stating that God is Commander, *M'tzaveh?* How does God command? Does God "speak"? How did Moses or others "hear"? Why *these* commandments as found in Torah and later tradition and not others?

Revelation, for that is what we are talking about, is a mystery. The character of a mystery, its very essence, precludes our ability to describe and analyze it with precision, in clearly stated detail. If we could so understand and describe it, it would no longer be a mystery. There is something impenetrable about a mystery, something that ultimately defies our human efforts at understanding in ordinary, day-to-day terms.

And yet, at the same time, we are fascinated and almost compelled to say something about it. And so we use ordinary, everyday words to hint at the impenetrable, to point toward, though never define, the mystery. And then we say "God speaks" and "man hears."

We should not forget, though sometimes we do, that we use the phrases "God speaks" and "man hears" in an approximate, vague, allusive, and nondefinitive way. Only when we forget are we misled into thinking that God speaks as we do (what language? Hebrew?) and that those who hear God do so as we hear each other (are there sound waves coming from God?).

Language is the problem here. We use terms such as "speaks" and "hears" when talking of God in the same manner as we do when talking of humans. We apply them to the mystery of encounter with God, to the unique and rare moments when a given person and the Divine Presence "meet," without making due allowance for the essentially different use and meaning of these words when they are applied to the mystery of revelation.

God becomes the "Speaker," the "Commander," the *M'tzaveh*, because Moses, in his extraordinary nearness to God, thus understood, thus interpreted, thus "heard," the impact and meaning of God's presence. God is *M'tzaveh*—Commander—because Moses experienced himself as *m'tzuveh* —commanded, summoned, directed. And this is why Moses transmitted what he "heard," why he expressed the meaning of God's presence in the mitzvot, the commandments to the people at Sinai and to their descendants ever after. This is why the Torah is both *Torat Adonai*, "God's Torah," and *Torat Mosheh*, "Moses's Torah."

This is why the Talmud can say, *Dibrah Torah bilshon b'nei adam*, "Torah speaks human language." Hebrew is a human language, like all languages. Torah, both written and oral, is a collection of human documents flowing out of the encounter of God and man, flowing out of the mystery of revelation. Torah is the recording by men in their language, their concepts, their ability to express and to articulate, what God's "coming down" (Exodus 19:20), God's making God's self present, means.

Why do we do mitzvot? Why should we do mitzvot? Because we are the descendants of those ancestors, the children of those parents who said at Sinai, *Naaseh v'nishma*, "We will faithfully do" (Exodus 24:7). All authentic Judaism until now has so understood itself, has so acted and so handed it on to hitherto faithful new generations. Thus the Divine Presence waits for us, and we for It. Thus the commandment comes to us in our time, asking to be heard, understood, and done.

Wouldn't we, then, have to do all of them? Why do non-Orthodox Jews not keep all the mitzvot? What entitles anyone to make selections? First off, no one, not even the most meticulous and strictly observant Jew, keeps "all" of the mitzvot as found in the Written and Oral Torah. Traditional Jewish authority, after the destruction of the Temple and the Diaspora, declared major categories of mitzvot to be inoperative. The scope of commandments, even for the most traditional Jews, has shrunk, for all practical purposes, to mitzvot concerning worship, learning, family life, kashrut, acts of human concern, and so on. But even within this shrunken perimeter, there is room for variant interpretations, even disagreement and conflicting opinions. This is one of the characteristics and undoubted virtues of the Jewish lifestyle.

It is built into the very definition and basic assumption of a mitzvah that it is the human response to the "Commanding Presence of God." That response is not, and cannot be, invariably the same. It depends on circumstances. It is not automatic. That response to the commanding God should never be altogether unthinking, routine. To be a genuine response of the person to God, it needs to take account of the condition, capacity, responsiveness, of the commanded one, that is, me. I cannot respond like an automaton, every time the same way. Nor should I be expected to. I must make my response freely, "with all my heart, with all my soul, and with all my might" (Deuteronomy 6:5). This means, surely, that I should not be negligent or devoted only to self-gratification. Such an attitude would surely indicate unwillingness to be "commanded." It would signify my withdrawal from mitzvah and from the *M'tzaveh*, the commanding God.

To be commanded—to "faithfully do"—must engage me, the doer, as what I am and can do and will do at the moment when the mitzvah confronts me or I seek it. There are times when I cannot or will not do the commandment, and I will know it and bear the consequences, perhaps standing in need of *t'shuvah* (repentance). And there will be mitzvot through which my forebears found themselves capable of responding to the commanding God that are no longer adequate or possible for me, just as there will be new mitzvot through which I or my generation will be able to respond that my ancestors never thought of.

Finally it all depends on whether I am ready to live my life in relationship to God, in response to God, in my acceptance of God's being Commander and of me as God's covenant partner, giving life to the *b'rit*—the covenant—by my mitzvah response. And while I have and retain the freedom of choosing my specific means of response at a given moment, the essential fact of my life will be my intention to respond. And once my feet are set on this road, then even what at one time appears opaque and incapable of eliciting my response may do so at another time. The number of mitzvot I thus choose to perform is not nearly as important as is the fullness of my awareness and intention, for it is likely that in time I may hear the authentic "voice of God" in many more mitzvot than at first I could have imagined.

The difficult, the decisive, step is the first one, to place yourself into the covenant with the commanding God. Thereafter, your own integrity and the joy of fulfillment will move you along the way. The important step is the first one. Therefore, begin!

RABBI DAVID POLISH *z"l*

History as the Source of the Mitzvah[1]

THE OBSERVANCE OF MITZVOT reflects a Jewish conception of history. This conception is composed of two elements. The first consists of historical events of which we are reminded by specific practices. The second consists of an outlook upon human events and the world that is embodied in a system of conduct and discipline, individual as well as corporate.

Mitzvot are related to historic experiences in which the Jewish people sought to apprehend God's nature and God's will. They are to be observed not because they are divine fiats, but because something happened between God and Israel, and the same something continues to happen in every age and land. Note the words of blessing preceding the performance of a mitzvah: *asher kid'shanu b'mitzvotav, v'tzivanu,* "who hallows us with mitzvot, commanding us." Mitzvot sanctify the Jewish people because they mark points of encounter by the Jewish people with God. They are enjoined upon us because through them we perpetuate memories of the encounters and are sustained by those memories. Since they are so indigenous to us, they are incumbent primarily upon us, the Jewish people, and they constitute the singularity of the Jewish religion.

Mitzvot thus emerge from the womb of Jewish history, from a series of sacred encounters between God and Israel. When we perform one of the many life-acts known as mitzvot to remind ourselves of one of those moments of encounter, what was only episodic becomes epochal, and what was only a moment in Jewish history becomes eternal in Jewish life.

---

1. A more complete development of Rabbi Polish's (*z"l*) concept of mitzvah can be found in *A Guide for Reform Jews* by F. Doppelt and D. Polish (New York: Bloch, 1957), pages 12–27.

Mitzvot are rooted in the biblical declaration "It shall be a sign for all time between Me and the people of Israel " (Exodus 31:17). Mitzvot are "signs" of the covenant, affirmed and reaffirmed through the ages at various turning points in which Jewish existence stood in the balance. Out of these turning points came hallowed insights, pointing to the pivotal moment and fashioning the mitzvah marking it. Thus, the Chanukah lights, marking Israel's rededication after near extinction. Thus, *milah* (circumcision), which began with Abraham and was invoked with special intensity during critical periods in Jewish history.

Moments in the life of the individual Jew are intimately related to Israel's historic career. To be sure, they are infused with the most intense kind of personal meaning, but they are at the same time bound up with the experiences of the people. Thus the mitzvot around birth, *milah*, naming, education, marriage, and death take on added meaning because in each case the individual is made conscious of his own role in Jewish history. *Milah* renews the covenant into which the individual enters with God and with all the generations of Israel who have been committed to a specific historical destiny. It is into that covenant relationship that the Jew of every generation reenters when personally participating in the mitzvah of *milah*. The *b'rit milah* service says it quite clearly: "to bring him into the covenant of our father Abraham." The same principle applies to the mitzvah of eating matzah on Pesach. It marks the encounter of our people with the God of freedom at the turning point in our history when we broke the shackles of Egyptian bondage. And it makes us sensitive to the modern bondages of which Egypt is a paradigm.

Jewish observance depends on the triune and inextricable encounter of Israel with God, Israel with the world, and Israel with its own destiny, and from this encounter it derives its meaning. It is the cryptic symbolism whereby we relive Jewish history and contribute to its continuity. This symbolism is predicated upon the summons to Israel to remember—to remember the roots of its being. The call to remembrance—*zachor, v'zacharta*—is as vehement and as consistent as any other imperative evoked by the Bible. Thus the *Kiddush* for

Shabbat and the festivals makes its demand on our memories of the Exodus.

K'dushah (sanctity) and mitzvah are vital components of this historical perception. Without them Jewish observance can have no real meaning. In the indispensable rubric *asher kid'shanu b'mitzvotav* are embodied the awareness of the inherent sanctity of Jewish existence and the divine imperative under which Jews live and to which they are subject. It is surely significant that so many Jewish observances are called by derivatives of the word *kadosh—Kiddush, Kaddish, kiddushin, K'dushah—*and God is referred to as *HaKadosh Baruch Hu,* "the Blessed Holy One."

It cannot be stressed too strongly that the observance of any particular mitzvah is a symbol of, and points to, a higher truth. Some symbols, because of their overpowering hold on us, endure; others change. Some fall into desuetude; new ones come into being. Thus, there is bound to emerge a compelling symbolism and observance that will someday speak to our people of the twin events of twentieth-century Judaism: the Holocaust and the establishment of Israel—catastrophe and rebirth. This new symbolism will capture the essential meaning of those events, a meaning that is fraught with the very elements that informed the Exodus and every one of its counterparts in our history—the presence of God in history, the struggle by Israel to preserve its being, and the confrontation of Israel with the world.

Jewish observance also reflects Judaism's moral verdict on history, a verdict that is hopeful, but also implacable in its redemptive expectations within history. This attitude and its counterpart are reflected in the second era of Christian-Jewish history. In 410 Rome was sacked by the Goths. At about the same time, the Jerusalem Talmud was completed and the Patriarchate came to an end. Each of these turning points represented a challenge and a response that Christianity and Judaism faced and dealt with in disparate ways. Christianity responded with Augustine's "City of God," which attempts to interpret history in terms of negation. Judaism responded by establishing a panoramic code of living within the structure of society and this life.

Augustine's view of society is predicated upon man's sinful and corrupt nature, from which there can be no earthly escape. The Talmudic response to the challenge of adversity is conscious of social corruption. Yet it is essentially resistant and pragmatic, and it is symbolized in a complex regimen of conduct. The regimen may no longer fully minister to our needs, but its underlying affirmation, that the incursions of evil in the world are to be met by a strategy of collective moral discipline and conduct, is as valid today as ever. The self-imposed discipline of observance, to which the Jew submits as a sacred mitzvah, thus becomes a symbol of the commitment of our faith and of our people to the unending struggle to enthrone God in the world within the bounds of human history. It is also a sign of the Jew's commitment to the covenant, which each generation renews and which each Jew reenacts in the regimen of Jewish living. By this discipline we not only renew the covenant, but we *choose* to renew it. We transcend time and stand with Abraham and with our ancestors at Sinai, to play our part in helping to perfect the world under the kingdom of God.

Finally, the mitzvah enabled the Jewish people to live creatively in cataclysmic times. Mitzvah was the defiant response of Jews to efforts at crushing their spirit. It helped preserve the Jew as a person, and it helped preserve the people. Together with all humanity, we are moving through apocalyptic times that may additionally test not only our people's *capacity* to endure but our *will* to endure as Jews. It would be an overstatement to say that mitzvot will guarantee our survival, but it can be said that our individual and collective decision to persist as Jews will be aided by cultivating a life of mitzvot.

Because of the apocalyptic nature of our times, mitzvot will also strengthen our resolve to retain our humanity and our moral strength when the foundations of the world are shaking. Many of the certainties of the past are shattered. The very future of civilization has become problematic. Mitzvot are our link with antiquity and eternity, both of which have enabled us to survive apocalypse before. We are called upon to be in the world. Mitzvot enable us momentarily to transcend the world and, strengthened, to return to it, as we must.

RABBI ROLAND B. GITTELSOHN *z"l*

Mitzvah without Miracles

WHAT CAN MITZVAH MEAN to a modern Jew who is a religious naturalist? Perhaps a prior question should be: what is a religious naturalist? Briefly, he or she is a person who believes in God but asserts that God inheres within nature and operates through natural law. A religious naturalist perceives God to be the Spiritual Energy, Essence, Core, or Thrust of the universe, not a discrete Supernatural Being.

What, then, can mitzvah mean to such an individual? Certainly more than custom or folkway, more than social covenant or mores. Mitzvah, by very definition, must be cosmically grounded; it must possess empyreal significance. For the religious naturalist, as for all believing, practicing Jews, in order to have mitzvah—that which has been commanded—there must be a *m'tzaveh*, a commander. That commander, moreover, needs to be more than human ingenuity or convenience.

In the mainstream of Jewish tradition through the centuries, this posed no great problem. The *m'tzaveh* was God. A mitzvah was God's will. It had to be performed because God wanted it. It may have made sense to the human mind or not; these things were not important. It had to be done, plainly and simply, because God had commanded it.

But how can an Energy or Essence, a Core or a Thrust, command? For the religious naturalist, who is the *m'tzaveh*? Answer: reality itself. Or, more precisely, the physical and spiritual laws that govern reality. Mitzvot must be observed because only by recognizing and conforming to the nature of their environment can human beings increase the probability of their survival in any meaningful way. Mitzvot are not man-made; they inhere within the universe. Our

Jewish mystics suspected this long ago. Mordecai Kaplan has summarized the view of the *Zohar* as holding that "mitzvot are part of the very process whereby the world came into being."

I agree with David Polish (see page 97) that mitzvot are binding upon us "because something happened between God and Israel, and the same something continues to happen in every age and land." What makes me a religious naturalist is interpreting the "something" to be a historic encounter between the Jewish people and the highest Spiritual Reality human beings have ever known or felt. No other people has been so persistent as ours in seeking that Reality and its moral imperatives.

It is easy to illustrate the cosmic nature of mitzvot on the level of physical reality. The universe is so constructed that, if I wish to survive, I must have adequate oxygen, nourishment, and exercise. God "wants" me to breathe fresh air, ingest healthful foods, and regularly move my muscles. These, therefore, are mitzvot.

No less is true in the realm of ethical mitzvot. Honesty is a compelling mitzvah. Human nature (which is, after all, nature at its highest level of development) is such that in the long run the individual or the social group that consistently flaunts the dictates of honesty risks disaster. The struggle for freedom is a compelling mitzvah. Ultimately only those who cherish their own freedom and grant it to others can achieve happiness. To love is a compelling mitzvah. Only the person who is capable of giving and receiving love will ever be fulfilled. These things are true, not because we want them to be and not because they were decreed by a human legislature, but because they are ineluctable aspects of reality. Hence the recognition, acceptance, and observance of them constitute mitzvot.

Most of the mitzvot spelled out in this guide, however, deal with ritual observance rather than physical law or ethics. Are they, too, related to cosmic reality? In a less obvious but equally binding sense than the physical or moral imperatives suggested above, yes. Human nature is such that we need to express our emotions and ideals with our whole bodies, not just our tongues. We need also to be visually and kinetically reminded of our noblest values and stimulated to pursue them. As otherwise lonely and frightened individuals, we need common practices and observances that bind us into meaningful and supportive groups. All of which adds up to the fact that we need ritual as something more than social luxury or convenience. For us as Reform Jews, a particular ritual may not be mitzvah. But the need for a pattern of such rituals, this—because it grows out of and satisfies our very basic nature as human beings—is mitzvah. And this we desperately need.

A concrete example at this point may be more instructive than further paragraphs of theoretical exposition. The most elaborate— and perhaps the most valuable—mitzvah in our tradition is the seder ceremony. A supernaturalistically oriented Jew celebrates at his seder God's miraculous intervention in nature and history.

The seder means no less, however, to the religiously naturalistic Jew, who rejects miracles. Plugging into centuries of his people's tradition as well as its unique pursuit of freedom, he visually, audibly, and dramatically commemorates that pursuit and rededicates himself to it. His *m'tzaveh* is triune: his very special human need to be free, both as a person and a Jew; his equally human need to augment speech with memory and motion in reinforcement of his highest values; and his specifically Jewish need to identify with his people's destiny.

Permeating our theological differences is the common understanding that God, however divergent our interpretation, is the Core Spiritual Essence of reality. In this sense, God is the *m'tzaveh* of the religiously naturalistic Jew, who eschews the supernatural not only in theological speculation but also in his approach to mitzvot. He responds naturalistically to his own essence and to that of his universal setting. Mitzvot for him represent the difference between talking or philosophizing about Judaism and *living* it. They bind him firmly, visibly, to his people and his tradition. They speak to him imperatively because he is Jewish and wants to remain so.

RABBI ARTHUR J. LELYVELD *z"l*

Mitzvah: The Larger Context

THE WORD *mitzvah* has been used by Jews for thousands of years with different levels of meaning, ranging all the way from the broad ethical injunction "You shall be holy for I, the Eternal your God, am holy" (Leviticus 19:2) to what in popular usage is a simple good deed: "Please go see your grandmother; it would be a mitzvah." But there is a core of steel in the word when used in its classic sense that is not there when it is used to mean an act of benevolence or a simple ritual act. The word *Mitzvah*, writ large and uttered reverently, means an act that I perform because God requires it of me.

The different levels of usage of the word *mitzvah* pose a problem for the liberal Jew who takes his Judaism seriously. In the view of our Orthodox brethren, God demands the fulfillment of all the commandments, both negative and positive, as recorded in the Torah and as seen through the spectrum of the oral tradition and its development down through the ages. For the strictly traditional Jew, the Talmud and the great medieval codes, as interpreted by authoritative rabbinic scholars, define what a Jew is expected to do. From the moment he opens his eyes in the morning to the moment he closes them at night, and to the moment that he closes them on his deathbed, his conduct is prescribed. But how do we liberals discern the divine demand? How do we train ourselves to respond with mitzvah (the deed) to mitzvah (the demand)?

We liberal Jews read Scripture not as the literal word of God, but as the work of members of the people of Israel seeking to *understand* the demand of God. Once we approach our Bible within that frame of reference, we necessarily become selective, for there are points in Scripture at which humans have broken through to an understanding of the highest, while there are also points that preserve primitive practices, anachronisms, or injunctions that long ago became obsolete.

The solution of our difficulty lies in the very fact that we use the word *mitzvah* in two distinct ways. We talk about specific mitzvot, and we also speak of Mitzvah in a more generalized sense, as enjoining upon us a certain attitude toward our fellows. Abraham Heschel makes clear this comprehensive meaning of mitzvah when he quotes Rabbi Nachman of Bratzlav, the great Chasidic sage, as having said, "Every act done in agreement with the will of God is mitzvah"; and George Foot Moore, the great Christian expert on the thinking of our Rabbis of the first and second centuries, says that the word *mitzvah* is most frequently used as meaning not a specific commandment, but any *particular* opportunity "to fulfill the comprehensive duty of man to his fellowman." Thus to do a mitzvah is to act in accord with God's will, in accord with God's demand upon humankind.

From this point of view, our liberal picking and choosing among the mitzvot makes sense. We are bidden to ask the questions "When does God speak to us? When does God make demands upon us?" In the answers to these questions we may find the larger Mitzvot—*Mitzvah* written here with a capital *M*.

Small-*m* mitzvot—the performance of ritual acts—have an aesthetic and affective function. They both beautify and enhance by religious drama the moral values and the ideals of our heritage. They become a structure on which the preservation of our people's tradition and its continuity may rest. We select the mitzvot we will perform, we shape our folkways, change our music, revise our prayers, eliminate customs, and add other and new customs. But Mitzvah is not the product of our human social engineering. Mitzvah is God's demand issuing in moral and spiritual values. Ceremonial mitzvot with their folk associations, their customs, and their symbolic objects and actions are the carrier of the values, the structural framework for the people's task of transmission. But large-*M* Mitzvah is the enduring essence to which the structure of small *m* testifies and pays obeisance.

This is a distinction made by the prophets of Israel as far back as the eighth century before the Common Era. When Amos proclaimed the words "I hate, I despise your feasts . . . but let justice well up as waters and righteousness as a mighty stream" (5:21, 5:24), he was making a distinction between formal adherence to practices of ritual observance and the response to the great Demand of God. When Isaiah cried out, "To what purpose is the multitude of your sacrifices unto Me? . . . Who asked you to trample My courts? . . . Cease to do evil, learn to do well, seek justice, relieve the oppressed" (1:11–12, 1:16–17), and when Micah summarized God's demand, "Wherewith shall I come back before the Eternal and bow before God on high? . . . Will the Eternal be pleased with thousands of rams or with . . . rivers of oil? . . . You have been told, O man, what is good and what the Eternal requires of you: only to do justly and to love mercy and to walk humbly with your God" (6:6–8), they were seeking the inner meaning of Mitzvah, the demand of God.

Contemporary, secular value-philosophy also supports this distinction when it recognizes the essential relationship between value and the enduring Demand to which we must bring a commitment. Henry Margenau tells us (*New Knowledge in Human Values*, ed. Abraham Maslow, 1959) that values are arbitrary choices unless they are related to "command." For example, life has no "value" to a person who is earnestly committed to its destruction, as in war. But Margenau says, "If you are committed to the prior maxim expressed in the Decalogue, *Thou shalt not fall*, then the value of life follows as a theorem follows from a postulate."

So it is with honesty, veracity, friendship, love of humankind, and every other ideal. They receive their "value" from a command, a directive to which the individual is committed. In other words, there can be no structure of values or of moral choice without Mitzvah.

In the last analysis, liberalism cannot escape its commitment to the supreme right and obligation of decision that is reserved to the individual soul. It is true that this makes the individual the ultimate authority as to what is Mitzvah and what is not Mitzvah. "I must distinguish in my innermost being between what is commanded me and what is not commanded me," says Martin Buber. But the awesomeness of this existential responsibility is mitigated for us as Jews by the fact that we stand in the midst of a covenant community and that we are bidden to hear the Mitzvah as informed and committed individuals within the informed and committed community.

Mitzvah, therefore, speaks differently to us than it did to our great-great-grandfathers. Cut off from the larger world, they retained the ideal of humankind's ultimate perfection, in their liturgy, in their aspirations, and in their obligation under the covenant *l'takein olam*—to perfect the world. The only task that was within their capacity as Jews was to be faithful, to observe 613 mitzvot and to practice *kiddush hachayim*, the effort to make the Divine Presence felt in the world. But the quarrels among kings and princes, the violence and the cruelty, the servitude of the peasants, were all part of the world of the gentiles. Even when our forebears recognized that the most stringent troubles were the troubles that affected *both* Israel and the world, they could not but feel that the only action required of them was personal witness and prayer.

We, in contrast to these ancestors, are part of the larger world. This is the precious and unhappy result of emancipation. We are participant, in destiny and in responsibility, with all people. We cannot even pretend to be building God's Kingdom by the faithful witness of personal discipline. For us, the demand of God that challenges us to compassion and to respect for the divine image in every human being must as Mitzvah eventuate in the Mitzvah that is performance: action in the world in behalf of human rights, justice, and peace.

This conception of the role of Mitzvah is not alien to our tradition. The midrash tells us that "the mitzvot were given to Israel in order to purify humankind" (*Vayikra Rabbah* 13:3). These particular and specific commands were given for a universal purpose—the perfection of *all* human beings. When we understand Mitzvah in this sense, we can begin to say what is expected of us as modern Jews. We are entitled to expect that we will act, that we will perform the Mitzvah, in response to the divine Mitzvah—the deed in response to the demand—and that we will do so as Jews within the context of the three-thousand-year experience of our people.

The ancient aphorism that tells us what it is that sustains the entire world also tells us how to be a Jew today. "The world stands upon three things: *Torah*, study; *avodah*, worship; and *g'milut chasadim*, deeds of loving-kindness." Under these three categories we can still bracket the primary Mitzvot and what a Jew must *do*.

Torah means that we will become part of the three-thousand-year experience that shaped our Jewish value-stance, by studying with our people, by devoting some part of our time to continuous Jewish learning. This is the foundation.

Avodah means that we will refine our sense of our people's aspirations by worshiping with the community, by practicing joyfully the richest of its distinctive mores: the *simchah* of Sukkot, the pride of Chanukah, the avowal of freedom in Pesach, the acceptance of the Torah and the covenant in Shavuot, and the weekly rededication and purification of soul in Shabbat.

G'milut chasadim means that we will concern ourselves with the needs of others, of our people and of our world. This response of loving-kindness is commanded and is Mitzvah. The traditional mitzvot of hospitality, concern for the sick and the bereaved, and the demand that we meet the human needs of the dispossessed are all fragments of the Mitzvah of *g'milut chasadim*.

The Jew must *act*. The Ten Commandments are not enough. As real Jews, we must actively love our neighbor, seek justice, and struggle against those practices and prejudices that stifle the image of God in human beings. These, as Leviticus 19 clearly shows, are the ways in which we demonstrate that we are *k'doshim*, reflections of the divine presentness.

Selections of Contemporary
Voices on Mitzvah

RABBI AARON PANKEN, PhD

Mitzvah and Halachah
A Dynamic Tension

BASED ON AN IMPORTANT distinction developed in the thought of Maimonides (1135–1204, North Africa), my teacher Professor Michael Chernick noted that the Jewish legal system is made up of two core parts: mitzvah and halachah. He defined the difference between them in the following manner:

> The *mitzvah* is the general decision, judgment or law; while the *halachah* is the practical program that actualizes the existence of the *mitzvah*.[1]

This distinction is crucial because it allows Jewish law to weave together a component that is eternal, inflexible, and unchanging—mitzvah—with a component that can grow and adapt to particular times, locales, and situations—halachah. I will attempt to flesh out the implications of this structure for Reform Jews as a way to develop a concept of mitzvah that is relevant and meaningful.

An example can best illustrate the division between these two components. Long before contemplation of the strict definition of these terms arose, the first occurrence of a mitzvah appears quite early on in the Torah, actually in the first chapter of Genesis. God commands Adam and Eve in Genesis 1:28 to procreate and fill the earth with their offspring. The mitzvah is named by the later Rabbis in Aramaic as *pirya v'rivya* (the commandment to "be fruitful and multiply"). Rabbinic tradition sees this mitzvah as applying equally to our edenic forebears as to all later generations, though it takes

---

1. Michael Chernick, "The Distinction between Mitzvah and Halakah in Maimonides' Thought" (Hebrew), *CCAR Journal* (Spring 1997), pages 108–122.

hundreds of years and numerous debates that continue until this day to define the exact parameters of its fulfillment.

In an early attempt to define the halachah, the actualization of this mitzvah, the Mishnah (written ca. 225 CE) shows two important schools, Beit Hillel and Beit Shammai, debating the precise obligations inherent in its observance. The Mishnah says:

> One may not desist from being fruitful and multiplying unless one has children. Beit Shammai say it must be [at least] two sons; Beit Hillel say it must be [at least] one son and one daughter, as it is written "male and female God created them" (Genesis 5:2).[2]

Such an attempt at defining the halachah that derives from this mitzvah is productive, yet instantly incomplete. Immediate questions arise for the Rabbis of this period and thereafter: How long must a couple try to fulfill this mitzvah? Why does the gender of the children matter? What if the couple is unable to bear children? How do divorce, remarriage, or the death of a spouse or a child factor in? How about surrogate parenthood, adoption, and methods of assisted reproduction? One can see, immediately, that the process of developing halachah from mitzvah is complex, incessant, and extraordinarily rich in intellectual breadth. In fact, thousands of pages have been written on the halachah on this mitzvah alone, in an unending chain that stretches back to the very first page of Genesis and forward to the most contemporary decisors from all streams of Judaism in every part of the world.

Reform Judaism can learn much from the dynamic tension built into this example. First, the distinction between halachah and mitzvah implies that the actualization of mitzvot changes radically over time. That is to say, what fulfilling a mitzvah meant to Adam and Eve (if they could even understand such a concept, aside from general questions of historicity) is different from what it meant to Beit Hillel and Beit Shammai, which is different from what it meant to Maimonides, which is different from what it means to us right now. The further implication is that the fulfilling of a particular mitzvah

---

2. *Mishnah Y'vamot* 6:6.

to contemporary Jews of one particular affiliation in one particular community must also differ, and rightfully so, from what it means to others in other places. And yet, the essential terms of the mitzvah as embedded in the Torah do not, in and of themselves, change. With this situation, it becomes incumbent on every generation and every individual in each historical moment to learn the initiating texts that define each mitzvah and to shape its halachic implementation based on the concerns and sensitivities of their own place and time. This becomes an enduring obligation for every Jew, for one cannot observe any mitzvah without learning something about it and contemplating its contemporary application.

Reform Judaism, more than any other movement in Judaism, has been particularly adept at managing what we might call a highly flexible version of this eternal-progressive boundary. We read our sacred texts for what is eternal—in this case the idea that procreating to produce the next generation of the Jewish people is a divinely motivated value we hold dear. And yet, we grapple with real-life constraints, pressures, and principles learned from surrounding culture and from reflecting on the trajectory of our own history, to create an innovative, new halachah for an ever-changing world.

Many Reform Jews term this process "progressive revelation"—the idea that divine revelation was not confined to ancient texts alone, but continues through the ages in a trajectory shaped by new human understandings. If revelation is progressive, then there was not a single moment at Sinai that defined everything to follow. Instead, what we learn from God progresses and changes as we grow in our ability to comprehend the world in new ways shaped by science, philosophy, history, ethics, and other fields of study. Rather than calling outside influences problematic or illegitimate, as some other approaches may, we thoughtfully incorporate them, deeming them to be desirable sources of vital and novel information. The result is a dynamic Judaism built on the eternal commandments that have always been a part of our people's lives, but shaped and improved by the ideas of feminism, GLBT concerns, new approaches to social justice, and a broad and beautiful spectrum of many other contemporary ideas—in short, a beautiful mélange of what is eternal and what is progressive, what is old and what is new, what is long-standing and what is ephemeral.

Philip Roth once famously said that Jews are to history what Eskimos are to snow. By actualizing mitzvot through this process of creating and renewing halachah, we also link ourselves to Jewish history—we insist that we are its extension, its manifestation in the current milieu, and we extend the well-trod paths that our ancestors marked for us, building upon their inspired linkage with God and all those who came before us. But we also creatively merge this history with new ideas and practices. We pair the ancient act of circumcising a son with the more recent ceremony of naming a daughter, to bring our children into a covenant creatively redefined by the ideas of feminist thought; we celebrate a child's coming of age with the long-standing act of reading from the Torah, while we celebrate this achievement in decidedly modern ways with new obligations never before imagined by our ancestors; we sanctify a couple's marriage with words recited regularly for more than a millennium, yet we write marriage contracts that reflect egalitarian sensitivities and, in some cases, even include non-Jews; and we mourn a relative's death with a subtle combination of timeworn Jewish customs and the latest in understanding the psychological process of mourning. In each case, the actions we take are determined along the axis of the eternal-progressive, binding ancient to modern.

At their core, life-cycle mitzvot mark the progression of individuals through their own private timelines, but they also signify far more than that. These acts can bring the wisdom of Jewish history to bear on each and every person in an individualized and spiritually meaningful way. To understand the beauty of individualizing the mitzvot of the Jewish life cycle, one need only watch the way joyous parents speak with reverence of an important familial name given their newly circumcised son; the way a thoughtful bat mitzvah interprets her Torah portion in a manner never before heard in the world; the joyous particularity of a newly wedded couple under the chuppah; or the acts of caring and loving tributes that surround the funeral and days of mourning. In each moment we celebrate or grieve in such manner, we punctuate our time on earth with beauty, gratitude, and reflection that enrich our lives and remind us that we do not simply exist—we grow from stage to stage and revel, as best we can, in being afforded the opportunity to do so.

Great sacred power, however, rests beyond the simple personal sacralizing of the individual timeline of any life. The celebration of Jewish life-cycle events forges a profound link between our lives and the greater continuity of the Jewish people in all times, places, and situations. To circumcise a son is to walk in the footsteps of Abraham our forefather, who brought Isaac into the covenant and is the timeless model for the expectation that rests on every Jewish parent on the eighth day of his or her son's life. To celebrate a bat mitzvah is to reflect on the fact that this celebratory recognition of adulthood for boys extends back into the Middle Ages, yet it was only in 1922 when such a ceremony was first celebrated by the family of a young woman, Judith Kaplan, daughter of the modern Jewish philosopher Mordecai Kaplan. To stand with a bat mitzvah is to know just how far Judaism extends back into the recesses of time and how much it has progressed and developed since the advent of modernity. To marry under a chuppah is to follow the path of the Torah's archetypical Adam and Eve, the first couple of Jewish tradition, whose acts of procreation filled the world with new life. And to mourn a loved one through burial, shivah, sh'loshim, and unveiling is to tread the meaningful communal track of hundreds of generations who expressed their sadness in like manner. Each individual mitzvah we enact in these moments links us, inexorably, to generations past, present, and future, in an unbroken chain of meaning, commitment, and commonality.

In addition to linking us with prior generations, the actualization of mitzvot links us with a God we can never fully comprehend, the source of holiness in the universe whose existence we affirm through acts of faith. If we were to hold ourselves to the standards of science, surely we would abandon these commitments—after all, no comprehensive proof exists of God's existence, let alone our obligation to fulfill commands that have been inscribed in books that may well reflect the wisdom of an inspired people, but contain challenging passages that sometimes contradict modern sensibilities and occasionally lack complete internal coherence. Acting in the face of such legitimate questions makes observing these mitzvot an undeniably meaningful act of personal faith. Actualizing mitzvot through practice allows us to act on our beliefs and affirm that there is deep and ineluctable purpose to our lives that transcends our own ephemeral existence. Beyond simple proof or disproof, in acting we elevate specific values and dedicate our days to making them present in our world.

Mitzvot, then, as developed into their particular halachic outcomes in each generation and community, meaningfully fuse the communal and the personal, the past and the present, the divine and the human. They testify to the continuation of a powerful chain of beliefs and commitments unbroken, though not unaltered, throughout the millennia. As Reform Jews, each time we act in this manner, we forge the next link in that chain and, in so doing, strengthen it and extend it. In connecting us with those links that came before and those links that will one day follow, actualizing mitzvot allows our ephemeral lives to transcend human limitations and to partake in the eternal.

RABBI DR. RACHEL S. MIKVA

Mitzvah

It Begins with Relationship

"The Stories of Which I Am a Part"

It begins with relationship. The Chasidic masters knew this when they reimagined the etymology of *mitzvah*, connecting it to an Aramaic term with the same root. Rather than the Hebrew sense of "commandment," they focused on meanings of attachment, companionship, joining together.[1]

Reform Jewish conversation about mitzvah used to circulate around questions of authority: Since we do not claim that God is the author of Torah, who exactly is the "commander" of the commandment? We have seen that the answer is multiple, fluid, occasionally hidden. I think our question is different now, perhaps: How do my relationships deepen my investment in mitzvah, and how does mitzvah deepen my relationships?

Many Reform Jews who choose to embrace additional mitzvot see them as opportunities to enhance the quality of their individual lives. They unplug for Shabbat. Torah study challenges them to think in new ways and engage in a lifelong course in moral development. A *b'rit* ceremony for their newborn daughter gives them a platform from which to shout for joy. Reading with inner-city kids instills a sense of virtue. Even as the praxis begins to make a claim on them, they see the emergence of a personal sacred discipline: the Rabbinic

---

1. The Aramaic term appears multiple times in the Babylonian Talmud, presenting this range of meaning (e.g., *Bava M'tzia* 28a, *B'rachot* 6b, *Sukkah* 52a, *Bava Batra* 80a). The Chasidic association can be traced back to the Baal Shem Tov, as cited in *Degel Machaneh Ephraim*. Abraham Joshua Heschel also alludes to it in *God in Search of Man* (New York: Farrar, Straus and Giroux, 1976), page 287.

insight "One mitzvah leads to another" (*Pirkei Avot* 4:2) defines a path of self-improvement.

Yes, the key phrase of blessing *asher kid'shanu b'mitzvotav,* "who sanctifies us with commandments," acknowledges that mitzvot open gateways to holiness all around us, providing chances to fall in love with our lives all over again and to draw closer to the person we'd like to see when we look in the mirror. But there is a grand irony in our careful instruction about the root *k-d-sh.* We make sure people understand it is about setting apart for sacred purpose, yet there is nothing that works more consistently to join beings together than sanctifying with mitzvot. It begins with relationship.

Lawrence Kushner, in a captivating little book where he deliberately mistranslates Hebrew words in order to get at something deeper, tells us that *mitzvah* means "response."[2] I think his insight lies at the core of my earlier writing on covenant and commandment:

> It does not matter whether the foundation of our Jewish relationship is a theistic concept of God, an abiding connection with Jewish history and culture, or nurturing a Jewish home; we internalize the claims made on us as mitzvah. As with our other covenantal relationships—as spouses, parents, and children—we know that we will often fall short and still the bond abides. We also know, however, that the relationship grows richer each time we can respond with the fullness of our being: *hineini,* here I am.[3]

The call is especially powerful around life's passages. God's presence saturates the membrane between life and death. Generations of family pack the marrow of our bones. The cells of our body reverberate with the tissue of Jewish history, and there is faith in the ancient wisdom for telling a human story. Judaism excels at investing moments with deep significance. After all, it can take a random day in the weekly calendar and transform it into a palace in time. In the construction and celebration of human becoming, our life-cycle

---

2. Lawrence Kushner, *The Book of Words* (Woodstock, VT: Jewish Lights, 1993), pages 91–94.

3. Rachel S. Mikva, in *Lights in the Forest,* ed. Paul Citrin (New York: CCAR Press, 2014), page 191.

rituals illuminate the passages so we can see the transcendent significance of where we are, where we have been, where we are going—and who is accompanying us on our journey.

Alasdair MacIntyre insists, "I can only answer the question 'What am I to do?' if I can answer the prior question "Of what story or stories do I find myself a part?'"[4] I am part of grand stories that shape my response to mitzvah. Exodus impresses upon my very soul the heart of a stranger and insists that whatever my evolving sense of the Divine, God is invested in human liberation. Sinai, the greatest mythic moment of Jewish religious imagination, establishes my place among this ever-aspiring people, tilling the inexhaustibly rich soil of Torah, straining still to hear the God who never shuts up. But our individual stories, the ones that mark life's passages, best reveal the dynamics of relationship as the nuclear, animating force of mitzvah.

Bat Mitzvah: The Claim of Family

Hugh Kerr cautions, "All wisdom is plagiarism. Only stupidity is original."[5] So as I pressed *b'nei mitzvah* to continue their Jewish education and to increase their sense of response-ability to Judaism, I borrowed trusty truisms as conversation starters. "Becoming bar or bat mitzvah is like getting a driver's license, not a diploma." I'm not sure where I heard that one, but it always caught their attention, eager as they were to reach driving age and get behind the wheel. Or I would invoke Arnold Jacob Wolf's image of walking down the street of Judaism, paved with precious jewels embedded in the stones. Each gem represents a mitzvah: Shabbat, civil rights, kashrut, honoring parents. Our task is to lift up and carry those that we can.[6]

"But why am I even walking down this street?" one too-bright-for-her-own-good student asked. "You tell me," I urged. "Because my

---

4. Alasdair MacIntyre, *After Virtue* (Notre Dame, IN: University of Notre Dame Press, 1984), page 216.

5. Hugh Kerr, "Preacher, Professor, Editor," *Theology Today* 45, no. 1 (1988): page 1.

6. See Wolf's contribution to the *Commentary* collection of Jewish thinkers answering questions of the day in *The Condition of Jewish Belief* (New York: Macmillan, 1966), page 268.

parents dropped me off there." It was a mildly subversive allusion to the fact that her parents were not all that learned or observant in their own lives. At the same time, she correctly identified the claim that the mitzvot had on her: her parents wanted them to mean something in her life.

"I feel Jewish; isn't that enough?" With adolescents, it is always a mighty struggle for me to ask good questions rather than preach. "When? When do you feel Jewish?" She identified the service at which she celebrated becoming a bat mitzvah, the funeral of her grandfather, holy day celebrations with her family. "Don't you see?" I exclaimed. "All those moments are constructed of actions. We are a people of doers."

An unstoppable mini-sermon came pouring out. I spoke of Abraham Joshua Heschel's brilliant charge to take a leap of action, to do more than we understand in order to understand more than we do. "In carrying out a sacred deed, we unseal the wells of faith." Heschel shows how mitzvah weaves us into a fabric of relationship. To do for the sake of Torah unlocks treasures of spiritual meaning. In the "ecstasy of deeds" we come into the presence of God.[7]

In the end we cut a deal. She was firm about leaving religious school but agreed to seek out one additional mitzvah that made her feel like she was making a difference in the world, one that whispered of something she might name as God, one that bound her to the Jewish people, one that she did just because it brought joy. She kept her end of the bargain, and when we checked in together, she reflected how, having begun the journey in response to the claim of family, she deepened her relationship with God, the Jewish people, Torah, the congregation, herself, and the patchwork quilt of humanity. "That was the point, wasn't it?" she asked.

Conversion: The Claim of the Most High

A bright twentysomething woman taught me something I have often shared. Speaking as a medical student, she said that all the selfish

---

7. A paraphrase of Heschel, *God in Search of Man*, pages 282–283.

behaviors of human beings make perfect biological sense. What gave her faith in God was the desire of human beings to be good.

She loved the midrash that tries to explicate the verse "You are beautiful, my darling" (Song of Songs 1:15) through the allegorical lens of God and Israel as lovers. How can the Divine be in thrall to this fragile, flawed creature? What beauty draws God near in intimate relation? On a path of conversion, she found the response of the midrash inspiring: You make yourself beautiful through the doing of mitzvot (*Shir HaShirim Rabbah* 1:63). Each new practice she engaged in made her feel closer to God.

But she did not feel connected to the Jewish people—just the one loving young man she planned to marry . . . and his parents, sometimes. "I am ready to become a Jew, Rabbi, but how do I become Jewish?" I asked her to describe the mitzvot she had been exploring; they all entailed sanctification of the home and mindfulness in daily life. "What about the mitzvot of community—worship, Torah study, singing in the Purim-spiel, or schlepping chairs for a synagogue program?" I suggested. "Then you'll see we were all at Sinai together."

"How about now?" I asked after the wedding. Those things helped, she acknowledged, but the real connection came from the service celebrating her conversion and from the wedding itself. At the service, she gave a brilliant *d'var Torah* on Maimonides's medical ethics (thanks to advice I adopted from Peter Rubenstein, to have Jews-by-choice become expert in a Jewish subject defined as knowing more about it than the rabbi), a congregant came to her with a query. Then as part of the *nisuin* ritual, their Jewish friends "translated" the seven wedding blessings in ways that spoke directly of the couple's relationship, values, and aspirations. "I wrote myself into the story," she said, "or the Jewish people got written into mine."

Reciting *Kaddish*: The Claim of the Jewish People

"525,600 minutes, how do you measure a year in a life?" This line from the musical *Rent* somehow nested in my mind while I was speaking with a man who recently buried his father. The father had been what Nachmanides would have graciously called "a scoundrel with the permission of Torah,"[8] a relatively observant Jew who nonetheless missed the point and managed to be a mediocre human being and a terrible father. The son was struggling with the mitzvah of reciting *Kaddish* for the (almost) year. "Why would I devote a year of my life to honor his memory?" I asked what pushed him to consider it. "Because that's what Jews do." And so he began the journey through loss and healing in the way that Mordechai Kaplan imagined, because of his relationship with the historical civilization of Judaism.

A few weeks in, I received an e-mail. "I'm not a theist, Rabbi. What do you suggest I make of the *Kaddish* prayer?" I responded with several possibilities, including the lovely interpretive rendering by Marge Piercy. It begins:

> Look around us, search above us, below, behind.
> We stand in a great web of being joined together.
> Let us praise, let us love the life we are lent
>   passing through us in the body of Israel.

I thought the emphasis on being woven together as the people of Israel would speak to him. Four months later, he revealed that it was a different line that made him catch his breath each time he read it:

> The past and the dead speak through us.
> We breathe out our children's children, blessing.[9]

"Our youngest son is so much like my father—but transformed into a mensch. It never occurred to me that my father had some hand in that, or that our son is the person my father might have been. I always imagined I had done it all despite him."

What had begun as a duty of the limbs, the mitzvah of reciting *Kaddish* for a deceased parent, ended as a duty of the heart.[10] The great kabbalist Isaac Luria insisted that mitzvot play a role in cosmic

---

8. Nachmanides's commentary on Leviticus 19:2.
9. Marge Piercy, "Kaddish," in *The Art of Blessing the Day* (New York: Knopf, 1999), page 138.
10. Bachya ibn Pakuda (eleventh century, Spain) wrote a work on spiritual ethics frequently translated as *Duties of the Heart*.

repair, each one composing a new harmony that reveals additional sparks of God's infinite light. The idea always seemed compelling, but I generally imagined it through the lens of social justice. Here it was what Kaplan once called "religious poetry in action," the transformative, redemptive power of connecting to forces larger than ourselves.[11] Initially motivated by the claim of Jewish tradition, this man reclaimed relationship with his father.

"525,600 minutes, how do you measure a year in a life? In truths that she learned or in times that he cried, in bridges he burned or the way that she died? . . . Measure your life in love." The closing line of the song used to seem a little simplistic to me. Perhaps I was wrong.

It begins, and ends, with relationship.

---

11. Mordecai Kaplan, *Judaism as a Civilization* (repr., Philadelphia: Jewish Publication Society, 1994), page 434.

RABBI A. BRIAN STOLLER

Mitzvah and Relationship
Honoring Our Beloved's Desires

TWO KEY PRINCIPLES lie at the heart of Reform Judaism. One is our belief that "the Jewish people is bound to God by an eternal *b'rit*, covenant."[1] The other is our commitment to "individual autonomy," the idea that each person has the absolute right to make his or her own religious decisions.

At first look, these two principles appear to contradict each other. On the one hand, saying that we are "bound" by the covenant implies that we are obligated by an external authority to engage in certain religious behaviors. Indeed, classical Judaism views the covenant as a hierarchical relationship in which God gives Israel authoritative mitzvot (usually translated as "commandments"), and we must either comply with them or face consequences for failing to do so. The binding nature of the covenant would therefore seem to limit our personal autonomy.

On the other hand, to be autonomous is to have the unfettered right to determine for ourselves how we will live as Jews. While we have long contended that Reform Jews should engage seriously with the tradition and make informed decisions as we chart our own Jewish paths, we remain insistent that the *individual*—not a book, or the tradition, or even God—is the final authority in his or her own Jewish life. Thus, the traditional definition of mitzvah as "commandment"—from the Latin root *mand*, meaning "to order"—lacks practical meaning for us because we do not subscribe to the view

---

1. CCAR, "A Statement of Principles for Reform Judaism" (Pittsburgh, 1999), s.v. "God," http://ccarnet.org/rabbis-speak/platforms/statement-principles-reform-judaism/.

that religious behavior can be mandatory. This would seem to preclude the possibility of a binding covenant.

How, then, can we say that we as Reform Jews are both completely autonomous *and*, at the same time, bound by the covenant? It only makes sense if we abandon the hierarchical view of the covenant and redefine it in terms that are more compatible with our religious outlook. We can look to the philosopher Martin Buber and contemporary Reform thinkers such as Eugene Borowitz[2] and Elyse Frishman,[3] who suggest that our covenant with God is better understood as a committed and intimate relationship between two beloveds, much like the relationship between spouses, or dear friends, or a parent and a grown child.

In these human relationships, each person is a fully autonomous individual who has the right and the freedom to decide how to relate to the other. Although our beloved may *ask* us to do certain things that are important to her, she cannot *force* us to do them. And yet, if we genuinely love and care for her, we are not inclined to dismiss or ignore her requests. On the contrary, we feel *bound* to try to honor them, even if it is difficult or inconvenient to do so, and even if they are things we would not otherwise choose to do had our beloved not desired them. We feel bound in this way not because we are *ordered* to honor her desires, but because, as Buber contends, our relationship has a "commanding power" that makes us *want* to do things for her to make her feel loved, valued, and happy. This is why, when the one we love expresses a heartfelt need or desire, we do not receive it as we would any ordinary statement from someone else; rather, we experience it as something that carries force in our life, something to which we are *obligated* to respond. It is ultimately our choice how to

---

2. See, for example, Eugene Borowitz, "The Autonomous Self and the Commanding Community," *Theological Studies* 45 (1984): pages 34–56; and Eugene Borowitz, "The Autonomous Jewish Self," *Modern Judaism* 4, no. 1 (February 1984): pages 39–55, including his discussion of Buber in both articles.
3. See Elyse D. Frishman, "The Power of God's Voice," in *Women Rabbis: Exploration & Celebration*, ed. Gary P. Zola (Cincinnati: HUC-JIR Rabbinic Alumni Association Press, 1996), pages 83–91.

respond, of course, but our decisions are not without consequence. While our partner may not punish us for ignoring or failing to honor her needs, inattention to them will, over time, create distance between us and erode our bond. By contrast, when we do things that we know bring our beloved joy and fulfillment, we strengthen our relationship and deepen our intimacy.

Our relationship with God is no different. We need to do certain tangible things for God in order to deepen our intimacy and keep our relationship strong. As our tradition understands it, the things God needs from us are expressed in a passionate love letter to the Jewish people: the Torah. Although Reform Jews have differing views on the origins and nature of the Torah, our movement's platform and liturgy affirm the idea that "Torah is a manifestation of *ahavat olam*, God's eternal love for the Jewish people and for all humanity."[4] As such, the mitzvot contained within it should be regarded not as mandatory orders but rather as heartfelt requests from one beloved partner to another. Each mitzvah expresses a longing of the divine soul, something God needs from our relationship and hopes we will do.

Although we have the right and the freedom to respond to these requests however we choose, we know that being in a committed relationship with God means we cannot dismiss or ignore them; rather, if we genuinely love God and value our connection, we will feel the commanding power of our relationship stirring in our souls, compelling us to listen sincerely to our beloved's longings and to try our best to fulfill them. We will autonomously *choose* to honor God's mitzvot—not because we are *ordered* to do so, but because we *want* to do so. Indeed, Rabbi Menachem Mendel Morgensztern, the Kotzker Rebbe, teaches that the mitzvot are opportunities to draw closer to God and strengthen our special bond. God cares what we do, and our actions, or lack thereof, have an impact on our relationship. As

---

4. CCAR, "A Statement of Principles for Reform Judaism," s.v., "Torah." See also the English rendering of the *Ahavat Olam* prayer in *Mishkan T'filah*, page 150: "Everlasting love You offered Your people Israel by teaching us Torah and mitzvot, laws and precepts."

the Kotzker puts it, "God desires and delights in our deeds,"[5] meaning that when we do mitzvot, we bring God joy and fulfillment.

Of course, no one can reasonably expect his partner, no matter how intimately connected they are, to satisfy his every wish. Sometimes God, like our spouse or friend or parent, will ask things of us we simply cannot do without being untrue to our own needs and convictions. But the covenant does not demand that we negate our own individuality for the sake of the other; quite to the contrary, it is premised on the idea that a healthy relationship is one that enables each partner to realize the full beauty of her individuality and to have it affirmed, without judgment, by her beloved. Therefore, in cases where honoring the request would require us to suppress our essential self, God—the source of our autonomy, our morality, and the souls that animate us—gives us the freedom to say we cannot do that particular mitzvah; indeed, the commanding power of our relationship *obligates* us to do so.

Yet, while our autonomy gives us the right not to do any of the mitzvot if we so choose, exercising this right simply because we do not feel like doing them, or because they are inconvenient, or because we judge them to be irrelevant or not meaningful will have the same ramifications as if we make that choice in our human relationships. Over time, inattention to the things God asks of us will result in a cold distance between us. The less we do, the greater that distance will grow and the weaker our connection will become. After all, a relationship in which the partners do little or nothing for each other is not much of a relationship at all.

In light of all this, our covenantal obligation as Reform Jews is

---

5. *Ohel Torah, Parashat Miketz*, 24. The Kotzker's statement is *sheHaKadosh Baruch Hu chafeitz b'maaseihem*. I have rendered the word *chafeitz* as "desires and delights in" because I am unable to come up with a single English term that accurately conveys both of these essential aspects of the Hebrew word's meaning. Additionally, I have quoted the Kotzker's phrase in the first person ("our deeds") rather than in the original third person ("their deeds") for the sake of rhetorical consistency with my first-person narration. The Kotzker is referring here to the deeds of the Jewish people, so the meaning is unchanged.

twofold. We must receive God's mitzvot as heartfelt expressions of need and desire that carry force in our lives, and honor them as best we can—even when it is hard, and even when we would not choose to do these things had our beloved not desired them. At the same time, we must assert our right *not* to honor a given mitzvah if doing it would require us to suppress our identity or core convictions. This is what it means to be an autonomous individual in a healthy, loving, committed relationship with God.

Let us see how this theory might play out in respect to three particular mitzvot: *t'filah* (prayer), kashrut (dietary practice), and *kiddushin* (marriage).

T'filah

It is a mitzvah to pray every day.[6] To understand this mitzvah in relational terms, we might think of God as a parent and ourselves as God's grown children who are living our own independent lives. Prayer is like calling home to have a conversation with our parent and let him know how life is going. Our parent cannot *force* us to call, but we know that when we do, it makes him happy and lets him know we care. If we call only when we feel like talking or when we need something from him, we make our relationship with our parent into what Buber calls "I-It"—meaning that it is all about *us* and our own personal needs, rather than about mutuality. By contrast, when we call because we know hearing our voice brings our parent joy, even when we do not have much to say, our relationship will grow deeper. So it is with prayer. If we pray only when we need something or because we want to feel uplifted, we make our relationship with God into "I-It"—one that serves *our* needs but not the needs of our Partner. Such a dynamic is unhealthy. God asks us to "call home" daily because God loves us and wants us to feel connected to each other. If we are willing to try to honor that mitzvah, even when it is hard or inconvenient to do, it can only benefit our relationship.

---

6. Maimonides, *Mishneh Torah, Hilchot T'filah* 1:1.

Kashrut

Our tradition teaches that God, as Creator and Owner of the world,[7] has set parameters regarding what we may eat.[8] To understand kashrut in relational terms, we can think of God as a friend and ourselves as a guest in her home. We might imagine our human friend saying something like, "Help yourself to anything in the pantry, but please do not eat the Oreos." Although she does not explain why the Oreos are off-limits, it does not really matter: we refrain from eating them out of respect for her and for the fact that we are in her home. It is the same with kashrut. We are guests in God's world, and God has asked us not to eat certain things in the pantry. Our autonomy surely gives us the freedom to eat whatever we want, but were we to do so, we would be saying that satisfying our appetite is more important than respecting our Friend's wishes in Her own home. If we value our relationship, we would do better to take Rabbi Elazar ben Azariah's approach and say that "I wish [to eat pork] . . . but what can I do? [God] has asked[9] me not to."[10] God's creatures are not ours for the taking just because we want them, and observing kashrut even to some extent is a way of acknowledging that truth. This show of restraint is a gesture of love and respect for the One who graciously welcomes us as guests in Her world and allows us to partake of its bounty.

Kiddushin

Jewish tradition teaches that a marriage is a trilateral partnership between the two spouses and God. The Sages say that when a couple conducts their marriage with respect for each other and reverence for God, "the *Shechinah* [God's Presence] dwells between them," but

---

7. See, for example, Psalm 24:1: "The earth is Adonai's and all that it holds, the world and its inhabitants."
8. See Leviticus 11:1–47.
9. Literally, "decreed" *gazar*. I have changed the verb to "asked" in accordance with the definition of mitzvah I have put forth in this essay.
10. Rabbi Elazar ben Azariah's statement is quoted by Rashi in his comment to Leviticus 20:26.

if they do not make God a partner in their relationship, the marriage cannot endure.[11] According to the traditional view, for those who decide to marry, it is a mitzvah for the man to betroth the woman through certain ritual and liturgical acts.[12] By doing so, he legally "acquires" her as a kind of consecrated property and gains an ownership right in her sexuality and in the fruits of her labors. Obviously, this mitzvah poses a significant difficulty for Reform Jews because it is based on a definition of the marital relationship that we simply cannot endorse. To perform these traditional rituals as they are prescribed would require that we act against our core values and thereby negate our essential selves. However, if the covenant is a relationship that validates the unique identity and truth of each partner, then it *obligates* us to exercise our autonomous right to say that "I cannot do this act—in terms of my present moral or communal understanding it seems . . . wrong."[13] This does not mean we should ignore the mitzvah altogether; rather, if possible, we should try to respond to it in a way that feels right to us. This is why Reform weddings, both same-sex and opposite-sex, typically include versions of the traditional *kiddushin* rituals that are modified to reflect our view of marriage as an egalitarian partnership.

As these examples aim to show, being in a committed and loving relationship with God, no less than being in such a relationship with another human being, comes with obligations—both to our Partner *and* to ourselves. When we sincerely try to honor our Beloved's needs and desires in a way that is true to our essential selves, then God "delights in our deeds," and our life-affirming relationship brings joy, meaning, and purpose to our existence.

---

11. BT *Sotah* 17a.
12. *Sefer HaChinuch, mitzvah* 522; *Shulchan Aruch, Even HaEizer* 27:1.
13. CCAR, "Commentary on the Principles for Reform Judaism," section I ("God"), s.v. "*Mitzvot*," http://ccarnet.org/rabbis-speak/platforms/commentary-principles-reform-judaism/.

RABBI AMY SCHEINERMAN

The Meaning of
Mitzvah for Reform Jews

How often do we think we know what a term means but upon close examination realize that the meaning is open to discussion and interpretation? *Mitzvah* is just such a term. Its root—*tz-v-h*—means "command," and therefore *mitzvah* is often translated "commandment," but there are many ways to understand it beyond "law" or "rule." The mitzvot are the paving stones of halachah (lit. "the way one walks").[1] Unfortunately, in the hands of the legal paradigm, halachah has come to connote a fixed set of rules in the minds of many people. A better understanding, one more in keeping with its origins in the Talmud, is that halachah is a thought system for discerning God's will through study and interpretation of sacred text, combining reason and logic with Jewish values and priorities in the interpretative process. In our time, our understanding of Torah, Talmud, and the process of halachah has grown; our understanding of God has broadened; and therefore a reexamination of the very meaning of mitzvah is in order.

Paving Stones and the Foundation Beneath

Mitzvot are the paving stones of the Jewish path through life, which for all its emphasis on ethical living is action-oriented: How do we live out our ethical values in our lives? How do we welcome a baby into the Jewish covenant? How do we celebrate a wedding? How do we say goodbye to a loved one? The very idea of mitzvah (commandment) suggests that there is a *M'tzaveh* (Commander). Hence

---

1. *Halachah* refers to the body of Jewish religious laws that derive from the Written Torah (the Five Books of Moses) and the Oral Torah (the Talmud).

beneath the behavioral paving stones of mitzvot lies the bedrock of God.

There is always a particular challenge in speaking about God: Are we to understand Torah's descriptions of God and God's will concretely or metaphorically? Torah speaks of God as a sovereign Ruler, supreme in power, who made a covenant with Israel that requires us to obey commandments (mitzvot) ordained from on high and who rewards our obedience to, and punishes our violation of, the covenant. There are other biblical metaphors describing God's relationship with Israel: Bride/groom; Doctor/patient; Husband/wife; Judge/plaintiff; Parent/child. Yet the paradigm of God as supreme Ruler (*Melech malchei ham'lachim*, "the King who is the king of kings") had the most sticking power in a world dominated by kings who promulgated law; God was conceived as the divine King who promulgated divine law. In turn, this gave rise to a complex Jewish legal system and a rich body of literature exploring and expounding the application of Torah in our lives.

Tradition holds that there are 613 mitzvot in the Torah. We find the first mention of *taryag hamitzvot* (the 613 mitzvot) in the Talmud,[2] where it is attributed to Rabbi Simlai, who lived in the third century CE. Mitzvot pertain to every aspect of life: criminal and civil law, religious practices and identity, family and personal relations, business ethics, social justice, and more. One way to understand them is as falling into three categories: *mishpatim*, self-evident mitzvot, such as the prohibitions against murder and theft; *eduyot*, mitzvot of remembrance, such as the mitzvot pertaining to keeping Passover to remember the Exodus; and *chukim*, mitzvot we would not have figured out on our own, such as the dietary mitzvot. Another way to think of these three categories is that *chukim* preserve our distinctive identity and relationship as the people Israel with God; *eduyot* preserve and celebrate our communal, religious history; and *mishpatim* are how we live out in our behavior the sacred values of our tradition, such as compassion, righteousness, and honesty.

---

2. BT *Makot* 23b–24a.

For many modern, liberal Jews, this conception is not a comfortable fit with our worldview, experiences, or beliefs. We are not alone in our discomfort. As far back as the period of the Talmud's composition[3] this understanding troubled the Rabbis. The Rabbis imagine God suspending Mount Sinai over the heads of the Israelites and threatening them, "If you accept the Torah, fine. But if not, your burial will be there!"[4] Rav Acha bar Yaakov asserts that the unilateral and coercive nature of the imposition of the covenant (contract) of Torah on the people Israel "is a great refutation against the Torah" because a coerced contract is invalid. Another sage, Rava, then asserts that at a later time in history, the Jewish people accepted the obligations of Torah of their own free will and volition. Clearly, there was a measure of discomfort with the metaphor and its implications.

Reconsideration of the Legal Paradigm

In the modern era, concerns about and objections to the legal paradigm and understanding of mitzvot has only grown. Judith Plaskow points out, "It is specific *halakhot* that have been questioned and *not* the fundamental presuppositions of the legal system."[5] But Rachel Adler goes much further. She says that the halachic system itself has become so calcified that it is inherently tainted and tantamount to a false god:

> The problems actually raised in the feminist critique, however, are *systemic* wounds too deep for liberal Band-Aids. As one of the originators of this critique, I have contended that members of a Jewish male elite constructed the categories and method of classical halakhah to reflect their own perspectives and social goals and have held a monopoly on their application. Borrowing a term from the post-Christian theologian Mary Daly, I have called classical halakhah a methodolatrous system. The method becomes a kind of false god. It determines the choice of questions, rather

---

3. The Babylonian Talmud was composed over the course of the second through the sixth centuries of the Common Era.
4. BT *Shabbat* 88a.
5. Judith Plaskow, "The Right Question Is Theological," in *On Being a Jewish Feminist*, ed. Susannah Heschel (New York: Schocken Books, 1983), page 224.

than the questions determining the choice of method. Questions that do not conform to the system's method and categories are simply reclassified as non-data and dumped out.[6]

The legal paradigm pervades historical Judaism and contemporary approaches to Jewish practice, and our tendency to sacralize history promotes this "methodolatrous system": it favors hierarchy, power, and control over spiritual exploration, innovation, and occasionally, even compassion.

In truth, there are many ways to understand the nature of God, the meaning and purpose of mitzvot, and our relationship to both.

Seeking a New Paradigm

Where can we find a new paradigm? To paraphrase the poet Muriel Rukeyser, the physical universe is made of atoms, but our lives are made of stories. Rachel Adler, in *Engendering Judaism*, provides us with sage insight and counsel. Drawing on the work of American legal theorist Robert Cover, Adler explains that nomos (law) is generated by "a universe of meanings, values, and rules, embedded in stories. A nomos is not a body of data to master and adapt, but a world to inhabit. Knowing how to live in a nomic world means being able to envision the possibilities implicit in its stories and norms and being willing to live some of them out in praxis."[7] One might think that Cover had Torah and Talmud in mind; the best place to begin is with the sacred stories that have defined and accompanied us since the beginning.

I offer three stories. The first comes from midrash.[8] Rabbi Levi tell us that God appeared to the Israelites at the Sea of Reeds in the guise of a virulent young warrior fighting on their behalf, and in the guise of a sage elder offering wisdom at Mount Sinai. God has no physical form, yet the Israelites envisioned God as they needed God to be in

---

6. Rachel Adler, *Engendering Judaism* (Philadelphia: Jewish Publication Society, 1998), page 28.

7. Ibid., p. 34. Robert M. Cover, "The Supreme Court, 1982 Term-Foreword: Nomos and Narrative," *Harvard Law Review* 4 (1983).

8. *P'sikta Rabbati* 21:6.

each predicament. How we conceive God—and God's mitzvot—has everything to do with religious, spiritual, social, and psychological needs. Mitzvot offer practices and principles that enhance and enrich our lives, enabling us to steer a path of righteousness through the shoals of life.

The second story is found in the Talmud.[9] The notion that there are precisely 613 mitzvot contributes to the sense that mitzvot are fixed laws, but Rabbi Simlai (mentioned above) explains that there are 365 negative commandments (prohibitions) corresponding to the days in a solar year, and 248 positive commandments (prescriptions), corresponding to the presumed number of parts of the human body.[10] This teaches us that every day we serve God by resisting the temptation to do something we should not and that we can serve God with every part of our being, opening the door to the notion that mitzvot arise from a value system by which we make conscious decisions about our behavior in order to elevate it to a level of holiness. And, indeed, the Talmud walks straight through that open door. We find next *not* an enumeration of 613 mitzvot, but rather six distillations of the *essence* of the mitzvot.[11] Each successive iteration is more concise and abstract than the previous one, ending with Amos, who reduced all 613 to one principle, "Seek Me and live" (5:4), and Habakkuk, who said, "The righteous shall live by his faith" (2:4).

The third story is from a commentary on *Parashat Lech L'cha* by the S'fat Emet[12]:

> Now surely [every] person was created for a particular purpose. There must be something that we are to set right. A person who achieves that is called *tzaddik* [righteous], walking a straight path of justice. But our father Abraham is called a *chasid* [lover

---

9. BT *Makot* 23b–24a.

10. The number 248 does not correspond with human anatomy; it is not clear whence the Rabbis derived this number. Perhaps because it is the difference between 613 and 365 helps them make their point about serving God by both doing and refraining.

11. Attributed to David, Isaiah (two formulations), Micah, Amos, and Habakkuk.

12. Rabbi Yehudah Aryeh Leib Alter of Ger, 1847–1905.

of God]; he went beyond the line demanded by the law. The one who serves God out of love can arouse a desire within God to let flow the source of his own soul in a way that cannot be comprehended by the human mind. Thus they interpreted the verse: *Those who fulfill His word to hear the voice of His word* (Psalm 103:20). By properly mending our deeds, we can come to hear more and more. This goes on forever. The *chasid* serves God in order to become attached to the root of the mitzvah, ever seeking to hear new things.[13]

Mitzvot both reflect how we see and understand the world, and how we make meaning of our place in it. The S'fat Emet understands the connection between each individual and God as deeply personal and intimate.

From Commandment to Commendation

In loving and committing relationships, the sense of obligation is both real and profound. We know this from our relationships with parents, children, spouses, and friends. This is true also for our relationship with God and the Jewish community. Rather than understanding mitzvah as "commandment," let us understand it as a commendation: something that, by doing or refraining, enhances and enriches important relationships: with God, with the people in our lives, and with the Jewish people.

Mitzvot afford us opportunities to create and recognize holiness through acts that bring spiritual meaning into our lives. It is we who ascribe meaning to the acts by doing them and interpreting them: *asher kid'shanu b'mitzvotav* ("who has sanctified us through the mitzvot"). The world we live in—time, space, actions, relationships—is the ordinary quotidian of life: not inherently bad; but not yet sanctified, or raised to a level of sacred purpose. When we ascribe religious significance and divine meaning to our acts, and through them embrace God's presence, and sacred meaning and purpose as we understand it, they become mitzvot. This occurs each week when

---

13. Adapted from *The Language of Truth*, trans. Arthur Green (Philadelphia: Jewish Publication Society, 1998), pages 19–20.

we declare the sanctity of Shabbat, which signifies both the creation of the universe and our redemption from Egypt, and hence institute holy time in our lives. Every moment is alive and open to holiness. Everything in the world can be sanctified, and it is the goal of living Jewishly to incorporate that consciousness into our being.

Mitzvot are expressions of identity and commitment to God of the universe, *Am Yisrael* (the people Israel), Torah values, and the God-within-each-of-us. Rabbi Mordecai Kaplan wrote, "A religion thus came to mean to me the sum of those habits and values which give a people the will to live in common, to perpetuate itself and to make the best use of its collective life." Mitzvot around the birth of a child, coming of age (bar/bat mitzvah), marriage, and death express both identity and commitment and bind us more closely to God and one another. Each time we consciously and purposefully perform a mitzvah, we express our Jewish identity and allegiance to the stream of tradition that defines us as a people.

Mitzvot are still paving stones of Jewish living, and we, living in the twenty-first century, continue to shape and polish them and to lay down new stones.

CHAPTER SIX

Expanding the Thinking

*Essays on Key Subjects
from the Jewish Life Cycle*

RABBI JOUI M. HESSEL, RJE

The Jewish Home

From the Physical to the Spiritual

A S CHILDREN, we find joy and peace within our bedrooms; we
play make-believe, build forts with bedsheets, and read books
with flashlights late into the night. As parents, we seek to transform
a house into a home, taking it from the profane and the ordinary to
the sacred and extraordinary. We infuse each room with our love for
those who live within the walls, and we build memories to last a lifetime by celebrating holidays, cooking delicious Shabbat dinners, and
nurturing special moments for our family.

Why is our home so special? What makes it a sacred space in
which we can find serenity and peace, joy and laughter? To find the
answer, we must go back in history thousands of years. At that time,
the place where God dwelled was thought to be the Temple, the
Beit HaMikdash, in Jerusalem. There, the High Priests on behalf of
the Israelites offered sacrifices, as a way to communicate with God
and to receive blessings. When the Romans destroyed the Temple
in 70 CE, the Rabbis were forced to consider whether God would
continue to reside with the Jewish people. And the answer was, yes.
Having decided that, the question was then where that would take
place without the central Temple available to God. At that time it
was believed, as we do today, that God would continue to be with
the Jewish people, but as they transitioned into a world without the
Temple in Jerusalem, God's presence would be found in two places:
the synagogue and the home. The home, therefore, became a small
sanctuary—a *mikdash m'at*, where God's presence would be felt and
the space itself would become holy.

According to the Talmud (BT *M'gilah* 29a), God will dwell in the holy spaces we create, for those creations are the Temple in miniature. How do we transform our homes into small sanctuaries? Perhaps it begins with shifting our viewpoint of our homes as places for storing material possessions to places for restoring spiritual connections. Instead of using an architect's blueprints, we are to use the blueprints found within the Torah, the mitzvot commanded us to make our homes physically, emotionally, and spiritually safe. Our homes should strive to be places of extreme hospitality, following our forefather Abraham's example in Genesis. Our homes should become places of gathering where friends come together for holiday celebration and ritual observance. Our homes should be locales of worship, not in lieu of synagogues but in addition to, where children can recite the words of *Sh'ma* at bedtime or roommates can share in the recitation of blessings at the table. Our homes should be places where we can meditate, communicate with God, and offer thanks for life's blessings we experience each day. Our homes should be places of study, whereby its residents become scholars of Jewish text.

The daily study of Jewish text is a fundamental part of Jewish living. The Rabbis long ago taught that each Jew was to study every day: "One should always divide their years into three parts, devoting one-third to the study of Scripture, one-third to the study of Mishnah [Oral Law], and one-third to the study of Talmud" (BT *Kiddushin* 30a). The Talmud thus concludes that the only certain way to fulfill this obligation is to do it daily. Early on (and still today in some communities), Jewish communities would study texts centered on sacrifices, viewing it as their own offerings, since their actual sacrifices were unable to be offered in the Temple once it had been destroyed. Today, Reform congregations recite a version of *Eilu D'varim*, which stems from the Talmudic passage in *Shabbat* 127a:

> These are things that are limitless,
> of which a person enjoys the fruit of the world,
> while the principal remains in the world-to-come.
> They are: honoring one's father and mother,
> engaging in deeds of compassion,
> arriving early for study, morning and evening,

dealing graciously with guests, visiting the sick,
providing for the wedding couple,
accompanying the dead for burial,
being devoted in prayer,
and making peace among people.
But the study of Torah encompasses them all.

Therefore, study in the home is a central part of modern Judaism and it is not just reserved for the synagogue any longer. *Shabbat* 127a teaches us about the obligations we have as Jews. But it is much more than an obligation, as the joy of helping others provides us with rewards that are beyond measure. The significance of the study of Torah (or of any Jewish text) being equal to any of these obligations underscores the importance of the value of *talmud Torah*, Jewish learning.

From *talmud Torah* to hospitality to guests, from honoring our parents to creating opportunities to fulfill deeds of compassion for others in our midst, all of these mitzvot stem from how we choose to live our lives and nurture others' lives within the home.

A Jewish home is recognized immediately upon gazing on the mezuzah, placed on the outer doorpost. The mezuzah contains a scroll of parchment within its casing, where the words of the *Sh'ma* are found painstakingly written in perfect calligraphy. These words recall the mitzvah from Deuteronomy 6 that speaks of writing these words and posting them on the doorposts of our house and on our gates. Traditionally, when we enter such a house, we lift our fingers and gingerly touch the mezuzah, recognizing its symbolism with a touch, and then we bring our fingers to our lips, allowing the words to become a part of us—a recognition of these ancient words becoming relevant to the modern day, reminding us of how we are to live ethically and morally, guided by the words of Torah.

Inside of the home, there are surely artifacts and treasures that reflect a sense of the Jewish calendar through ritual objects displayed in cabinets and on counters. Challah platters and seder plates, Shabbat candlesticks and Chanukah menorahs (*chanukiyot*), dreidels and groggers, and *tzedakah* boxes can be found in addition to Jewish books that serve as resources and guides to our daily questions that arise. The usage of these ritual objects and the synthesis of ritual with commandment is what transforms Judaism from a religion of learning to a religion of doing. And it is in *doing* that we actively participate in Jewish life with those around us, beginning in our homes.

But it is not only through ritual that a Jewish home exemplifies a *mikdash m'at*, a small sanctuary. Indeed, Judaism is lived not only through the physical space and the use of physical objects, but also in the spiritual realm through the adherence to Jewish values, *midot*. For it is the way in which we treat our loved ones with whom we share living space that illustrates the synthesis of *talmud Torah*, the study of Torah, with that of practice. The Jewish philosopher Martin Buber taught that we should each strive to move from an I-It relationship of superficial objectification to the true deep connection of I-Thou. Recognizing the holiness that exists within each of us is how we are able to make that transition from text to reality, from ancient words to modern actions. The relationships and the Jewish values that serve as each relationship's foundation is what the prophet Micah (6:8) commands of us—to do justly, to love mercy, and to walk humbly with our God.

> May our homes be filled with the light of Torah.
> May our homes be overflowing with words and deeds of love.
> May our homes be complete with the blessings of family and
>   of friendship.

Tzedakah

*T*ZEDAKAH is the Jewish principle of giving money for the purpose of *tikkun olam*, "world repair." The word *tzedakah* itself is not derived from the Latin *caritas*, which is the root of the English word "charity," but rather from the Hebrew root for "justice." That is to say, the fundamental task of giving *tzedakah* is to rectify social imbalances in the world that exist between rich and poor, between people who have and people who are in need.[1]

The origins of *tzedakah* are found in passages from the Torah that describe how ancient farmers were expected to leave the corners of their fields (called *pei-ah*), gleanings that had been neglected or dropped (*leket*), and rows of crops that they had forgotten to harvest (*shich'chah*) for poor and hungry people to come and gather (Leviticus 19:9–10; Deuteronomy 24:19–20). These parts of the landowner's property *did not belong to the landowner anymore*; they legally belonged to the most desperate and hurting members of society. From this, the later sages of the Mishnah and the Talmud derived the laws of *tzedakah*.[2]

What is it that is so special about money? Why not give our time, our skills, or our love in lieu of money? In terms of mitzvah power, or the impact of our giving, we tend to attribute to money both *more* and *less* power than it deserves. In fact, there simply are things that

---

1. Meir Tamari, *With All Your Possessions: Jewish Ethics and Economic Life* (Northvale, NJ: Jason Aronson, 1998), page 248.
2. For more about this evolution, see Frank M. Loewenberg, *From Charity to Social Justice: The Emergence of Communal Institutions for the Support of the Poor in Ancient Judaism* (New Brunswick, NJ: Transaction Publishers, 2001); and Moshe Weinfeld, *Social Justice in Ancient Israel and in the Ancient Near East* (Jerusalem: Magnes Press, Hebrew University, 1995).

money can do that even infinite reserves of goodwill and good intentions cannot accomplish. It takes money to build a wing of a cancer hospital, or to buy food for a family that has none, or to support the needs of a synagogue and a Hebrew school. Conversely, all the money in the world cannot hold the hand of someone in a hospital bed, or comfort someone who is alone and scared, or heal a broken heart. That is why our tradition gives us two categories of mitzvot: *tzedakah* (giving money) and *g'milut chasadim* (volunteering our time and energy). Both are essential Jewish ways to do the work of *tikkun olam*.

How is a person expected to do the mitzvah of *tzedakah*? Maimonides describes the commandment this way:

> When a poor person comes and asks for his needs to be met, and the giver cannot fulfill them all, he should give what he is able to give. How much? One-fifth: this is the mitzvah par excellence. One-tenth: this is average. Less than one-tenth is *ayin raah* [stinginess, but see below].
>
> A person should never give less than one-third of a shekel in a year. A person who gives less than that has not fulfilled the mitzvah. Even a poor person—one who is sustained from the *tzedakah* fund—is obligated to give *tzedakah* to another person.[3]

Maimonides teaches us several things in this passage. First, our primary obligation is to look and listen carefully to the other person's needs. So often we presume that we know what is best for others. Instead, we should pay closer attention to what the needy person is asking for.

Second, Maimonides acknowledges that the needs in the world are so great that each of us, with our limited resources, cannot solve them all. But we shouldn't let that stop us from being actively engaged in *tzedakah*-work. So he provides a range of 10 to 20 percent of our earnings that we should be giving away. At different times in our lives, we may be able to give closer to the upper or lower limits of that range.

---

3. Maimonides, *Mishneh Torah, Hilchot Matanot Aniyim* 7:5.

Third, Maimonides somewhat surprisingly provides an upper limit to the amount we should give away (20 percent). It is not a Jewish ideal to impoverish ourselves while we support others. However, that upper limit is removed for very wealthy people.

Fourth, Maimonides asserts that people who do not give enough to *tzedakah* (10 percent) are guilty of *ayin raah*. The rabbis take this expression, based on the words for "eye" and "bad," to mean "greediness." However, we might create a midrash here and interpret the phrase to mean, "bad eyesight." In other words, people who are not involved in enough *tzedakah*-work don't see certain fundamental truths: they fail to observe the real need that is all around, the power that each of us has to make a real difference, and the potential that our own contribution has (small as it may seem when compared to the enormity of need) to bring about change.

Finally, this passage tells us that even a person who receives *tzedakah* in order to survive needs to give a portion away to *tzedakah* as well. Why? Perhaps because there is something quintessentially Jewish, and human, about helping others, and we have no right to deny anyone of the fundamental act of caring for and supporting other human beings.

For many of us, the hardest part of giving *tzedakah* is setting priorities. Should I give my money away locally or to a worthy cause overseas? To people I know or to an organization? To Jewish causes or universal ones? Here or in Israel? It is worth struggling with these questions. In truth, how we choose to distribute *tzedakah* money says more about our priorities and values than almost anything else we say or do. (Consider: What does your checkbook say about what is important to you? Is it consistent with the values you speak?) Halachic sources suggest that when it comes to the essential needs of food, shelter, and clothing, one's family comes first, followed by the needs of the local community, then more distant communities, and then communities overseas.[4] However, we are warned not to

---

4. See BT *Bava M'tzia* 71a; *Tanna D'Vei Eliyahu* 27; and *Shulchan Aruch, Yoreh Dei-ah* 251:3. See also the discussion in Cyril Domb, *Maaser Kesafim* (Jerusalem/ New York: Feldheim, 1980), pages 100–106.

neglect the secondary needs simply because there are local recipients that come first.[5]

How we give *tzedakah* is nearly as important as *how much* we give. In a well-known passage, Maimonides describes eight levels of giving *tzedakah*. The best way of giving *tzedakah*, he writes, is to enable someone to become self-sufficient, "by giving a gift or a loan, entering into a partnership, or finding the person a job so that, by strengthening him or her, the recipient will no longer need to ask for support."[6] The next highest level is anonymous giving, where the giver does not know the recipient and vice versa. With each subsequent level that Maimonides describes, a degree of anonymity of the receiver is lost, and thus so is a measure of dignity. The primary goal is to preserve the dignity of the recipient in every way possible and to avoid humiliation at all costs.

Rabbinic tradition is full of examples of creative *tzedakah* giving with a careful eye on preserving this sense of dignity. The Talmud describes a secret chamber in the Temple in Jerusalem, where wealthy people could give in secret and people in need could come and take what they needed anonymously and without humiliation.[7] Some of the sages would carry their *tzedakah* money on their backs, distributing it to needy people in a manner that would keep the recipient anonymous.[8] In our time, the author and Torah teacher Danny Siegel coined the term "mitzvah heroes" to describe people who do the mitzvah of *tzedakah* in creative, powerful, and grassroots ways.[9]

Giving *tzedakah* is a tremendous responsibility, and thus we have to be extremely careful when we give. *Tzedakah* organizations must

---

5. *Aruch HaShulchan, Yoreh Dei-ah* 251:4. See also Domb, *Maaser Kesafim*, page 105.

6. Maimonides, *Mishneh Torah, Hilchot Matanot Aniyim* 10:7.

7. BT *Sh'kalim* 5:6. In fact, the Talmud describes these recipients as people who had once had money but had now fallen on hard times—and would thus be especially vulnerable to embarrassment or humiliation.

8. Rabbi Abba is described this way in the Talmud, *K'tubot* 67b.

9. See, for instance, the myriad stories of mitzvah heroes in Danny Siegel, *Heroes and Miracle Workers* (1997), *Good People* (1995), and *Giving Your Money Away* (2006). All are published by Town House Press, Somers, NY.

be absolutely scrupulous in their work, and givers have the right to be sure that those organizations are trustworthy and efficient. If an organization will not divulge its annual reports, for instance, or if it seems to have an unusually high amount of overhead, a giver should be wary, even if the cause seems just. Many websites offer useful guides for measuring the effectiveness and reliability of *tzedakah* organizations.[10]

When is the appropriate time to give *tzedakah*? Certainly, as often as possible. That said, there are many specific times when it is especially fortuitous to give:

- Whenever a need presents itself
- In celebration upon hearing good news
- To soften the impact of bad news
- In honor of a happy occasion
- In memory of someone who died
- In celebration of someone who achieved a milestone
- In gratitude of another's support or hard work
- Just before Shabbat begins, to end the week on a note of giving
- Immediately after *Havdalah* at the conclusion of Shabbat, to begin the new week with a mitzvah
- Before praying
- At each significant moment in the life cycle
- At the arrival of a holiday
- When an opportunity to make a difference suddenly falls into your lap
- On any given day, for no reason at all except that it's the right thing to do

Furthermore, most every Jewish holiday has a specific *tzedakah* dimension to it. For instance, on Purim it is a special mitzvah to give gifts to poor people (*matanot la-evyonim*). On Passover, one should give food to people who are hungry (*ma'ot chitin*). On Chanukah, many families devote a night for making donations to organizations

---

10. For instance, Charity Navigator, www.charitynavigator.org.

that reflect their values. And many synagogues throughout North America participate in food drives on Yom Kippur.

In a home or office, *tzedakah* is often collected in a special piece of Judaica called a *pushke*. (An entire generation of twentieth-century American Jews were raised with ubiquitous blue-and-white *pushkes* in their homes, *tzedakah* boxes from the Jewish National Fund, which collected donations to strengthen the nascent State of Israel.) Strategic placement of *pushkes* can help emphasize the primacy of *tzedakah* in Jewish life, and they can help cultivate a *tzedakah* reflex.

Ultimately, *tzedakah* is a primary spiritual value of Judaism. *Tzedakah* is a way of life: by cultivating a *tzedakah* reflex, we become generous people. In a pedagogical moment, Maimonides asks, which is better—giving one thousand coins to *tzedakah* once, or giving one coin one thousand different times? He concludes that the second way is better, because we cultivate a habit of giving and thus become accustomed to hearing voices of people in need and to seeking out *tzedakah* opportunities wherever they appear.[11] Generous living is spiritual living, and this is embodied by a life of *tzedakah*.

---

11. Maimonides, *Commentary on the Mishnah, Avot* 3:15. Rambam was being dramatic in order to teach this lesson. Other commentators have challenged his point, saying that each *tzedakah* situation is different and money should be used in the way in which it has maximum impact.

RABBI SIMEON J. MASLIN

An Introduction to Kashrut
You Shall Not Boil a Kid in Its Mother's Milk

KASHRUT, the system of Jewish dietary regulations, has long been the single most recognizable aspect of Jewish behavior. There were eras in Jewish history when Jews were persecuted and even executed because they adhered to certain features of kashrut, most notably the avoidance of pork products. But even today in the open societies of the Western democracies, where Jews often choose not to observe kashrut, virtually everyone, Jew and non-Jew alike, is familiar with at least two main features of the historical Jewish dietary regimen, that is, the avoidance of pork products and the separation of milk and meat.

Possibly the best known of all the dietary laws is the very cryptic "You shall not boil a kid in its mother's milk" (Exodus 23:19, 34:26; Deuteronomy 14:21). This injunction was interpreted by later generations of Jewish authorities to forbid the eating or preparing of dairy products and meat together. Whether or not that was the original intent is open to question, as we shall see below, but whatever its interpretation, it is an essential pillar of the structure of kashrut.

Almost equally familiar is the prohibition against the eating of animals that do not have cloven hooves and do not chew their cud (i.e., ruminants) in Leviticus 11:3. This injunction allows for the eating of most domestic animals, including cattle, sheep, goats, and deer, with the notable exceptions of pigs, horses, camels, and donkeys. The same chapter in Leviticus lists twenty birds (one of them actually a rodent) or species of birds that are prohibited. The chapter also enumerates those insects that may or may not be eaten.

Somewhat less familiar to most people and, curiously, less

observed today is the prohibition against all sea creatures that do not have scales and fins (Leviticus 11:9). Although this prohibition is no less prominent than the ones above, it is not unusual to find Jews who avoid nonkosher animals and who do not mix milk and meat but who yet partake of such shellfish as lobster and shrimp.

Even less familiar to most people are the prohibitions against the eating of animal fat and blood (Leviticus 3:17, 7:23) and the prohibition against the eating of any animal that has died of natural causes or that was "torn by beasts" (Exodus 22:30; Leviticus 22:8). The term used by the Torah to indicate "torn by beasts" is *t'reifah*, and somehow over the centuries that word was expanded by popular usage to include all nonkosher food. For most Jews, whether or not they are familiar with the prescriptions of kashrut, food is either kosher or *treif*.

Having now reviewed the basic laws of kashrut, I pose four questions:

1. Should the eating habits of Jews today be delimited by a set of laws and taboos that originated in the sacred texts of a prescientific society?
2. Should the eating habits of reasonable people be determined by any considerations beyond health?
3. Shall we cede to medieval sages and to those who claim to be their successors today the right to determine how a cryptic ancient text should be interpreted?
4. Shall we also cede to these sages the right to determine what constitutes the humane treatment of animals?

The first of those four questions is clearly the most essential, for if one believes that the Torah in its entirety was written or dictated by God, then no human being has the right to dispute even one letter of it. If, on the other hand, one believes that the Torah and the subsequent prophetic and early Rabbinic writings were the products of God-inspired but fallible human beings, then one has the right and even the obligation to examine those writings and to subject them to critical analysis. This essay is intended for readers who reverently think of God as the creative spirit of the universe and who equally reverently think of human beings as endowed by God with the intelligence and critical faculties to differentiate between what is sacred and timeless and what may be the product of human beings who, however well-intentioned, were influenced by the mores, rites, and taboos of their times.

I believe that we have every right to reconsider the laws of kashrut and to determine, with due respect for history and tradition, which of those laws should be determinative for us today. But I believe equally that every sensitive human being, Jew or non-Jew, should evolve a personal dietary regimen that accords with the basic meaning of the word *kasher* (or kosher), that is, "fitting and proper."

And so to the second question: should our eating habits be determined by any considerations beyond health? I respond with an emphatic yes. In eating, as in every other human activity, there are ethical questions that must be considered. Should food be considered kosher if its production involves pain to animals or the despoliation of natural resources? If it is eaten without any indication of gratitude? If it is not shared by other human beings or animals?

There are those who consider the eating of any animal, fish, or fowl to be unethical because it involves the killing of living creatures. I have no argument with vegetarians and vegans. Vegetarianism could be considered a form of kashrut, but this essay is directed primarily to the vast majority of people who do eat meat and/or fish and fowl.

Whether one eats meat or not, those who do are obliged by consideration of ethics to see to it that whatever they eat has been produced with the least possible pain to animals. One of the great ethical teachings of Judaism is *tzaar baalei chayim* (relieving the pain of animals). There is no shortage of verses in the Torah that require sensitivity to the feelings of animals. A few examples should suffice:

> You shall not muzzle an ox while it is threshing. (Deuteronomy 25:4)
>
> When an ox or a sheep or a goat is born, it shall stay seven days with its mother, and from the eighth day on it shall be

acceptable as an offering. . . . No animal from the herd or from the flock shall be slaughtered on the same day with its young. (Leviticus 22:27–28)

If . . . you chance upon a bird's nest . . . with fledgling or eggs and the mother sitting over the fledglings or the eggs, do not take the mother together with her young. Let the mother go, and take only the young, in order that you may fare well and have a long life. (Deuteronomy 22:6–7)

When you see the ass of your enemy lying under its burden and would refrain from raising it, you must nevertheless help raise it. (Exodus 23:5)

While there is no law in the Torah that states specifically that one must treat animals humanely, it was quite clear to the Sages of the Talmud that this was the intent of the passages above. "Relieving the pain of animals [*tzaar baalei chayim*]," they ruled, "is commanded by the Torah" (i.e., it supersedes Rabbinic law) (BT *Bava M'tzia* 32b; BT *Shabbat* 128b).

Certainly, personal health should always be a major factor in determining one's eating habits. Furthermore, it could be argued that it is gluttonous to eat any food without at least pausing to acknowledge the source of that food. For some, this will mean a prayer of thanks to God before breaking bread, while for others it might mean a simple moment of reflection. We should remind ourselves each time that we participate in this most bestial act of eating that we are, in fact, not beasts.

In this regard, I will always remember a lesson that my father taught me as a young boy. We were studying the passage in Genesis that tells of how Esau sold his birthright to his brother Jacob for a bowl of lentil stew. The text reads, "[Esau] ate, drank, got up, and left. Thus did Esau disdain his birthright" (Genesis 25:34). In what way, my father asked, did Esau demonstrate that he despised the sacred birthright? In that he ate, drank, got up, and left, without taking even a moment to thank God for his food. From that day to this, I have never been able to eat a meal without at least pausing to consider the source of my nourishment.

And of course, a further proof of our humanity in the act of eating is our resolve to provide food for those who are not as fortunate as we might be. Every moral human being must either give food directly to needy people or contribute regularly to organizations that provide food for the hungry and homeless. And a related consideration must be a proper regard for the toil and the rights of those laborers who participate in the harvesting and production of our food. Examples of the exploitation of seasonal farm workers are numerous and notorious. We should carefully avoid buying foods that are seasoned by the sweat of exploited workers. These two elements must also be features of any ethical system of kashrut.

And there is yet another consideration beyond health in our determination of what foods we should or should not eat. I alluded above to periods of persecution when Jews were either forced to eat pig flesh or executed because of their refusal to do so. It is very likely that it is historical memory, rather than the Torah text, that keeps a large proportion of the modern Jewish community from eating pork.

As to the third question, about the interpretation of a cryptic text from the Torah, we come to that well-known verse on which the Rabbis of old based the prohibition on the eating meat and dairy products together: "You shall not boil a kid in its mother's milk." This very familiar law has absolutely nothing to do with the mixing of milk and meat but is another of those injunctions that were intended to teach *tzaar baalei chayim*. This matter has been widely argued over the centuries, but the most telling proof that this law has nothing to do with the dietary prohibitions is the fact that it does not appear in the exhaustive list of dietary laws specified in Leviticus 11.

"You shall not boil a kid in its mother's milk" appears three times in the Torah, in Exodus 32:19 and 34:26 and in Deuteronomy 14:21. In the first two instances, it occurs at the conclusion of passages that have to do with festival sacrifices. In the third instance, which does indeed deal with dietary laws, it is appended to the concluding admonition "You are a people consecrated to the Eternal your God"

(Deuteronomy 14:21), and it is clearly disconnected from the dietary laws that precede it. The twelfth-century biblical commentator Rashbam (Rabbi Samuel ben Meir) argued that "it is disgraceful and voracious and gluttonous to consume the mother's milk together with its young. This law is comparable to Leviticus 22:28 and Deuteronomy 22:6–7 [see above]. The Torah gave this commandment in order to teach you how to behave in a civilized manner." Maimonides, in his *Guide for the Perplexed*, suggested that one of the reasons for this prohibition is "because it is somehow connected with idolatry" (*Guide* 3:48).

Few people will ever boil a kid in its mother's milk, not because that law has anything to do with the mixing of milk and meat but because to do so would be as callous as killing a mother bird together with its babies or muzzling a working animal. These are all ethical dicta and have absolutely nothing to do with drinking milk or eating cheese along with meat or fowl. It is purely and simply a law intended to encourage civilized behavior.

Proceeding to the fourth and final question, about the humane treatment of animals, we must address the issue of *sh'chitah* (ritual slaughter) as it is practiced today. The fact that both the U.S. Department of Agriculture and the organization People for the Ethical Treatment of Animals have raised questions about the humaneness of kosher slaughter (particularly in the notorious slaughtering plant in Postville, Iowa, described in the book *Postville* by Stephen G. Bloom, 2000) should be an embarrassment to the Orthodox kashrut authorities who give their approval to such slaughter.

These same Orthodox authorities certify the kashrut of butcher shops that sell foie gras and "milk-fed" veal with no consideration whatsoever of the pain of the animals involved. It should be an embarrassment not only to the Orthodox authorities but to all who buy kosher meat that the U.S. Humane Slaughtering Act of 1978, which requires the stunning of animals before they are killed so as to avoid unnecessary pain and the sensing of impending slaughter, must make an exception for *sh'chitah*. Yet, the laws of *sh'chitah* require that an animal be killed as swiftly and painlessly as possible.

Just a few words about that anomaly that is generally referred to as *glatt* kosher. According to the laws of *sh'chitah*, the lungs of a kosher animal must be examined to be sure that they are smooth, that is, free of adhesions. But there are various types of adhesions that may be found in the lungs of animals, some of which are minor and do not render the animal unkosher. However, those who impose more rigid standards of kashrut on themselves will insist on eating only those animals whose lungs are absolutely smooth, that is, *glatt*.

I believe in kashrut, and I heartily recommend it to all who want to participate in the richness and the blessings of Jewish tradition. I consider our family dining table to be a *mizbei-ach m'at*, a miniature or a proxy altar. On the Sabbath and festivals, our table is graced by wine, candles, and challot; it is a sacred space that connects us to God and to the history of our people. Even on ordinary days, one's table should represent something more than catering to our basest animal instinct: eating.

But the kashrut that I recommend and that I observe is not the kashrut of the Orthodox establishment. It is a dietary regimen that derives from an enlightened understanding of the ancient admonition "You shall not boil a kid in its mother's milk," and its primary requirements are as follows:

- Sensitivity to the pain of animals
- Acts of *tzedakah* to the hungry
- Expressions of gratitude for sustenance
- The avoidance of gluttony
- Consideration of the food taboos of previous generations
- The avoidance of foods that are reminiscent of historical persecutions
- The avoidance of foods that are the produced through the exploitation of laborers

This is kashrut, choosing to eat only that which is fitting and proper for an observant ethical Jew.

RABBI MARY L. ZAMORE

Jewish Value Meals

IN AMERICAN ADVERTISING, a value meal is one that provides a
lot of food for a little money; in Judaism, it instead embodies the
best of our ritual and ethical values. While it is certainly appropriate to serve celebratory or comforting communal meals at life-cycle
events, these meals must not be a reflection of the worst of Western materialism, consumption, and waste. Instead, we must create
meals, parties, and gatherings that reflect the Jewish values we strive
to uphold every day. Moments of transition, such as welcoming new
family members, entering into adulthood, dedicating ourselves to
a life partner, choosing Judaism, or letting go of the ones we love,
should spur us to evaluate our lives and rededicate ourselves to lives
of meaning. The food we serve at these life-cycle events must reflect
our best practices as they relate to the Jewish rituals and ethics of
food and its production. In short, our life-cycle meals should be Jewish value meals.

Commanded Meals
Whether a happy or sad occasion, we usually want to feed the people
who have congregated for our sake, often sacrificing personal time
and traveling to do so, and as a result, the food has become a great
focus of our life-cycle events. Jewish tradition, in fact, recognizes
the parties and meals that accompany our life-cycle events as integral parts of our rituals. It may be hard to believe that eating a bagel
is an obligation, but the meal that follows a happy life-cycle ritual
(and other festive Jewish occasions like the completion of a course
of Jewish study) is referred to as *s'udat mitzvah*, "a commanded
meal." Therefore, it is beholden upon the host to provide the meal
and upon the guests to attend it. The more sober counterpart to the

s'udat mitzvah is the s'udat havraah, "meal of consolation," which is served to the mourners when they return from the cemetery and begin sitting shivah.

The meals of celebration and sorrow both have deep roots in our tradition. The origins of the s'udat mitzvah can be traced back to the feast that Abraham hosted marking Isaac's weaning (Genesis 21:8). Interestingly, in the Rabbinic period, the midrash draws a connection between the weaning meal and bar mitzvah repast by musing that Isaac was thirteen when weaned, and therefore the feast was his bar mitzvah meal (B'reishit Rabbah 53:10). Revealing early roots, the s'udat havraah is linked to II Samuel 3:35, in which David mourns Abner and the people comfort him by giving him food to eat, and Jeremiah 16:7, which refers to the practice of comforting the bereaved with food. Meals associated with marriage rituals are well documented in the Talmud (BT K'tubot 8a; BT B'rachot 31a).

Hidur Mitzvah: The Beautification of the Mitzvah

Raised to the status of mitzvah, or commandment, these life-cycle meals are a necessity. However, how elaborately we design the culinary experience (and accompanying party, if applicable) is up to us and our financial means, time, and energy. The value of hidur mitzvah, "beautification of the mitzvah," guides us toward putting time and care into any mitzvah with which we engage.[1] For example, after a bris, we are commanded to serve food to our guests. However, we could put out a few day-old bagels salvaged from the bargain bin and a pitcher of lukewarm water. Yes, we have fulfilled the commandment of serving a s'udat mitzvah, but we have missed the opportunity to rejoice in the mitzvah by presenting the food in a caring and enticing manner. Yet, on the other hand, striving for a meal infused with hidur mitzvah does not require us to take out an

---

1. The concept of hidur mitzvah is derived from the verse "This is my God and I will glorify Him" (Exodus 15:2). The Rabbis are troubled by the idea that human beings could increase God's glory. They navigate that theological problem by explaining that we glorify God by performing mitzvot in the most beautiful manner possible (p. 164 M'chilta, Masekhet D'shirah, Parasha Gimel, ed. Horowitz-Rabin, p. 127).

extra mortgage. For mitzvot that require a financial commitment, we are expected only to spend within our means. Unfortunately, we do not have to urge members of our communities to have festive meals and parties, as our generation is not witnessing a phenomenon of under-spending on life-cycle parties, but of gross over-spending. Even if every culinary indulgence is within our financial means, it may not be appropriate to create the most expensive party ever seen. Our *s'udot mitzvah* must also embody restraint, and most importantly, the meals must not overshadow the reason for gathering, the ritual itself. Again, when we allow our Jewish values to guide the food choices we make for life-cycle meals, we move away from mere materialism toward value meals.

Charitable Giving of Money and Care

Since the meals linked to the life cycle are commanded, if there is a family in our community who may not be able to afford to throw a party, it is the obligation of the community to assist the family make a meal. Clearly, this should be done with great sensitivity in order not to embarrass the family or bring their financial situation into public discussion. However, working with one's rabbi, support can be offered to the family quietly. Friends can even offer to host a festive potluck with homegrown entertainment.

The other outlet for charity concerning life-cycle meals is to include in our party budgets a line for *tzedakah*, giving money to the needy. In premodern times, it was expected that the poor of the community would be invited to the life-cycle events of the well-off. A modern adaptation of this practice would be giving a donation to a local feeding program in honor of the happy event. By including the giving of *tzedakah* in our budgets or to-do lists every time we enjoy a festive communal meal, we build the expectation that helping the hungry is a normative part of our celebrations, not a mere optional add-on.

When we throw appropriate, more modest parties, we also help our friends and community by not furthering an endless competition to outspend each other. By keeping our parties to a reasonable level, we also allow the meal to complement our happy occasion, not hijack it. Therefore, these repasts should be planned not only with social mores in mind, but with Jewish values at the forefront.

Unfortunately, as much as the bris, bar/bat mitzvah, and Jewish wedding meals are in danger of being defined by conspicuous consumption, the *s'udat havraah* is overrun by the impulse to play host and entertain guests. At its best, the *s'udat havraah* should set the tone for the community's goal to care for the mourners from the time that they leave the cemetery and return to their home to the end of shivah (or even beyond, if appropriate). The synagogue should have a caring community group whose members offer to help set up the mourner's home for shivah; lend items like a large coffee urn or hot water kettle, chairs, folding tables, and so on, to accommodate those who will visit at the home; and bring a round of food to feed the mourners, their family, and friends. It is customary for those making a shivah call to bring food and therefore contribute to the *s'udat havraah*. However, those food gifts can arrive erratically and not cover all food needs. Rather than leaving the mourners in a position where they need to run out to get milk or make a salad, the caring community or a trusted friend can also help coordinate food gifts. This can be especially important if among the mourners there are those with specific dietary restrictions. Too often the mourners feel as if they must set up their home as if a party is about to take place; this is a burden that should not be added to their loss. Of course, as with any other type of *chesed* (act of kindness), the recipients always have the last word and should never feel like help, no matter how well meaning, is being forced upon them. Friends or a caring community group can also offer to help clean up after each day of shivah, especially keeping an eye on the storage of leftovers. Sometimes, so much food is brought to the mourner's house that it is impossible to refrigerate or eat everything. Each community should be prepared to help remove leftovers, store them when needed, and find an appropriate repository for them, like a local feeding program.

Kashrut: Jewish Food Value Menus

When we allow kashrut, the Jewish dietary practices, to influence our eating habits, we affirm our Jewish identities and connect to our greater Jewish community, our sacred tradition, and God. As we discussed, our life-cycle meals are an extension of the rituals themselves. Therefore, families should consider menus reflecting our ritual and ethical food laws to connect the life-cycle event and meal fully. The Jewish dietary laws exclude nonkosher foods like pork, shellfish, and nonkosher[2] meats and require separating milk and meat foods and their related products. While we may or may not keep kosher during the rest of the year, we can sanctify our life-cycle events by following some or all of the Jewish dietary laws at those special moments. Making a kosher-style meal is a good place to start for Jews who do not regularly keep kosher. Keeping some or all of the laws of kashrut will distinguish our life-cycle meal from other gatherings; it will connect us to Jews throughout the world; it will model living Judaism for our families.

Another way to bring kashrut to our tables is to use kosher wine. While some Jews look forward to the unique taste of kosher wine labeled "heavy Concord grape," others will appreciate the wonderful variety of fine kosher wines. While it is acceptable from a Reform Jewish perspective to say *Kiddush* over any wine, Jewish festivities are wonderful times to serve kosher wine. In particular, Israel produces an amazing variety of kosher wines in many different price ranges. We can connect to and support Israel by especially buying Israeli kosher wine.

B'rachot: Blessings

It is very common to start festive life-cycle meals with the recitation of *Kiddush* and *HaMotzi*, the blessings over wine and bread. Caterers and hosts, in fact, often provide an oversized challah for

---

2. Nonkosher meats can refer to those cuts of meat that are not deemed kosher, like the hindquarters of cattle, or meat that is not butchered by a certified trained kosher butcher, a *shochet*.

this purpose.[3] Among liberal Jews, it is less common to include *Birkat HaMazon*, the blessings after we eat. While this may not be part of our individual daily practice, these after-the-meal blessings can help us reflect in gratitude for the gifts of food and company and connect to God in thanksgiving. These potentially lengthy blessings can be recited according to the gatherers' ability. If no one knows the full blessing, it is fine to sing the parts known in Hebrew and then read the rest in English. For life-cycle events like weddings, a bris, and even the house of mourning, there are specific insertions to *Birkat HaMazon*. Otherwise, we can add some personal, even spontaneous, prayers that are tailored to the specific life-cycle event and the people in the room.

The additions to *Birkat HaMazon* for weddings is referred to as the *Sheva B'rachot*, the "Seven Blessings," which echo the seven blessings recited over the glass of wine under the chuppah, the wedding canopy. In most traditional Jewish communities, friends and family hold festive meals for seven days after the wedding for the bride and groom. These are also referred to as *Sheva B'rachot* meals, because the *Birkat HaMazon* recited after the meal includes again the *Sheva B'rachot* additions. If the bride and groom are not following the secular American custom of leaving immediately after the wedding for a honeymoon, it is certainly joyful and meaningful to take a cue from our Jewish traditions and host small, festive meals in their honor and, if possible, to sanctify them with blessings before and after the meal.

Bal Tashchit: Environmentalism

While it can be easy to follow what is modeled by our communities, offered by caterers, or expected by our relatives, it is important to check in with our Jewish ethical values before we plan a communal meal. Beginning with the Torah, Jewish law has commanded us

---

3. It should be noted that one does not require a challah in order to say *HaMotzi*, the blessing over any type of bread. It is merely a custom to use this beloved egg bread, reminding us of the Shabbat table.

not to be needlessly wasteful and instead to be astute stewards of our earth. The Rabbinic term *bal tashchit*, literally meaning "do not destroy," is rooted in the biblical commandment *lo tashchit* (Deuteronomy 20:19–20), meaning the same. Today *bal tashchit* is often used synonymously with *shomrei adamah*, "guardians of the earth," a term that describes humanity's relationship to the earth. Both terms become the heading under which environmental issues are addressed. The application of the value of environmentalism to Jewish eating is boundless, but for life-cycle meals we can focus on two parts of our meal: what we serve and how we serve it.

For festive meals, we like to bring out the best of our culinary culture. However, we must remember that human consumption has a profound impact on our environment. We can make menu choices that minimize that impact by eating lower on the food chain; reducing the amount of meat we serve; avoiding fish that are endangered through overfishing or are produced through poorly regulated and highly polluting fish farms; choosing local, organic, and/or seasonal foods.

Today's life-cycle celebrations, especially weddings and bar/bat mitzvahs, often include several meals, the main festive meal and one or more small meals for family and out-of-town guests. As plastic plates, glasses, and flatware are designed to convincingly mimic their reusable counterparts, it is increasingly common for disposable food service items to be used at many of these meals. Given that we frequently are hosting many people at life-cycle meals, high-quality disposable food service may seem like an easy and even affordable choice to make. However, it does so at the expense of our environment by adding to our overstuffed landfills. A Jewish life-cycle value meal should strive to be as green as possible within the financial and logistical ability of the host. Since festive meals are usually planned well in advance, we have the opportunity to think ahead in order to reduce our dependency on disposable serving pieces. We can budget for and request that our caterers use real service items; we can borrow items from family and guests in order to reduce the use of disposables; we can organize volunteers to wash dishes in order to share the burden of reusable dishes. Our festive meals can celebrate our highest ideals.

Tzaar Baalei Chayim (Animal Rights) and Oshek (Workers' Rights)

In addition to planning a menu that seeks out green choices, we can also live the Jewish ethical value of *tzaar baalei chayim*, the prevention of suffering to animals. This is a Rabbinic value, based on the biblical commandment "When you see the ass of your enemy lying under its burden and would refrain from raising it, you must nevertheless help raise it" (Exodus 23:5).[4] We can choose sources for our meat, dairy, and eggs that are dedicated to the humane treatment of animals. We can also shun foods like veal and foie gras, which are technically kosher, yet violate the value of *tzaar baalei chayim*.

For life-cycle events, especially the ones with big parties, it is likely that we will be hiring a caterer, paying for help at our home, or going to a restaurant. The rights of the workers who produce our food and help serve our food are, unfortunately, rarely discussed in the context of life-cycle events, when we are frequently concerned with our budgets and centered on our celebrations. Yet, we must remember that we are often an employer at these occasions. *Oshek*, the oppression of a worker, is expressly forbidden in the Torah, as defined by several primary texts. The Torah instructs, "You shall not oppress your neighbor. You shall not commit robbery. The wages of a laborer shall not remain with you until morning" (Leviticus 19:13). In addition, "You shall not abuse a needy and destitute laborer, whether a fellow Israelite or a stranger. . . . You must pay out the wages due on the same day" (Deuteronomy 24:14–15). In a modern context, *oshek* commands us to treat and pay our help fairly whether they work in our Jewish institutions, homes, or restaurants or for our caterer. Being clear about work duties, hours, and pay is important. Making sure those who work for us have a safe way of getting home, especially at night, is also vital. Thanking our employees privately and

---

4. BT *Bava M'tzia* 32a–b.

publicly is also respectful of their role in creating a beautiful event.

We can also support the rights of agricultural and food workers when we buy our food, both groceries and prepared foods, by looking for certifications that assure that those involved in its production have been fairly paid. There are a growing number of secular and specifically Jewish certifications that attest to food workers' conditions. These include Fair Trade, a secular agency that certifies the payment of living wages to workers, especially in the notorious coffee, tea, chocolate, and nut industries;[5] Magen Tzedek (originally named Hechsher Tzedek), created by Rabbi Morris Allen through the Conservative Movement to certify that kosher products adhere to additional ethical guidelines, including *oshek*;[6] the Israeli Orthodox social justice organization Bemaaglei Tzedek, which awards its "*Tav Chevrati*, a seal of approval, granted free of charge to restaurants and other businesses that respect the legally-mandated rights of their employees";[7] and the American Orthodox social justice organization Uri L'Tzedek's Tav HaYosher, which seeks to certify kosher restaurants that uphold "the right to fair pay, the right to fair time, and the right to a safe work environment."[8] While it is extremely difficult to find a large range of food products with these certifications, we can support this value by seeking out such products, especially when we buy coffee, tea, and chocolate.

Sh'mirat HaGuf: Preserving Our Health

Life-cycle moments may seem like a time to forego dietary health concerns, but some thought should still be given to healthy menu offerings. In the Torah, we are taught that we were created *b'tzelem Elohim*, "in the image of God" (Genesis 1:27), from which evolves the value of sh'mirat haguf, the value of caring for our bodies. In other words, when we work to preserve our own health, as well as that of others, we are honoring God's handiwork. The food choices we

---

5. http://www.transfairusa.org/.
6. http://magentzedek.org/.
7. http://www.mtzedek.org.il/english/TavChevrati.asp.
8. http://www.utzedek.org/tavhayosher.html.

make as hosts directly affects our health and our guests' health; it indirectly affects the agricultural workers. For example, if the food one serves is produced with chemicals, we should have two concerns—the effect of the chemicals on our own health and on the agricultural workers' health. Emphasizing organically produced foods will benefit our personal health and that of our guests, the workers' health, and the environment.

S'udot mitzvah and *s'udot havraah* often include indulgent food designed to celebrate or comfort. While some treats are certainly called for, sh'mirat haguf directs us to lighten the health impact of our life-cycle meals by choosing lighter versions of our favorite recipes, emphasizing fruits and vegetables in our menus, and avoiding the message that everyone must eat with abandon in order to celebrate fully. The modern host will offer lighter and vegetarian choices, as well as inquire about guests' dietary needs, especially allergies, and do the best to accommodate them. If a loved one's diet is too complicated, it is perfectly fine to invite that guest to bring his or her own food.

B'tei-avon, Enjoy the Meal!

There is no such thing as a perfect meal, whether it is designed to rejoice or comfort. However, we can shift away from meals that embody the worst of food culture and instead make better food choices, connecting us to our Jewish ritual and ethical laws. It is virtually impossible to create a life-cycle meal that includes all of the above values, but we can host meals exemplifying the values we strive to uphold every day. At the most important moments of life we can serve Jewish value meals.

For a more complete discussion of Jewish ritual and ethical dietary laws, see *The Sacred Table: Creating a Jewish Food Ethic*, ed. Rabbi Mary L. Zamore (New York: CCAR Press, 2011).

RABBI LISA J. GRUSHCOW, DPhil

A Jewish View of Sexuality

ADAM AND EVE, not Adam and Steve!" So goes a chant against
equal rights for people who are LGBTQ (lesbian, gay, bisexual,
transgender, and queer). A biblical scholar might reply, "But how
about Jacob, Leah, Rachel, Bilhah, and Zilpah?" (the patriarch, his
two wives, and his two concubines).

As evident from the biblical period through to our own times, sexuality is not simple. But Judaism in general, and progressive Judaism
in particular, sees sexuality as one of the greatest and most powerful
gifts we have as human beings. Judaism is known as a sex-positive
religion; in this chapter, we will explore what this means.

First and foremost, sexuality is seen as something worth talking
and learning about. It is not shameful, and it is not taboo. In this
surprising story from the Babylonian Talmud (*B'rachot* 62b), we see
how much this is so:

> Rav Kahana once went in and hid under Rav's bed. He heard him
> chatting [with his wife] and joking and doing what he required.
> He said to him: One would think that Abba's [Rav's] mouth had
> never sipped the dish before! He said to him: Kahana, are you
> here? Get out, because it is rude. He replied: This too is Torah,
> and I must learn it.

In Rabbinic Judaism, to which we are heirs, sexuality is firmly
set within the system of mitzvot. Celibacy is neither expected nor
required. There are things we should do and things we should not
do; there are good and bad forms of sexual expression. Sex itself,
however, is neither inherently good nor inherently bad. This is in
keeping with the notion that each of us has within us *yetzer hatov*, an
inclination toward goodness, and *yetzer hara*, an inclination toward
evil. When it comes to sexuality, Jewish teaching is meant to help us

direct our desires in positive ways.

Two stories can help illustrate the importance of positive sexuality in Judaism, on the communal level and on the personal level. First, communal:

> You find that in the time when Israel were in forced labor in Egypt, Pharaoh decreed against them that they could not sleep in their houses, in order to stop them sleeping with their wives.
>
> Rabbi Simeon bar Chalafta says: What did the daughters of Israel do? They went down to draw water from the Nile, and the Holy Blessed One would arrange for them tiny fish inside their buckets. They sold some of the fish and cooked the rest, took wine, and went to the field. There they fed their husbands. . . . Once they had eaten and drunk, the women took mirrors and showed them to their husbands. She would say, "I'm more beautiful than you," and he would say, "I'm more beautiful than you," and through this they became accustomed to desire once more and were fruitful and multiplied, and God visited them straight away with children. . . .
>
> Through the merit of these mirrors that the women showed their husbands and re-accustomed them to desire in the midst of the slavery, were established the hosts [tz'vaot] of the Israelites. . . .
>
> When later God told Moses to build the Tabernacle, all of Israel stood up and gave voluntarily. Some brought silver, others gold or bronze. . . . But the women said, "What do we have to give as an offering to the *Mishkan*?" They arose and brought the mirrors to Moses. When Moses saw the mirrors, he was furious. He said to Israel, "Take sticks and smash them. What do we need mirrors for?" But God said to Moses, "Moses, you think these are worthless? These mirrors established all the hosts in Egypt. Take them and make a basin of brass and its base for the priests, for through it the priests will sanctify themselves."[1]

In this fascinating story, Moses is told to accept the mirrors that the women offered, precisely because they were instruments of desire. The ability to arouse sexual desire is seen to be essential to the redemption of the Israelites from Egypt. Some of this, of course, is connected to procreation. But there also is an acknowledgment that

---

1. *Tanchuma, P'kudei 9.*

desire can be difficult in the context of oppression, and that regaining one's desire—and awakening the desire of one's partner—is part of what it means to be free. Aside from being what we could see as an endorsement of the use of sex toys or other creative means to keep a marriage full of passion, this story makes a profound link between sexuality and human freedom.

Next, a more individualized story:

> In Sidon it happened that a man took a wife with whom he lived for ten years and she bore him no children. When they came to Rabbi Simeon bar Yochai to be divorced, the man said to his wife, "Take any precious object I have in my house—take it and go back to your father's house." Rabbi Simeon bar Yochai said, "Even as you were wed with food and drink, so you should separate with food and drink." What did the wife do? She prepared a great feast, gave her husband too much to drink [so that he fell asleep], then called to her servants saying, "Take him to my father's house." At midnight he woke up from his sleep and asked, "Where am I?" She replied, "Did you not say, 'Whatever precious object I have in my house—take it and go back to your father's house?' I have no object more precious than you." When Simeon bar Yochai heard what the wife had done, he prayed on the couple's behalf, and they were remembered with children.[2]

Although both these stories end with the birth of children, they also show that procreation is not the sole reason for sex in Judaism. In numerous places in Rabbinic law and lore, we see examples of non-procreative sex. Independent of conception, sex is seen as an essential part of relationships, something to which the woman in particular is entitled within a heterosexual marriage.

Although there are varied biblical examples of relationships (e.g., polygamy, concubines), Jewish sexuality today is focused on the marital model. At its best, marriage is, as it is known in Hebrew, *kiddushin*: something holy that two people choose to create with one another as they establish their Jewish home. It is worth noting that if that covenantal holiness is broken, divorce is not only allowed but encouraged. Relationships, and sexuality within them, are never to

---

2. *P'sikta D'Rav Kahana* 22:2.

be coercive or abusive, and appropriate boundaries are essential to what it means to be an ethical, sexual human being.

In progressive Judaism, the model of marriage has been both expanded and challenged. It has been expanded to include the sanctification of same-sex relationships on a completely equal level to heterosexual relationships. We find biblical precedents—for example, in the passionate friendship between David and Jonathan—but most importantly, we find precedent in the inherent dignity of every human being and the recognition that intimate relationships have fundamental value. When one looks at the rituals and liturgy of egalitarian Jewish marriage, it is striking how little change is required to include same-sex couples. When different treatment based on gender (for example, a man acquiring a woman in marriage, or impurity determined by a woman's menstrual cycle) is rejected, then marriage is open to same-sex and opposite-sex couples alike. Much has been written on the traditional prohibition on sex between men, found in the Book of Leviticus. Here, we may simply note that we understand that prohibition as coming from a place and time very different from our own and that our approach is based on more enduring Jewish ideas of human dignity and wholeness.

It is also worth noting that there are countless Rabbinic texts that recognize diverse gender identities and acknowledge that not everyone is clearly male or female. We hold firmly to the belief, as expressed in Genesis, that each of us is created in the image of God. In all our diversity, we mirror the Divine.

Beyond the expansion of marriage to make it more inclusive, we recognize that marriage itself is not the only model within which sexuality resides. As people get married far past puberty (a significant difference from ancient times) or sometimes never get married, we take Judaism's principles of healthy sexual relationships—consensual and communicative—and apply them to all sexual choices. With new challenges posed by dementia and aging, we explore how one might find ongoing intimacy and companionship without sacrificing loyalty to a spouse.

All these issues highlight how the covenantal model between

ourselves and God is also expected of our interactions with each other. Ideally, these covenantal relationships are characterized by shared commitment and the joy that comes from intimacy. In Judaism, adultery is seen as analogous to idolatry, because both involve betrayal of that intimacy—the shattering of something sacred. The area of sexuality is one in which we can experience profound connection and also one in which we can experience profound pain. Throughout, our interactions are meant to be shaped by a deep recognition of the existence of the other, whether it is the lover passionately searched for in the Song of Songs or the partner with whom one weathers the ups and downs of life.

Just as there are mitzvot related to holidays and life-cycle moments, to prayer, and to food, there are mitzvot related to sex. How often a couple can expect sex from one another and how to keep passion alive, what boundaries prevent exploitation and abuse, how to make space for sexuality beyond fertility—all these are questions on which Judaism can guide us. This too is Torah, and we must learn it.

Table for One

TABLE FOR ONE? Yes.

It is great to be single, but at times, it can also be hard to be single. There are times when you want to go out and do something fun, like eat a lovely meal at a restaurant or go to the movies late at night, and you don't particularly feel like doing it alone. None of your friends or family are around when you decide you want this experience, so you consider what it might look like if you do it by yourself. And, perhaps, you decide that having the experience by yourself is better than not doing it at all. So you venture out on your own, have a lovely time, and realize that it's okay to be single or by yourself and do what makes you happy.

The same is true of Jewish ritual. Judaism will always emphasize the importance of engaging in ritual with families and in teaching generations to come about the history of our rituals and the necessity to engage in them in order to keep our traditions alive. But that doesn't mean that the opposite cannot be true—that if you don't have a family or you don't have children or a spouse, you cannot also engage in meaningful ritual or begin new traditions by yourself. In fact, one of the best things about being on your own is getting to dictate what you do in your life and how you do it. It is the perfect time for experimenting in meaningful Jewish rituals and figuring out and adapting the rituals that are most meaningful to you into the regularity of your life. In fact, by consciously choosing which rituals are significant to you, you will likely strengthen your desire to engage in ritual and even strengthen your relationship with Judaism at the same time.

But it can be overwhelming, and even intimidating, to try and explore the world of ritual all on your own. It might be hard to know where to begin and what to choose to do in order to make space for ritual to be part of your life. To make it a little less daunting to begin thinking about new practices, it is important to break apart, into steps, the process of beginning and trying new rituals.

The first step in creating and finding your own personal ritual practice is figuring out what rituals you are drawn to in Judaism that you can see making a real part of your life. What is it about Judaism that you love and would like to incorporate more of in your own life? Now is the time for you to really brainstorm and explore the areas of Judaism that you love, without being tethered to anyone else and their notions of ritual practice. There are a myriad of things you can do to celebrate and practice Judaism, and nothing, except saying a prayer that requires a minyan, is impossible to do on your own. Ritual can be as big as keeping kosher and saying prayers daily, or it can be as simple as baking challah once a week, affixing a mezuzah to the doorpost of your home, or saying *Kaddish* on the anniversary of a family member's death. Ritual becomes a real part of our lives when we look forward to engaging in that which we find to be most meaningful and in practicing that ritual on a consistent basis. Whatever it is that draws you to Judaism will most likely have a ritual associated with it. Now is the time to discover what those rituals are and which you are most interested in exploring.

The next step in developing your own ritual practice is to be realistic about how you will consistently make the rituals you love within Judaism a priority in your life. Some people who are single have very structured and regimented lives, whereas others live a more carefree and unstructured existence. This is true of couples, families, and family systems as well. No matter who you are, be true to yourself when making a decision about trying a new ritual. If you are never home on Saturday night, then celebrating *Havdalah* every week probably would not work for you. If you know that you have extra time in the morning and prayer is important to you, try starting your day off with a few daily morning prayers. Rituals in Judaism are often time-bound, but not all of them. So, if your life demands a little more flexibility than structure, try exploring rituals that offer that flexibility, such as saying a blessing before or after you eat, which you have the opportunity to do at least once or twice a day. There are some rituals within Jewish practice that can be done once, many times, or daily. Whatever it is that you choose to do, be sure that it makes sense for the schedule and rhythm of your life, as well as something that you'll want to incorporate as a regular part of how you live your life—no matter what your schedule.

Next, don't be afraid to go outside of your comfort zone. This doesn't just mean trying new rituals; it means making time to try new rituals. Often, it's easy to want to push aside something because we are fearful we don't have enough time to commit to it. People often want to get in shape but claim that they have no time to exercise, so they don't even begin a workout regime. Or, hobbies can go by the wayside when it becomes clear that it takes more time than one is willing to put in. But that doesn't have to be the case with ritual, especially as you are discovering and settling into new rituals that may or may not be right for you. It is okay to try out a ritual once or twice and then get bored with it or drop it. That is usually a sign that it's not the right fit for you or that it doesn't fit well into the rhythm of your life. Learning how to weed out rituals that don't work for you, on your own, is hugely important to finding and practicing the ones that do. Once you do find a ritual that works for you and that you love, you will be surprised at how easy it is to regularly incorporate it into your life. Just be patient and comfortable with experimenting, trying, and making time for new things.

Finally, once you've tried different rituals and maybe even found a few that you really enjoy, never be apologetic for being single and making Jewish ritual and practice a priority in your life. Being unapologetic applies not only toward the judgment of others, but also to your internal justification for making ritual a priority. Don't be afraid of embracing ritual and making it your own. Like going out alone, it can seem fearful, at first, to try new things on your own and to continuously do them on your own. But, in the end, it will make your personal connection and the connection you have to others within Judaism more significant and meaningful.

Being single is a lot of fun. And, it is also a time to really discover who you are and what you want out of your life—what is it that is most important to you? There are times when it can seem easier to do nothing or to do what you have always done, rather than explore new options and experiment with new ideas, especially because no one is holding you accountable for your actions. And, perhaps, it even seems like a lot of work to try out new rituals and ritual practice. But this is true for nearly everything you do as a single person. Making a meal on your own, for example, can seem like a lot of work, but it is worth it in the end, because you get exactly what you want. Jewish ritual is the same—it might take a little more work than doing nothing, and it might be easier to use the excuse of being single to justify not needing or wanting to engage in ritual. Why go to all that effort, if it's just for yourself? The investment of time can enable you to create something for yourself that you enjoy and that brings meaning to your Judaism. In the end, understanding what ritual is like for you, individually, will be worth it in creating a life and a Jewish practice that is filled with purpose, significance, and importance to you.

RABBI HERBERT BRONSTEIN

Kiddushin

A Jewish View of Marriage

MARRIAGE HOLDS a special place in Jewish tradition. It is the place where love, the creation of a family, and the perpetuation of Judaism in the holy space we call a home all coalesce. The home is designated as a *mikdash m'at* (a miniature temple). Marriage is a sacred covenant—a sacred partnership between two people. One of the primary metaphors for marriage in Judaism is the giving of the Torah at Mount Sinai, which is imagined as a wedding ceremony between God and the Jewish people, in which the Torah is understood to be the *ketubah* (the wedding contract). Nothing clarifies the Jewish attitude toward marriage quite as well as the traditional name for the wedding ceremony, *kiddushin*, derived from the Hebrew *kadosh*—holy. As we come to understand the deeper meaning of *kadosh*, we may begin to appreciate why Jewish tradition reserved the word *kiddushin* for marriage.

In Jewish thought, all existence is derived originally from God and is, therefore, potentially holy. Time and space, God-given, are sacred but can also be desecrated by idolatry—the worship of things or of self. In consequence, we set special times and places aside for respect, for reverence, so that they may be kept apart from the realm of the profane, from exploitation for material gain and utilitarian usage. In time, the Sabbath; in space, the synagogues are instances that come to mind. The prayer in which we set aside the Shabbat *day*, a time of value in and of itself and not for further gain or use, we call *Kiddush*, "Sanctification."

Humanity lives, however, not only in the dimensions of time and space, but also, from birth, in the dimension of relationship. And while all relationships, like all time and space, should be considered sacred, certain relationships are especially exalted. In Judaism, the holy of holies of all relationships, to which the poetic genius of the Hebraic spirit turned most often for the paradigm of the covenant between God and Israel, was and is the covenant between husband and wife (see, for example, Hosea 1 and 2). Today Reform Judaism recognizes same-sex marriage to be the equivalent of opposite-sex marriage, a sacred commitment by two loving partners. A sacred entity, the newly united couple, comes into being in Jewish marriage. As in the *Kiddush* of Shabbat we set apart a period of *time* as holy, in *kiddushin* the partners set themselves apart from others and commit to a sacred bond that is only for each other. Historically Jewish tradition considered the woman who married as *m'kudeshet*—"made holy," set aside and apart for her husband, consecrated and thus inviolate. In the view of contemporary Reform Judaism, this "setting aside" is mutual; both spouses (of any gender) are consecrated to each other. They create a sacred entity in the act of *kiddushin*—consecration.

In the Jewish marriage service, in the very act of consecrating a *particular* relationship as holy, the potential sanctity of *all* relationship is asserted. The couple represent the bond between God and humanity, the ideal toward which all human relationships should strive. *Kiddushin* is the rooting of the human in the realm of the sacred, with the goal that all our relationships become holy, bearing the blossom and fruit of life.

A Jewish marriage, then, takes place when a couple, in the presence of at least two adult, competent witnesses, make a commitment to one another that their union will be inviolate. Each says to the other, "Behold, you are consecrated to me . . . according to the tradition of Moses and Israel." It is as if each were saying to the other, "I will do everything that I can to make our relationship sacred."

Since Judaism looks affirmatively upon marriage, including its physical aspect, *kiddushin* is not "given" as a concession or as a required channel of salvation. Nor, strictly speaking, does a rabbi "marry" a couple; the couple marry each another. Because of the dignity and joy of this most important personal religious observance in Judaism, the rabbi is asked to speak the blessings in behalf of the community. But the rabbi does not "do" the *kiddushin*. The rabbi is, in the careful Rabbinic definition, the *m'sadeir* or *m'saderet kiddushin*, the one who "arranges *kiddushin*" and helps the couple through their act of consecration one to the other, as they begin together to form the sacred relationship of marriage.

Traditional Jewish worship was designed around the three overarching biblical motifs of Creation, redemption (as in the Exodus), and revelation (that occurred at Sinai). The entire round of Jewish observance is suffused by these same three themes. Thus, in the holiday cycle, Rosh HaShanah is clearly associated with Creation; Passover with the Exodus; Shavuot with Sinai. For *kiddushin*, the act of marriage, the Rabbis of our classic period chose the theme of Creation around which to design the celebratory blessings. These are known in our tradition as the *Sheva B'rachot*, the "Seven Blessings of Praise."

Indeed the *Sheva B'rachot* contain in brief compass the entire sweep of the Jewish conception of existence, from the miraculous glory of the original panoply of Creation to the sublime perfection of Creation in the messianic completion. Both the evocation of paradise and the affirmation of the messianic celebration are comprised in a seven-versed poem on the theme of Creation, which bears the luster of that crystallization that is the mark of poetry of genius. Even the *number* of blessings, *seven*, which is the numerical symbol of the cosmos, emblematic of the seven days of Creation, of the spheres, of light (the menorah), is meant to convey the unified theme of Creation.

Of the three major motifs of biblical Judaism, why did the Rabbis choose the theme of Creation for the blessings of *kiddushin*? For the couple, in choosing to join their lives together, a new world comes into being. Undoubtedly, also because historically the miracle of Creation is renewed in procreation. Out of the very substance and spirit of husband and wife, created in the image of God, is spun the perpetual, miraculous fabric of life. That is why, in the Jewish folkloristic conception, partners are seen as newborns in marriage; they are, as it were, sinless, blessed with a whole new start in life. In today's world, the broadened understanding of marriage to include same-sex couples challenges that historic paradigm, but all Jewish couples, whether opposite-sex or same-sex, are tasked with the same communal responsibility, should they so choose—to create a new generation.

Further, the purpose of Jewish existence is the partnership with God in the maintenance, the harmonization, of Creation. And every good marriage is considered to be a *tikkun*, a "putting in order," for each good marriage lifts existence to a state of higher harmony. Within the tradition, especially among the mystics, can be found the idea that every true act of love in marriage is itself a *tikkun*, uniting the transcendent and immanent aspects of divinity, an analogy to spiritual and physical union in married love.

Thus, the consecration of a marriage is a cause for great rejoicing. Of all relationships, the marriage relationship is *kodesh kodashim*—the holy of holies; and the wedding, among all the rejoicings of life, is the *simchat s'machot*—the celebration of celebrations. Indeed, in traditional Jewish life, the union of two lives was the occasion for celebration by the entire community. It is as if the framers of the wedding service gathered from the garden of the Hebrew language a whole cluster of words signifying happiness and joy and put them together in the blessings, like a floral bouquet for the couple, thanking God for being "the Creator of love and companionship, laughter and song, pleasure and delight, harmony and celebration, peace and friendship." And further: "May these loving companions rejoice together with the joy You have set aside for them since the days of Creation. Blessed are You, Adonai, who grants joy to this couple."

And yet, while certainly expressing an ethos of pleasure in life, the *Sheva B'rachot* do not encourage the couple to relinquish social obligations or, through self-isolating privatism, to endeavor escape from the ills of the world. The text of the blessings also evokes the messianic hope. The couple is encouraged to look beyond their private Eden toward the vision of Zion rejoicing with *all* her children.

In the reference toward the end of the blessings to Jeremiah's vision (33:10–11), which sees beyond the terrors of the world to the ultimate wedding celebration in the peace of Zion, the couple are reminded of the Jewish commitment to the work of redemption for all.

As the couple begin to create their own world, they know that together they must bring something to the perfection of God's Creation, so that the time may soon come when God, as it were, will rejoice with the people of Israel.

RABBI NANCY H. WIENER, DMin

The *Ketubah*

THE VAST MAJORITY of Jewish wedding ceremonies around
the world include a Jewish marriage document, known as a
ketubah. The *ketubah*, with its ancient origins, links the couple to
countless generations of Jews. For liberal Jews, it also serves as a
spiritual adjunct to a civil marriage license, providing couples an
opportunity to articulate and affirm, in writing, their shared hopes
and commitments. Modern, liberal *ketubot* (plural of *ketubah*) represent the continuation and reinterpretation of an age-old Jewish
marriage practice.

More than two millennia ago, Jews adopted the custom of preparing and signing what is essentially a prenuptial agreement. The
ketubah (a Hebrew word that refers to any written document used
in legal transactions) became a mainstay of Jewish weddings. Long
before women were accepted as independent agents, the *ketubah*
was a revolutionary means of ensuring a woman's ongoing financial
stability. Originally written in Aramaic (the *lingua franca* of Jews in
antiquity, and therefore the language of business transactions and
literature for many centuries), the *ketubah* delineated the details
worked out by two families related to the transfer of the bride from
her male relative's household to her husband's. It included the date
and location of the transaction; the woman's status, that is, virgin,
divorced, or widowed; the value the groom or his family paid for
the bride (once known as the bride's price); the value and content
of the dowry the bride planned to bring with her into the marriage;
the responsibilities the husband assumed for his wife's maintenance
and welfare; and the amount the bride would receive in the event of
a divorce. The bride played no part in its preparation, nor did she
sign it. At its inception, the *ketubah* represented a noteworthy legal

innovation: a guarantee that a woman would have ongoing financial security, even in the event of a divorce; with the dissolution of her marriage, her return to her father's household would not represent an additional financial burden for him. Two "kosher" male witnesses (men who followed Jewish laws, customs, and teachings) signed the *ketubah* following the wedding ceremony, attesting to the fact that the transaction had been completed. To this day, some Jewish communities use the same Aramaic *ketubah* described above, and their religious courts continue to recognize it as legally binding.

In the early nineteenth century, finding the economic aspects of this signed agreement objectionable, the first Reform rabbis began to perform Jewish weddings without requiring this type of *ketubah*. They introduced a *ketubah* written in the vernacular, so that both members of the couple and all those in attendance could understand it. As an expression of their commitment to egalitarianism, these early Reform rabbis allowed both men and women to serve as witnesses and sign the document. References to the virginity and prior marital status of the bride were removed from the text, as were all references to money. It simply attested to the fact that a binding religious ceremony had occurred.

For over one hundred years, some Reform rabbis felt that it was unnecessary to have a specific Jewish marriage document at all. They reasoned that since in modern nations Jews needed to register their marriages with the state, the civil license was sufficient evidence that a valid marriage had taken place. By the middle of the twentieth century, therefore, many Jews in the United States did not include a traditional Aramaic *ketubah*, or any other specifically Jewish document, in their wedding ceremony. Those that did had them written in English.

In the late twentieth century, the inclusion of *a ketubah* at Jewish weddings again became a common practice across the Jewish spectrum. In the late 1960s and early 1970s, groups of young, non-Orthodox Jews began to create their own *ketubot*, focusing on the spiritual and religious commitments they saw themselves making at their weddings, rather than on the economic obligations their families promised in the traditional *ketubah*.

Most Reform rabbis today expect a couple to have a *ketubah*, though its form and content are not fixed. For many contemporary Jewish couples, the *ketubah* is both an expression of their personal pledges to each other and a piece of personally meaningful Jewish art that will adorn their home. Others wish to have a *ketubah* but do not intend to display it. Still others have adopted the custom of leaving room on the *ketubah* for the addition of hopes and pledges that arise in the days and years to come.

Today, *ketubot* have many forms. They come in different languages: English, Hebrew, Aramaic, or any combination; they range from simple printed documents to elaborately designed works of art with expert calligraphy. A couple may select the design, form, and content that reflect their tastes and personal predilections. While Judaica stores and websites sell *ketubot*, many couples choose to design their own. Some couples work together and design their *ketubah* on their computers. Others either involve artistic friends and family in designing and preparing their *ketubah* or hire professional calligraphers and artists.

Couples regularly use the selection or preparation of their *ketubah* as a way to articulate the meaning they ascribe to their relationship and to their wedding day. Since this document marks their spiritual transition, rather than a legal transaction, it can include anything they choose. Many couples spend time together exploring their thoughts and feelings about key issues, such as what they most value in each other and in their relationship; what marriage means to them; the type of support and nurturing they hope to offer and receive; special talents or aspects of their personalities they hope will flourish in their home; and the emotional, spiritual, and religious tones they hope their home will embody and convey to friends and families.

Ketubot still tend to include information affirming that the Jewish wedding ceremony took place on a specific date, in a specific place, and for a specific couple. They identify the members of the couple by their English or Hebrew names or both. While Hebrew names traditionally identified people as the sons or daughters of their fathers, today the vast majority of contemporary liberal Jews use both of their parents' names to construct their Hebrew names. For example, traditionally a Hebrew name would have been Joseph son of Samuel; now it is Joseph son of Samuel and Rachel. Some people choose to include on their *ketubah* the names of non-legally-recognized parental figures who helped raise or nurture them, placing these names either alone or alongside the names of biological or legal parents. Hebrew is a gender-based language, and until recently the information on a *ketubah* always reflected that reality. Today couples can find a growing number of non-gender-based alternatives in stores and on the Internet. There are also many premade *ketubot* and templates of *ketubot* designed specifically for members of the LGBTQ community.

At most liberal Jewish weddings, the couple, two Jewish witnesses (who are not blood relatives of either member of the couple), and the officiant(s) sign the *ketubah*. Some clergy and couples sign the *ketubah* in both Hebrew and English and ask their witnesses to do the same. Other couples choose to invite everyone who attends the wedding to sign it.

The *ketubah* signing is often included as another element of the public wedding ritual. Since the signatures attest to the witnessing of a wedding ceremony, it is often signed immediately after the ceremony has been completed. Some couples choose to incorporate the signing into the wedding ceremony, often preceded by the officiant reading all or part of it aloud. Another popular option is to create a separate ceremony around the signing of the ketubah, to take place either immediately prior to or immediately after the wedding ceremony. Sometimes all of the guests are invited to witness the signing. More often, a smaller group gathers, creating a more intimate atmosphere. Some officiants have created their own rituals around this moment that include having the officiant or members of the couple read the *ketubah* aloud; having the officiant ask the couple if they are ready and willing to sign; having the couple hand the document to each other as a symbol of all that they are offering to each other; having each member of the couple sign the document; and finally, having the witnesses and officiant sign. Some couples display their *ketubah* on an easel during and/or after the ceremony.

Many couples find that their *ketubah* holds special meaning for them as a couple, well beyond the day of their wedding. Some couples hang their *ketubah* on a wall, as a piece of art and as a daily reminder of the hopes and aspirations they shared at the time of their *kiddushin*. Many adopt the custom of reading their *ketubah* aloud to each other each year as part of their anniversary celebration. The *ketubah* then becomes a document that adds special meaning to their relationship: in the months prior to the ceremony as the couple prepares it; while standing under the chuppah as it is read; and throughout their lives in the years to come as they pass it daily, review it, or recollect it.

RABBI HOWARD L. JAFFE

Intermarriage

THE HEBREW WORD for marriage, *kiddushin*, comes from the root of the word that means "holy." Marriage is considered the holiest state that two people can enter. Reform congregations seek to celebrate and strengthen the marriages (and families) of all of our members, including, of course, those households in which one adult member identifies as Jewish and one has a different (or no) religious identity.

The prophet Isaiah said, "My house shall be called a house of prayer for all peoples." (Isaiah 56:7). We know that from the very beginning, there have been individuals who have been part of the Jewish community but were not themselves Jewish. More than just houses of prayer for all peoples, our Reform congregations strive to be places of meaning, gathering, connection, and growth for all who choose to be part of our communities.

Worship is, of course, the centerpiece of the synagogue community, and everyone is welcome to participate in the worship of every Reform congregation. Each congregation has its own practices regarding certain specific rituals and leadership of the service, but all are invited to participate fully in the communal worship experience. I am often asked by non-Jews in our community if they may attend our services. I always tell them that it would not only be all right, it would be wonderful!

There is often a concern about following along and understanding what is happening, especially since some percentage of the service is done in Hebrew. While that amount varies from congregation to congregation, almost every Reform congregation worships from a prayer book that includes translation of all of the Hebrew and, most often, transliteration of the Hebrew (a phonetically written rendering). Most of the Hebrew prayers are repeated week after week, and many of them are set to tunes that become familiar, so that participation in worship services is accessible to anyone who is interested.

Involvement in the life of the congregation is open to all who are interested. I am often asked what percentage of the members of my congregation are not Jewish, and I always answer, as I must, that I do not know. I do not know because that statistic is unimportant. What is important is the quality of the Jewish community that we are always building and the effort we make to include everyone who wants to build that community.

Each congregation has its own policies and norms around leadership roles for those who are not Jewish, but there is not a Reform congregation in North America in which non-Jews will not find welcome and an invitation to participate fully in the life of the community. I still recall the time many years ago, when, in preparation for a bat mitzvah, I noticed that the form the parents had filled out listing the names of those who would partake in certain honors in the service did not include the father's Hebrew name, while it did include the mother's. He was one of the most active members of our congregation, a regular at worship services, a participant in a host of activities, and someone well identified as a leader in our congregation. I asked why he left out his Hebrew name, and when he told me that he did not have one, I expressed surprise. He wondered why I would have thought that his parents would have given him a Hebrew name, seeing as he was not Jewish. I had no idea and was gratified to realize there was no reason that I would have known that. He had found a comfortable place for himself in our synagogue community, and both to him and to me, that was what mattered.

In fairness, it is important to note that this kind of openness is a relatively recent phenomenon. If you go back just a generation or two and ask intermarried couples with their experience was, it would not be surprising to learn that it was quite different from the scenario that I am describing. The great concern then was the potential for assimilation that intermarriage once represented. Jews are, after all, a tiny minority in North America, a little over 1 percent of the population in Canada, and a little over 2 percent of the population in the United States (worldwide, Jews are just 0.2 percent of the world's population).

There was also particular concern about the religious identity of the next generation, especially when a Jewish man married a non-Jewish woman, which was for a time the case in the majority of intermarriages. Historically, religious identity was (and in Orthodox and Conservative Judaism, still is) determined in the Jewish community by the religious identity of the mother. A child born of a Jewish mother was considered Jewish, and a child born of a non-Jewish mother was (and again, in Orthodox and Conservative Judaism, still is) considered non-Jewish. Genuine fear about Jewish continuity fueled the belief that the marriage of a Jew to a non-Jew might well mean the end of Jewish identity in that family line.

As we know, the rate of intermarriage between Jews and non-Jews has increased dramatically. In the 1960s, it was estimated that about 7 percent of Jews married non-Jews. A 2013 study by the Pew Research Center put the number at 58 percent. And along the way, the entire North American Jewish community, and especially the Reform Movement, has reconsidered and reshaped its thinking about not only the consequences but the opportunities that this trend provides and inspires.

One of the most dramatic and impactful decisions ever made by the Reform Movement was a 1983 resolution of the Central Conference of American Rabbis regarding the Jewish status of a child of a Jewish father and a non-Jewish mother. In a bold decision, recognizing that it is not biology but upbringing that is the proper determinant of religious identity, the resolution stated that the identity of a child of either a Jewish mother or a Jewish father who is raised and educated exclusively as a Jew "is to be established through appropriate and timely public and formal acts of identification with the Jewish faith and people," such as *b'rit* and naming, bar/bat mitzvah, and confirmation.

The last part of that resolution is important and often lost. Traditional Jewish practice holds that a child that is born of a Jewish mother is Jewish, regardless of education, practice, or identity. Reform Judaism, on the other hand, explicitly requires Jewish education, engagement, and affirmation of a Jewish identity.

No one expects a non-Jewish parent to give up their own identity, nor to diminish or sever ties with his or her family of origin (heaven forfend!). There is, however, an expectation that parents who commit to raising Jewish children will nurture their children's Jewish identity and not confuse them by raising them with conflicting religious ideas (such as suggesting that they can be both Jewish and Christian). Making this kind of commitment is a gift to one's Jewish partner and, in turn, to the Jewish people. It entails great sacrifice, and I am not certain that we do a good enough job of acknowledging that gift and especially that sacrifice, even though that appreciation is always present.

As for weddings, many, but not all, Reform rabbis will officiate at wedding ceremonies when one of the partners is Jewish and one is not. It is always best to speak with a specific rabbi about his or her practice and availability. It is important to note, however, that what matters most is the warm welcome that anyone who wants to become a part of one of our congregations and communities will experience, that he or she might find a spiritual home and bring their own gifts and contributions to our sacred efforts.

RABBI BARRY H. D. BLOCK

Welcoming Converts

WELCOMING CONVERTS is a mitzvah!

Jewish tradition regards Abraham and Sarah as the first converts. Raised in idolatrous families, they respond to God's call to travel to the land of God's choosing, that they might be a blessing. Like Abraham and Sarah, those desiring conversion to Judaism in our own day are embarking on a journey—albeit a spiritual, rather than a geographical, sojourn.

Abraham and Sarah are also understood to be the first Jews to receive converts. The Torah teaches that when they set out for the Promised Land, our patriarch and matriarch brought "the souls that they had made in Haran" (Genesis 12:5). The medieval commentator Rashi understands those "souls" to be proselytes whom Abraham and Sarah "had brought under the wings of the *Shechinah* [Divine Presence]. Abraham converted the men and Sarah converted the women and Scripture accounts it unto them as if they had made them."[1] We may even say that receiving converts is the first mitzvah ascribed to our original patriarch and matriarch, concluding that welcoming converts is a most exalted religious obligation.

We may puzzle, then, at an unfortunate reality: many people, including many Jews, believe that Judaism does not especially welcome converts. Yes, in addition to Abraham and Sarah, the *Tanach* tells of Ruth, the Moabite, who becomes a loyal daughter of Israel and ultimately an ancestor of King David. Yes, the Talmud, written in the earliest centuries of the Common Era, lays out a procedure

---

1. Rashi on Genesis 12:5, *Chumash with Targum Onkelos, Haphtaroth, and Rashi's Commentary*, A.M. Silberman in collabortion with M. Rosenbaum, translators and annotators (Jerusalem: The Silberman Family, 5745).

for receiving converts.[2] Still, the suspicion remains that Jews don't enthusiastically welcome converts.

In 1978, in an address to the Board of Trustees of the UAHC, Rabbi Alexander Schindler, then the president of the UAHC (now URJ), explained the sad historical reality that led Jews to be reluctant to receive converts:

> After Christianity became the established religion of the Roman Empire, and later, again, when Islam conquered the world, Jews were forbidden to seek converts or to accept them. The death penalty was fixed for the gentile who became a Jew and also for the Jew who welcomed him [or her]. Many were actually burned at the stake, and the heat of the flames cooled our conversionist ardor. Even so, it was not until the sixteenth century that we abandoned all proselytizing efforts; only then did our rabbis begin their systematic rejection of those who sought to join us.[3]

Centuries of necessity-driven discouragement of conversion continue to weigh on the Jewish people, even now, as we live in free lands, where men and women of conscience can and do freely choose to adopt new religions. Rabbi Schindler urged Reform Jews to adopt a new attitude, to embrace converts with joy, and to serve as their guides along the way: "Newcomers to Judaism, in short, must embark on a long-term naturalization process, and they require knowledgeable and sympathetic guides along the way, that they may feel themselves fully equal members of the synagogue family."[4]

Rabbis play a special role in receiving prospective Jews-by-choice. The rabbi is charged with providing a warm welcome while at the same time maintaining standards for conversion. Rabbis are conscious of this dual role and of the vulnerability that many conversion candidates understandably feel in relation to the authority figure who must ultimately accept them for conversion. In the words of the CCAR's "Guidelines for Working with Prospective *Gerim*,"

---

2. See, especially, BT *Y'vamot* 46–47
3. Address of Rabbi Alexander M. Schindler, president of the UAHC, to the Board of Trustees on December 2, 1978, in Houston, Texas, http://www.urj.org/rabbi-schindler-1978-speech-establishing-outreach
4. Ibid.

"Relationships between rabbis and prospective *gerim* [converts] pose a particularly sensitive set of circumstances of which rabbis must remain aware."[5] Therefore, rabbis eagerly seek lay partners to serve as mentors and guides, providing the most unfettered embrace of the conversion candidate.

Rabbis will typically meet privately with individuals soon after being approached about conversion. The rabbi will then describe the requirements for conversion, emphasizing that each person is on an individual journey and that the timetable for the process cannot be predicted at the outset.[6] Throughout the rabbi's work with a prospective convert, the rabbi may raise questions about the candidate's fitness for conversion. While many people are aware of a traditional requirement that prospective converts be turned away three times before being accepted,[7] the CCAR has affirmed, "The Reform Movement . . . has formally rejected the traditional practice of strongly discouraging prospective *gerim* [converts] three times."[8] Many people choosing Judaism are initially inspired by Jewish theology. Exploring Judaism through family or friends, through books or the Internet, they find that our faith fits the belief system they have always held. In the case specifically of Reform Judaism, others are attracted to our movement's commitment to social justice, often exemplified by a local rabbi and congregation.

Still, the process of becoming a Jew is essentially one of beginning to live as a Jew by taking on the performance of mitzvot. The ancient Rabbis called that requirement *kabbalat ol mitzvot*, literally, "acceptance of the burden of the commandments." Reform Judaism views the performance of mitzvot not as a burden, but rather as an opportunity to come closer to God and the people of Israel, bringing the world closer to the messianic ideal.[9]

---

5. "Guidelines for Working with Prospective *Gerim*," CCAR, June 2001, "Initial Contact," https://www.ccarnet.org/rabbis-communities/professional-resources/guidelines-for-rabbis-working-with-prospective-gerim/.
6. Ibid.
7. *Ruth Rabbah* 2:1.
8. "Guidelines for Working with Prospective *Gerim*," "Initial Contact," 1b.
9. Ibid., 6.

Conversion is a journey. The preparation includes intellectual learning, spiritual direction, and participation in the community.[10] Each encounter—in an introduction to Judaism course, in the rabbi's study, or in community celebration—introduces the prospective convert to new opportunities to explore mitzvot that will most meaningfully enrich that person's life.

In each area of Jewish observance—from Shabbat and holy days to personal ethical conduct, from affixing a mezuzah to the doorpost of one's home to considering some degree of Jewish dietary discipline, from *tzedakah* (righteous charitable giving) to selecting ritual garb for worship—becoming a Jew requires studying traditional Jewish text and practice, discussion with one's supervising rabbi, and prayerfully considering how mitzvot will best ennoble the individual's journey.[11]

When the conversion candidate and the rabbi agree that the time is right, the performance of mitzvot will mark the individual's entry into the covenant, the *b'rit*, with God. Each person seeking to become Jewish will appear before a *beit din* (Jewish court), made up of three knowledgeable Jews, arranged by the supervising rabbi. Upon acceptance by the *beit din*, male candidates will usually be asked to enter *b'rit milah*, the covenant of circumcision. Those previously circumcised enter *b'rit milah* through a ritual called *hatafat dam b'rit*, drawing a drop of blood from the site of the original, non-ritual, circumcision.[12]

The crowning moment of the conversion process is immersion in the mikveh, the ritual bath. Witnessed by an appropriate person of the same gender, the candidate enters the mikveh with blessing. Rabbi Rachel Cowan, describing her own immersion in the mikveh, writes "that it had helped me reach a new level in a spiritual journey that would last the rest of my life."[13] The person who emerges from

---

10. Ibid., 2–4.
11. Ibid., 6.
12. Ibid., 8.
13. Rachel Cowan, "A Personal Story of Conversion," in *Embracing Judaism*, by Simcha Kling (New York: Rabbinical Assembly, 1987), page 179.

the mikveh is a Jew in every respect.[14]

Each Jew-by-choice will receive a Hebrew name, chosen by the individual in consultation with the rabbi. That name will include *ben* (son of) or *bat* (daughter of) *Avraham v'Sarah* (Abraham and Sarah). The connection to the original matriarch and patriarch of Judaism emphasizes that the new Jew is to be considered a lineal descendant of the first man and woman to choose to follow the God of Israel.

The first conversion ceremony I ever attended was my aunt's, in 1968, ten years before Rabbi Schindler called for renewed enthusiasm for conversion. I was only five years old, but two aspects of the event remain emblazoned on my mind: First, I do recall that the ceremony was joyous and attended by our entire family. By contrast, though, I was told that we must never speak of the fact that my aunt had converted to Judaism. Her conversion was to be kept secret, making me imagine it to be shameful.

Today, conversion is celebrated publicly. Some time after the private moment at the mikveh, the new Jew is welcomed by the congregation—with an *aliyah* (blessing over the Torah), with a public blessing before the holy ark, or with a full conversion ceremony in the presence of all gathered for Shabbat worship. The congregation is inspired by the devotion of the newest Jew in its midst, reminding all assembled that whether we be Jews by conversion or "by birth," we can all be "Jews-by-choice," Jews who continually choose to perform mitzvot and embrace our covenant.

---

14. BT *Y'vamot* 47b.

RABBI ARIANA SILVERMAN

Jewish Parenting through the Life Cycle

Enduring Technologies for Living

LIFE-CYCLE RITUALS allow us to express our gratitude and embrace change as we pass through times of transition in our lives. While some of our life-cycle ceremonies are ancient rites and others are new, they help us to imbue significant life moments with Jewish meaning. They can also be opportunities for confronting fear and anxieties. They are, in a sense, technologies for living, giving us tools to process and contextualize life's many stages.

The experience of bringing a new child into our home, for example, can be both exciting and terrifying. Whether the child came into your lives expectedly or unexpectedly, quickly or after years of struggle and heartbreak, once a child enters our home, we assume a monumental and sacred mission. And in this moment, how can we feel the love and support of the community, knowing that it stands with you and is prepared to welcome and help the child grow? Further, in this moment of extreme import and vulnerability, how can we connect to a source of power beyond ourselves?

Covenantal Welcome and Naming

Judaism provides us a rich repository of ritual and practice. Some rituals feel nourishing and immediately relatable. Some are more archaic and difficult to understand in our day. Sometimes, identity and tradition ground our ritual decisions. Other times, modern considerations outweigh these. These decisions are complex; they merit thoughtful consideration and consultation with rabbis and other Jewish experts.

The welcoming rituals of *b'rit milah* and naming ceremonies bring our community together to assure us we are not alone. They give us a forum to affirm our desire to raise a Jewish child. And they give us language to begin speaking to God as we enter a new stage of our lives.

Some parents have conflicted feelings about *b'rit milah*, feelings centered around questions of pain and body modification. For many Jews, *b'rit milah* is the right choice because it binds this generation to past generations. It has endured for millennia as a symbol in each generation of the significance of joining the Jewish story, and the power of doing so in partnership with other Jews and with the Divine. It places our child firmly within the Jewish narrative. It is not an easy thing to do, and no one does it because it is easy. We do it in part *because* it is hard; it is a symbol of a deep, though at times challenging, commitment to the Jewish past and future.

Marking a daughter's entrance into our lives, the life of the Jewish people, and the covenant with the Divine is also a sacred responsibility, not of any lesser significance than what we would do for a son. Naming ceremonies for girls, a relatively recent innovation, grew out of the reality that Judaism is constantly evolving. Judaism, like a living being, continues to adapt to a changing world in order to survive. We do not practice Judaism the way Jews did centuries ago. With each life-cycle ceremony we enact, we are perpetuating not just the Jewish people but the very evolution of Judaism itself. Naming ceremonies and *b'rit milah* provide us with an opportunity to connect to past generations and articulate our hopes and dreams for the new life in our world. It is also one of the first times we practice making informed Jewish choices for our children in partnership with Jewish teachers and texts.

Bar and Bat Mitzvah

We continue to need these technologies for living Jewish lives as our children grow. In the twenty-first century, *bar/bat mitzvah* ceremonies do not mark entry into adulthood as they once did. Yet, they are an important way to mark the challenging transition into adolescence. It is easy to get swept up in the minutiae of party planning and biblical trope. But feeling the support of the community as a child begins the adventure of life as a teenager is an incredible gift, both for the parents, who are suddenly on a new leg of the parenting journey, and for the child, whose life is in flux. Through ritual, our children are given the opportunity to mark this fraught time in their lives with hard work, Jewish exploration, and special encouragement.

Lifelong Learning

Every parent of a Jewish child is a Jewish educator. Whether we are Jewish or not, trained as an educator or not, confident in our Jewish knowledge or not, in love with Judaism or not, our children look to us as they form their Jewish identity. It is an awesome responsibility.

In order to be a teacher, every parent of a Jewish child must also be a student of Judaism. We must give ourselves, and our children, the gift of becoming adult learners—not simply so we can respond to the questions of our children, but so we can engage with our own questions. Judaism is not just for kids; its truths are deeper, its challenges more profound, its rituals more transformational when we wrestle with them as an adult.

And if children see their parents learning about Judaism, they are more likely to want to do so themselves. If we treat Jewish education as something only kids do, we send a message that tradition, community, and God can be outgrown. If we want to transmit the power and meaning of Judaism to our children, they need to see us going to Jewish classes, reading Jewish books, checking Jewish websites, and asking Jewish questions.

This is especially important when our children are teenagers. Getting a child to prepare to become bar/bat mitzvah, planning the service, and, in some cases, planning a party for friends and family can be overwhelming. But, *b'nei mitzvah* cannot be the end of a child's immersion in Jewish learning. *Bar/bat mitzvah*, rather, is an acknowledgment that a child is ready to take that learning to the next level. I doubt that many of us would be happy to see our child completing a secular education at eighth grade graduation. Similarly, we need to instill the understanding that Jewish learning through high school and beyond enriches our lives and provides tools for adulthood. Leaving a child with a pediatric understanding of Judaism stunts any ability to develop an adult understanding of God, Judaism's strengths and flaws, and how tradition can help inform ethical decision-making.

Fortunately, we and our children grow into and develop a relationship with Judaism as part of a community, with the care and attention of friends, family, and professionals. Regardless of where we live or where we are in our family's Jewish journey, Jewish clergy, Jewish educators, Jewish camp counselors, and youth group advisors are ready to become part of the team.

The Sacredness of Intimate Time

In addition to the life-cycle ceremonies that punctuate transitional times and the formal and informal education we can provide, it is also in the weekly and daily moments of living that our children learn what it means to live a Jewish life.

Developing a family Shabbat practice is a way to sanctify time and relationships. Lighting candles, saying blessings, having a special meal, joining with Jewish community in celebration, taking some time away from electronic devices, going on a walk as a family—these have the power to create meaningful practices and memories for our children.

And Judaism need not just be a weekend activity. Mealtimes provide a remarkable opportunity to delve into Jewish identity. Regardless of whether we have a kosher kitchen or are in the habit of making kugel, hummus, jachnun, or bagels and lox, our food choices can reflect our Judaism and Jewish history. Jewish values from labor rights to environmental protection are important considerations in our food choices. Explaining why our family does or does not eat certain foods instills a sense of how we make ethical decisions. And saying a blessing or simply expressing gratitude before eating as a family sanctifies something we do every day.

In seemingly mundane moments, having a child can change our relationship with God. I have prayed in spectacular sanctuaries with exultant music. And yet, it was often when I was exhausted, changing the dirty diaper of a crying, resistant, baby, that I felt closest to God. As a new parent, I frequently worried whether my child would still be breathing in the morning. So when my child awoke, I sang *Modah Ani*, a prayer thanking God for restoring our souls. I was grateful to be alive but also deeply grateful that my child had survived the night. I now delight in singing it with her.

Whether lighting Shabbat candles, working for social justice, saying the *Sh'ma* before our children go to sleep, making ethical decisions throughout the day, or fielding the unexpected question from the backseat of the car, as parents we teach Judaism to the next generation. Fortunately, we don't have to already be experts. Our life-cycle ceremonies reflect the wisdom and timeless longings of parents across millennia, as well as the constantly evolving nature of Judaism. As teachers, we also become learners. And we begin to find the ritual moments in our daily lives that reinforce our Jewish values.

Judaism is an incredible gift to give our children. It is worth the effort. When a child's eyes light up as the Shabbat candles are illuminated, when a child asks a deep question about morality, when a child teaches us to see our tradition in a new way, it is a gift for us as well.

RABBI ELYSE GOLDSTEIN

B'rit Milah
Covenant and Controversy

PERHAPS NO COMMANDMENT in the Torah is more difficult, more divisive, more perplexing, and more male-exclusive than circumcision. Some Reform Jews have cast it aside, choosing to reject it as a primitive and oppressive ritual. Yet in the spirit of choosing and understanding (*naaseh v'nishma* [Exodus 24:7]) upon which Reform Judaism is based, it is possible for feminism to "save" *b'rit milah*, to inject into this male covenantal ceremony some sense of meaning other than the lame jokes and awkward silences. If we allow ourselves the power of modern midrash and expand our understanding of symbolism and metaphor in the ceremony, we can reimagine *b'rit milah* as a contemporary and significant milestone.

The Practice
Scholars agree that circumcision may be one of the most ancient tribal practices we have on record. We know from biblical and other sources that the Egyptians, Ammonites, Edomites, and Moabites all practiced it. Among most peoples it was done at marriage or puberty, as a sacrifice to ensure fertility. The Talmud calls both a groom and a baby ready for the circumcision by the same word—*chatan*. The ancient link between removing the foreskin and marriage is further established in the biblical account of Zipporah and Moses. In Exodus 4:25, after circumcising their son to ward off supernatural danger, she flings the foreskin toward Moses and cries, "You are truly a bridegroom of blood [*chatan damim*] to me!" What is significant in the Hebrew manifestation is the move from *adult circumcision* to *infant circumcision*. The connotations of sexuality and fertility are

now enlarged by levels of spirituality. What was once a tribal rite to ensure fruitfulness now becomes a divine command, incumbent even upon those who may not live past childhood into marriage, even upon those who may prove to be infertile. The foreskin is the extra piece that defiles, that is fruitless, non-useful. Like the "uncircumcised" fruit of trees that cannot be eaten for the first three years in Leviticus 19:23, called *orlah*—the same word for "foreskin"—the foreskin is an unripe fruit.

Women and the Commandment: A Female Covenant of Blood

Women are neither commanded to circumcise nor to be circumcised. If the cutting of the genitals was meant to ensure fertility, then surely women—for whom fertility is the guarantor of status—should have to undergo something similar.

Sarah shares in the blessing granted to Abraham after circumcision but does not have to undergo a physical sacrifice. Abraham's circumcision will signal new fertility, and Sarah's name change in Genesis 17:15 signals the end of her barrenness. As he will be the ancestor of multitudes, so too will she.

From Sarai to Sarah entails dropping one letter, *yod*, and replacing it with *hei*. This change was not seen as arbitrary by the commentators. The Hebrew letter *hei* preceded by the vowel *kamatz* (the "ah" sound) is a symbol of the feminine ending, as in, for example, *yaldah* (girl) or *naarah* (young woman). The commentator Kli Yakar suggests, "Before this episode Sarai was barren, not able to give birth, like a man. The masculine *yod* was exchanged for the feminine *hei*."

Here we see the possibility of a *b'rit* of the womb. In Genesis 17:15–21, God reiterates just how crucial it is that the Jewish covenant be founded through the offspring of Sarah, not Hagar: "It is with Isaac, whom Sarah will bear . . . that I will establish My covenant" (Genesis 17:21). This is directly juxtaposed with Abraham's circumcision, a few verses before. *B'rit milah* then is only half of the covenantal picture; lineage through Sarah, the mother, is the other. We could suggest that in its matrilineal state, Judaism ascribes to the womb a sense of covenant: a child born through a Jewish womb is

Jewish. Just as *b'rit milah* "covenants" the male child, birth through a Jewish womb "covenants" all children. That is why when a person converts, he or she must be "reborn" through the water of the mikveh, symbolizing the Jewish womb. Therefore, since the blood of menstruation leads to birth through the womb, could we not suggest that women have a *b'rit* already inscribed in their flesh every month?

Another possibility is that women are considered *already circumcised*. In the Talmud (BT *Avodah Zarah* 27a), the question of whether women may perform a *b'rit milah* arises. Rabbi Yochanan says yes. To understand this controversial answer, Rashi does a wordplay on Genesis 17:13, where it says *himol yimol*, "surely one must be circumcised," to read *hamol yimol*, "one who is circumcised must/can circumcise." The Rabbis, seeing female anatomy as open, exposed, and uncovered—as the penis is after circumcision—imagined that women were born circumcised. In fact, we could go so far as to suggest that male circumcision makes men more like women by removing the foreskin and "opening up" or revealing the genital. Women bleed monthly from their genitals and do not die. They experience the power of life and death within their own body. Men get to do it just once, at a "woman-like" moment.

Men and the Commandment: The Male Birth Experience

Women already know the incredible bonding moment that occurs through the act of giving birth. From our own body comes forth new life, born in water and blood, a primordial encounter with Creation itself. No matter how sensitive, how involved, how sympathetic, a man can never physically participate in that mystical encounter. Or can he?

Myriel Crowley Eykamp, in an essay entitled "Born and Born Again," suggests that nearly every religious culture in the world—both Eastern and Western—have some sort of initiation ceremony in which there is "a reappropriation or taking-over of the birthing act by the male priest. . . . One must not only be born again, but born again of the male."[1] Ritual rebirth by males is almost a universal

---

1. Myriel Crowley Eykamp, "Born and Born Again," in *The Sacred Dimensions*

religious phenomenon. Perhaps this points to a deep longing by some men to be birthers themselves. Most societies enact ritual "re-birth" by water, baptism, sacred immersion, or the like. Jews do it by blood, parallel to the blood of the actual birth, through the very male act of *b'rit milah*.

While that reappropriation can be seen as threatening to women, we can also reexamine it from a spiritual viewpoint. There ought to be a moment when the birthing experience is shared, when men birth through blood, when they bond as powerfully physically as women do. If we see childbirth as a metaphor for nurturing and car-ing in relationship, males can experience that firsthand. If a father "gives birth" by circumcising his child or even symbolically by allow-ing someone to do it in his place, he is taking equal responsibility as a giver of life.

Men and the Commandment: Male Sexuality Defined and Limited

Anita Diamant, in *The New Jewish Baby Book*, writes, "If God had asked Abraham to remove a flap of skin from his elbow and the el-bows of all males of his household, bris would probably not be the emotionally loaded commandment it is. . . . The fact that the mark of the covenant is surgically imprinted on the penis dramatizes the fundamental importance of the act."[2]

Seen within the context of metaphor and interpretation, circumci-sion is a symbol of disciplined sexuality; this idea is not new. Already Maimonides saw the rite as reducing sexuality to a manageable level. It is today that we sorely need this idea reintroduced. Jewish views of sexuality are in accord with the notion that sexual pleasure is mutual, that force is violence and not love, and that human sexual encounters must be based on sanctity and not strength. Therefore we can suggest that circumcision functions not only as ritual initiation but also as the communal setting of boundaries to male sexuality.

---

of Women's Experience, ed. Elizabeth Dodson Gray (Wellesley, MA: Roundtable Press, 1988), page 61.

2. Anita Diamant, *The New Jewish Baby Book* (Woodstock, VT: Jewish Lights, 2005), page 88.

Zalman Schachter-Shalomi writes in *How to Deal with a Jewish Issue: Circumcision*: "Perhaps something destructive and 'macho' gets refined by a bris, directing a man away from pure instinct and toward prudent judgement. . . . Maybe Freud was right about the dominating power of the libido: if so, it makes sense to take that absolute power away from the penis. . . . So much of what happens in sex is covenantal. Perhaps this is why Covenant has to be imposed on this organ from the very start."[3]

We cut the organ that can symbolize love or terror, endearment or violence. Here is a ceremony in which we metaphorically pronounce the limits of the male organ, to all gathered, publicly. It is as if we say to this child, "We who are gathered here charge you—as your father used his organ in love to produce you, so you too are expected to sanctify yourself, to restrain the power of your maleness." And it is fitting that men do this to men. That message can help make women feel safe—at the very least symbolically—that our community, in theory, rejects an unbridled masculinity. We publicly acknowledge that male sexuality is moved from the specter of casual, hurtful, or noncommittal to the sphere of the holy, the whole, the good.

That is why an equivalent ceremony for girls of drawing blood, from whatever place has been suggested, does not work as a meaningful parallel. In our society, male violence is still the norm, based on phallic authority and the fear that the phallus can instill. It is the male organ that needs "bloodletting" and not the female. I suggest those few drops of covenantal blood be seen as *kaparah* (atonement) for male control and male sexual violence still so accepted and prevalent in our society. Let men teach men—father to son—of vulnerability, of exposure.

In other words, let our boys be entered into a circumscribed world of men whose sensitivities are increased as their phallic-centered power is decreased.

---

3. Zalman Schachter-Shalomi, *Learn Torah With...1995-1996 Torah Annual: A Collection of the Year's Best Torah* (Los Angeles, CA: Alef Design Group, 1999), page 25.

The Commandment and the Reform Movement: Yes, But . . .

So why keep this controversial ritual intact within Reform communities? We find ourselves divided into camps. On the one hand, there are those who take *b'rit milah* as a given even as feminists understand the gender divide it causes and the other reasons to reject it: genital mutilation, the birth of a "perfect" child who is now surgically altered, and so on. Our leaders are often reluctant to discuss this divide with congregants or students. On the other hand, there are those who reject *b'rit milah* and are prepared to face the communal consequences of counseling against it and creating alternatives but who may patronize the aforementioned camp as "not real feminists." And, on the third hand, there are those who, like me, start with *b'rit milah* as a valuable, powerful, and public ritual to mark—literally—the limitations of male sexual power but who recognize the wishful thinking of hoping this idea would actually be incorporated into a *b'rit* ceremony.

Thus even with "rescuing" *b'rit milah* through creative and revisionist thinking, I still call my own and other feminist attempts at reading *b'rit milah* through a feminist lens as arriving at a "yes, but."

Yes, but: *b'rit milah* may be our oldest Jewish ritual whose very power, like that of a ram's horn as opposed to a trumpet on Yom Kippur, lies in its primitiveness and in its ancient symbolism and enactment to evoke primordial connections. Like a funeral, we need not "pretty it up" but instead value its evocative reality.

Yes, but: if we approach *b'rit milah* as *tikkun* (repair) for male violence inflicted by the very same organ and for male predisposition to sexual carelessness, this can be seen as an attack on men and maleness in general. Let's consider these ideas in their purest theoretical form and not as condemnations.

Yes, but: the very maleness of *b'rit milah*, this moment of visceral Jewish male bonding, may be its most meaningful asset, especially in a Reform setting, which is already female-conscious and female-heavy—as difficult as this is to hear as women.

Yes, but: the implicit patriarchal notion is that men are created "whole" and perfect, and circumcision negates that. In Judaism it is just the opposite: men are born imperfect, and removing the foreskin makes them whole. In losing some male power, in "sacrificing" some of the male ego, in uncovering and revealing themselves in their most vulnerable parts, men are made more "soft."

If we can reappropriate and reinvent both the covenant of the womb and the covenant of the penis, we can keep a tradition ancient yet modern, bounded yet open, gender-specific yet rich with sexual import.

RABBI SARI LAUFER

Be Fruitful and Multiply
The Challenge of Infertility

Be fruitful and multiply, we are taught—the very first commandment in Torah. (Gen. 1:28)

Teach them faithfully to your children, we recite daily—a sense of
our purpose in Jewish life. (Deut. 6:7)

From generation to generation, we say proudly—explaining our
commitment to Jewish education and Jewish continuity. (from
the prayerbook)

TODAY, one in eight couples[1] will have trouble getting pregnant
or sustaining a pregnancy. One in eight couples will wait month
after month, staring at home pregnancy tests, waiting and praying
for a positive sign. One in eight couples will, after six months or a
year, sit in a doctor's waiting room, get poked and prodded, hoping
and praying for an easy fix. For some of those couples, time alone
will do the trick. For some, the road will lead to hormone pills, to
injections, to sterile operating rooms and pristine laboratories. For
some, the road will lead into a complicated web of sperm donors,
egg donors, embryo donations, and surrogates. Approximately 65
percent of women who seek medical intervention of some kind or
another will, at some point, give birth to a child.[2]

But statistics only tell part of the story. They cannot express the
pain of the woman, still bleeding from her last miscarriage, deflect-

---

1. The language of "couple" is challenging, of course. Single men or women looking to become parents face their own challenges; some will be fertility related.
2. "Fast Facts about Fertility," RESOLVE: The National Infertility Association,
http://www.resolve.org/about/fast-facts-about-fertility.html.

ing the question from a sweet, curious older woman at synagogue: "So, when are you going to have kids?" They cannot convey the emotion of the woman, at yet another *b'rit milah*, tearfully asking for a blessing from the *sandak*.[3] They cannot convey the powerlessness of the man fighting tears as another baby—not his—is blessed from the bimah at a naming ceremony.

A fact sheet published by RESOLVE: The National Infertility Association deals with religious perspectives about infertility. Amid the biblical quotes and Christian perspectives and before a brief overview of the halachic concerns and decisions around assisted reproduction, there is a paragraph of emotion, of experience, a paragraph that tries to capture living with infertility in the midst of life in a religious community:

> Every weekend, infertile couples sit quietly in church and synagogue pews throughout the country. Most of their pastors or rabbis are unaware of the pain and suffering of those couples trying desperately to have a child. Although many church and synagogue members have immediate family and friends experiencing infertility, religion, for the most part, doesn't acknowledge infertile people. The secrecy of the infertile, their inability to voice their pain and their quiet disappearance from church and synagogue rolls, has deepened the problem. To be involuntarily childless is an ever-present struggle with grief. A most natural place to go for solace and healing is their place of worship. Yet the overwhelming emphasis upon family, and upon rituals revolving around family, makes some services particularly painful.[4]

I like to believe that the questions, the teachings, the reflections come from a loving place. The man who asks how many children you have is simply trying to start a conversation. The rabbi who frames a sermon as a letter to his daughter is trying to connect Jewish lessons to what he understands to be the lives of those around him.

---

3. There is a tradition that receiving a blessing from the *sandak* at a *b'rit milah* is a *s'gulah*, or a sign, for fertility.

4. "Collection of Religious Perspectives about Infertility," RESOLVE Fact Sheet Series 13, http://familybuilding.resolve.org/site/DocServer/13_Religious_Perspectives.pdf;jsessionid=90D36649D3CC753DFEB82AC6C620CEC3. app260b?docID=5703.

The woman who asks if you are pregnant is genuinely hopeful for you. Synagogues and Jewish communities are supposed to be our safe spaces, but they often feel anything but safe for those who are, silently or not, suffering with and through infertility.

Anyone who has sat in a synagogue, whether on a Shabbat morning or a festival evening, has encountered Judaism's focus on and concern with family, with children, and with the next generation. We celebrate at *b'rit milah* and baby-naming ceremonies, we smile at consecration ceremonies as sweet young children are formally welcomed to their Jewish education, we rejoice as adolescents are called to the Torah as *b'nei mitzvah*. It is built into our liturgy, into our life cycles, into our psyches. "Be fruitful and multiply," God commands—and most of us listen, dreaming of the day we will become parents.

A congregant of mine is fond of telling a sweet story about looking for a neighborhood synagogue when his daughter was a (rambunctious) toddler. Wandering the neighborhood in which he lived at the time, he stumbled into a storefront *shtiebl*; the only people inside were old, German men. My congregant sat down, and soon—as toddlers are wont to do—his daughter wanted to run and play. Like so many parents in synagogues, he tried everything—distracting her, shushing her, maybe even bribing her—but she would not quiet down. Flustered, he turned to the men sitting closest to him and said, "I'm so sorry." These old, German men—Holocaust survivors—turned to him and said, "Uch, it's good noise. Such good noise."

It is, most of the time, good noise. It is the noise of continuity, of Jewish life, of joy and hope and commitment to the future. But, for our congregants, our friends, our neighbors, ourselves—it can be the hardest noise to hear. It is the noise of a dream deferred or shattered. The noise of a heart broken. The noise of a hope that feels as if it might never be fulfilled.

"Be fruitful and multiply," God commands—as if that's all it takes. But, just a couple of generations later, our Torah suggests that perhaps this family-building quest is not as easy as a simple command. Sarah, the matriarch, Abraham's partner in forming the Jewish people, is the first biblical woman we see facing fertility challenges. She turns first to a complicated surrogacy situation and eventually conceives a biological child through what we would now call assisted reproductive technology—the assistant being God. And while each path looked a little bit different, as it does for modern couples and individuals trying to conceive, Sarah's story sets a tone; hers is what scholar Robert Alter calls a biblical type-scene. Sarah, Rebekah, and the beloved Rachel all struggled to conceive; all needed God's assistance to get and stay pregnant. The story of Hannah and her desperate, pleading prayer is offered as the haftarah on Rosh HaShanah morning. Jewish tradition and its most sacred texts deeply acknowledge the reality of infertility. Our biblical ancestors do not silence the pain of wanting to be parents and not being able to make it happen.

For most of the biblical women, the announcement of their "barrenness" is followed—with no narrative break—by the announcement of their pregnancy and subsequent healthy birth. God plays a direct role in the reproductive lives of our ancestors. For most modern Jews, it is a theology that is hard to swallow at best and insulting at worst. We praise God as *pokeid Sarah*, the One who took notice of Sarah, but perhaps feel ignored, forgotten, even punished. When Sir Jonathan Edwards, the British doctor who pioneered the technique of in vitro fertilization, died, Rabbi Lord Jonathan Sacks eulogized him by saying:

> Though towards the end of his life Edwards received the récognition of a Nobel Prize, he had to face a barrage of criticism at the time. People conjured up fears of Aldous Huxley's brave new world and the manufacture of human beings as if they were machines. There were also some religious groups who saw him as trespassing into the sacred mystery of life itself, of "playing God."
>
> As Jews we saw things differently. We didn't see it as the sin of playing God. To the contrary we saw it as responding to God's invitation to become, in the ancient rabbinic phrase, "God's partners in the work of creation" and in a particularly moving way.[5]

---

5. Rabbi Lord Jonathan Sacks, "The Sacred Gift of Life," *Thought for the Day*, BBC Radio 4, April 12, 2013, http://www.rabbisacks.org/thought-for-the-day-the-sacred-gift-of-life/.

We are blessed to live at a time of incredible science, when doctors, nurses, and practitioners can partner with God in this work of Creation. We live in a time of unprecedented information and connection; wherever you are, literally and figuratively, in your family-building journey, you can find someone to share stories, give advice, and support your choices and your challenges. We are, as modern Jews, also lucky to live in a time and a place where families come in all shapes, colors, and sizes; the word "family" does not have a monolithic definition. Our communities pride themselves on being open and inclusive, and that inclusivity—and sensitivity—can and should expand to include all of those struggling to build the family of their hopes and dreams.

The midrash *B'reishit Rabbah* (45:4) asks the question: "Why were the matriarchs made barren?" And the answer? From Rabbi Levi and Rabbi Chelbo: Because the Holy Blessed One desired their prayers and their whispers. Much of the theology of biblical and Rabbinic teachings on fertility is challenging, most particularly to those going through their own fertility struggles. But this small teaching, this bit of Rabbinic wisdom, also suggests that the struggle need not be a silent one—not for God and not for us. Our communities, our rabbis and cantors and educators, our synagogues, and our friends can hear our prayers, our whispers, our hopes, and our pain. And, we pray, those same communities and same people will be there with us when we reach the end of our family-building road, whatever that looks like and wherever it may take us.

RABBI LISA S. GREENE

Jewish Divorce

D IVORCE IS PERMITTED within Judaism, though it is not desired. It is, according to Jewish tradition, "a legitimate procedure but one which should be employed only in the case of unavoidable necessity."[1] Divorce is viewed with sadness but, at the same time, understood as a reality. Mentioned in our texts since biblical times, its procedures and rules laid out for centuries, we see that Jewish divorce is in the mainstream of Jewish legal discussion—not shunned to the sidelines as something Jews don't do. The challenge for Reform Jews is how we approach those proceedings.

Historically, a husband would grant his wife a *get* in order to become divorced. A *get* is a writ of Jewish divorce created according to Jewish law and then given by the husband to the wife in a precisely scripted ceremony. It is enacted by and in front of a *beit din*, a rabbinic court of three Orthodox rabbis. The wife's role is to just accept the document granted by her husband. The process has multiple repetitions of questions asking the husband and wife to confirm that both consent to the divorce process. These repeated inquiries make certain that neither person is participating under duress—that both are there of their own free will.

In traditional contexts, a *get* is required before either party can remarry. While that halachic (Jewish legal) requirement to have a *get* is not one that most Reform Jews feel obligated to fulfill, it is one that we respect. Thus, rabbis and cantors may not require a *get* from a divorced couple but respect the tradition and encourage couples, especially those with Conservative or Orthodox connections, to seriously consider a *get*. Many rabbis will suggest a *get* as protection to

---

1. *A Rabbi's Manual* (New York: CCAR Press, 1988), page 244.

any couple who might find themselves marrying again. A *get* is not in place of a civil divorce, but is attained subsequently and in addition to a civil divorce. Ultimately, across the Jewish spectrum, the civil divorce in the country in which the parties live is the binding document.

For liberal Jews, however, the *get* is rife with challenge. There is for some the obligatory nature, which contrasts living a life of autonomous Jewish choice in which one may not be bound to traditional Jewish law. And at the heart of the *get* transaction is its inherent inequality. While both the husband and wife must consent to the *get*, the wife's role is simply to accept the document. She must wait for her soon-to-be-former-husband to grant this document; she is essentially a passive recipient. It is worth noting that this Jewish legal procedure was not created to be discriminatory; rather, it is reflective of a different time and practice. Still, many of us wrestle with this process that seems out of step with our modern lives.

Ultimately, though, the reality for many non-Orthodox Jews going through divorce is that they might never approach their rabbi or cantor for Jewish ritual in the face of their civil divorce, not knowing that there is something Jewish to do or not seeing a need or opportunity to Jewishly mark the end of their marriage—a (once) sacred relationship originally marked by Jewish ritual under the chuppah. Herein lies the paradox: we begin a marriage with a wedding, a Jewish ceremony, but we end it in a civil courtroom, devoid of Judaism.

But this is also the great opportunity in divorce despite the inherently negative reality—namely, to create meaningful Jewish moments in this situation. What can we do? First, realize you can go it alone, but asking a rabbi or cantor or even a friend to help will make the journey an easier one. And, consider what it is that you are seeking—closure for yourself, a ritual with your former partner, or legal closure on the matter. As to what path to take, there are options.

You could take the path of a *get* or *get*-like document. You could seek an Orthodox *get* or work with an organization like Kayama that facilitates the *get* process, framed in a meaningful way by your rabbi or cantor. Or you could select a Reform ritual using the Document of Separation that makes the process more egalitarian but is not legally binding in the larger Jewish community. In the new *CCAR Life-Cycle Guide* we find a contemporary adaptation of the traditional *get* ritual that offers a modern, thoughtful ritual with which to end a marriage. Each partner affirms that he or she is releasing the other from their marriage, and a Document of Separation is signed and torn, pieces given to both people. This ritual concludes with readings and a prayer of escape, *Birkat HaGomeil*, closing with the Priestly Blessing, spoken to each of the two people. It is an egalitarian ritual involving both members of the couple and could easily be done by two people alone or with a friend, rabbi, or cantor facilitating.[2]

Another way to approach this moment of ending a marriage is to create or participate in a new ritual, alone or with friends, or with your rabbi or cantor helping to create and facilitate, sharing resources of our tradition that can be re-engendered with new meaning and given our own voices as well. Here the opportunities for sacredness and Jewish meaning are limited only by your willingness to explore. You could create the ritual on your own or guided by a knowledgeable teacher. Examples of new ways to mark what can be sacred time are perhaps lesser known but are rich. The website Ritualwell (www.ritualwell.org) posts many rituals to use for yourself or to learn from in order to create your own. Some examples of thought-provoking, accessible rituals include the following:

› A *tashlich*-based ritual created by one woman who wanted to affirm her new wholeness and cast off the brokenness and uncertainty of her past. She brought her own *beit din* of sorts—three women friends—to Lake Michigan before Rosh HaShanah and participated in a ritual that she and her rabbi created, culminating in *tashlich*. The woman wrote her own statement of affirmation, read it, and cast bread into the waters to mark the casting off of her old

2. *L'chol Z'man v'Eit: The CCAR Life-Cycle Guide*, section 4.1. (New York: CCAR Press, 2015).

status.[3] This is a ritual that could easily be adapted and done for yourself, bringing friends to support you and, before going to a moving body of natural water, writing a reflection on what your are casting off and/or what you are affirming in a new or renewed status post-divorce.

> One couple implemented a ritual together that emphasized their split, and included their mutual release and forgiveness. They each drank from their own cup of wine—in contrast to drinking from the same *Kiddush* cup at their wedding. They spoke of the split of their partnership, but they affirmed their partnership in parenting even and especially after divorce. They participated in a scripted ritual together, facilitated by a witness who guided the ritual, reading parts of the ritual script. This ritual mirrored part of the traditional *get* ritual in that there was a document of release, but in this case different from a traditional *get*. Here there were two documents of release, one written by each partner and then dropped into the hands of the other. This ritual, too, could be adopted by other couples who are divorcing, either as is or adapted.[4]

> One woman created a ritual for herself after going through the *get* transaction, which she found wanting. She surrounded herself with her own symbolic *beit din*—friends who represented her loving community rather than a legal body—and immersed in water, marking her transformation. This ritual incorporated an outdoor natural body of water in which the woman immersed three times and included some traditional Jewish prayer, but prayer that is

3. Lisa Greene and Laura Milsk Fowler, "*Tekes Ishur V'shleimut*: A Ritual of Affirmation and Wholeness after Divorce," Ritualwell, https://ritualwell.org/ritual/tekes-ishur-v%E2%80%99shleimut-ritual-affirmation-and-wholeness-after-divorce.
4. Rachel Barenblat, "A Ritual for Ending a Marriage," Ritualwell, http://ritualwell.org/ritual/ritual-ending-marriage.

from other contexts, such as *Elohai N'shamah*, the morning prayer affirming the purity of one's soul, at the outset, and *Shehecheyanu* after the three immersions. This ritual was not scripted but organic and included Jewish prayer, singing, and the Israeli Progressive Movement's separation document read and signed by those friends.[5] Again, this ritual could be adopted by others, though it is less scripted and so requires some comfort in independently choosing the words of prayer.

The opportunities abound, allowing a technical legal ending of a civil transaction to be infused with community, Jewish words, warmth, and maybe even the Divine. Such rituals afford the opportunity to affirm emotions for which signing a courtroom document may not open the door and to make the ending and new beginning of divorce a Jewish ending and new beginning.

5. Lisa Greene, "What Do You Wear to Get Divorced?," *Huffington Post*, July 26, 2016, http://www.huffingtonpost.com/rabbi-lisa-greene/what-do-you-wear-to-get-d_b_11207284.html.

RABBI LAURA GELLER

Lech L'cha, Go Forth
Growing Older and Gaining Wisdom

IN *PIRKEI AVOT* (5:21) we read, "At five years old, you begin Torah. At ten, Mishnah. At thirteen, you are responsible for mitzvot. At fifteen, for Talmud. At eighteen, you get married. At twenty, you are ready to pursue a career. At thirty, for strength. At forty, for understanding. At fifty, for advice. At sixty, for *ziknah* . . ."

Ziknah is hard to translate. Old age? Maturity? Some commentaries read the word as an acronym for *zeh skanah chochmah*, "one who has acquired wisdom."

The stages of a life are measured differently now than in the days of *Pirkei Avot*. In the middle of the twentieth century the stages were childhood, adolescence (invented in the early twentieth century), midlife (when the task was the building of career and family), and then old age. Now there is a new stage between midlife and old age. This stage, where people realize that there is less time ahead than behind, heightens people's longing for meaning and purpose.

One way Judaism teaches about meaning and purpose, and acquiring wisdom, is through ritual. Ritual marks the important moments where a culture both wants to reflect and to teach what is important to its members. What messages do we want our tradition to teach about this new stage? What are the moments that ought to be noticed, marked, and celebrated that could both reflect and teach what is important?

Some moments relate to significant birthdays; others to transitions like retirement, becoming a grandparent, taking off a wedding ring after the death of a spouse. Some relate to moments of joy; others to difficult times that might lie ahead. The messages embedded in marking these moments through ritual remind us that divinity is present at every stage of our life and that growing older presents opportunities as well as challenges. This view disrupts the vision of aging as just one of decline and pushes back against the ageism and negative stereotypes about aging that are so deeply rooted in our culture.

An example: Not long ago, I got a call from a congregant on her way with her sister to clean out her mother's home after having moved her mother to an assisted-living facility. She asked, "Rabbi, what is the prayer you say when you begin to close up the home you grew up in?" I thought, "Yes, there should be a prayer!" I found one online, in an article by Rabbi Jack Reimer, which we adapted slightly:

> Holy One, as we enter the home of our beloved mother at this moment of transition in her life, please guide our actions to be in accordance with Jewish tradition as well as in accordance with her wishes.
>
> Help us to move through her home, which so enriched our lives, in a manner that is a tribute to her teachings and her values. May we perform this poignant duty with reverence and with dignity.
>
> May we do so with generosity to others in the family, acknowledging their desire for some of these mementos, and with generosity to others in the community who might benefit from these possessions.
>
> Kein y'hi ratzon—May this be Your will.[1]

They said this prayer before they began the work, and it helped them experience their task as a sacred one. And it made the ritual of putting up a mezuzah in their mother's new home much more meaningful for all of them.

Another more personal example is related to what could be called "the sacred conversation," that difficult conversation about what we want at the end of our life. My husband and I brought our children together and shared with them a document we had prepared called "The Five Wishes." It asks five questions: Who is the person or who

---

1. http://www.reformjudaism.org/home-dismantled-devotion.

are the people I want to make care decisions for me when I can't? What kind of medical treatment do I want or don't want? How comfortable do I want to be? How do I want people to treat me? What do I want my loved ones to know?

Some of what we each wanted is the same; some of it is different. If I were in a situation close to death and life-support treatment would only delay the moment of my death, I don't want that treatment. My husband would want it if his doctor thought it could help.

The kids asked lots of questions: "What if you change your minds? Would the situation be different if this happens before you get really old?" The kids and their partners talked about their grandparents' deaths and their feelings about how they had died. And then they asked for blank copies of "The Five Wishes," because they realized it would be good for them to think about these questions for themselves.

The hardest part for me, surprisingly, was the wish for what we wanted our loved ones to know. My husband was clear that he wanted his family, friends, and others to know that he has forgiven them for when they may have hurt him in life. I am not yet ready to issue a blanket statement on forgiving everyone who has hurt me, which led us gently into a conversation about forgiveness and reminded me that I have a bit more work to do around the issue. We also talked about organ donation, and burial versus cremation, and whether the children thought "visiting" a cemetery where we were buried would be important to them. And we talked about how we would want to be remembered. Finally, we talked about Alzheimer's and dementia. We told our kids that if one of us no longer could recognize the other, our understanding of love meant that we would want the healthy partner to be free to live a full life.

Later in the week, just before we lit the Shabbat candles, we turned "the sacred conversation" into a short ritual. We read out loud our B'rit Ahuvim, the promises we made to each other when we married. And then we added a new provision to our covenant:

Now, ten years after we first entered into our *B'rit Ahuvim*, we reaffirm the commitments we made then, and, in the presence of our children, we add another:

We declare that if one of us should become ill with such serious dementia or Alzheimer's disease that it becomes impossible to recognize our partner, and that this condition is attested to by two doctors and one rabbi, the other one of us should feel free to live as full a life as possible, including having other intimate relationships. That freedom in no way compromises the promise we have made to honor and to care for each other physically and financially as we grow older. We make this declaration because each of us believes that loving each other includes granting this freedom to pursue new intimate relationships even as we honor our commitment to be present to each other as we age.

Then we lit Shabbat candles as we do each week—one for each of our children and their partners, along with the traditional two. And then we blessed our children, not in absentia as we do each week, but in their presence, our hands on their heads, whispering the blessing that each of them is to us both.

Thinking about new ritual for this new stage of life evokes the story of God's call to Avram and Sarai, which is in fact the beginning of the Jewish narrative, in the Torah portion called *Lech L'cha*. They too were older adults, called by God to go forth (*lech l'cha*) from their safe and familiar place to a place where God would send them, with the promise that this new journey would lead to their becoming a blessing. After God calls to Avram and Sarai, three important things happen. The first is that their names are changed by adding the letter *hei*, one of the names of God. Avram becomes Avraham; Sarai becomes Sarah. The second is that they make a covenant, a new promise to God. And the third is that they offer a sacrifice. These actions suggest questions that can help us think about creating new rituals for this new stage.

First, in what way are our names changing as we transition to the new stage? From mother to mother-in-law? From parent to grandparent? From full-time professional to retired? From salaried employee to volunteer? From spouse to widow or widower? From child to orphan? From adult to elder? In a classic text about *t'shuvah*, Maimonides teaches, "Among the paths of repentance [*t'shuvah*], is for the person to change his name, as if to say 'I am becoming a different person now.'"[2] In what ways might we be becoming different people now? Who do we want to become? How could the ritual we create reflect those changes?

Second, is there a new covenant, a new promise, that we want to make at this stage of our lives? For Abraham and Sarah it was a covenant with God that clarified their life purpose. This is a moment to try to be clear about ours. The only way to get clear is to look back, understand what we have achieved and where we've made mistakes, and think about how we want to do things differently. This might suggest a commitment to renew our wedding vows, or to reappropriate the long-standing Jewish tradition of writing an ethical will, a letter to our children and their children, about how we want to be remembered and what we hope our legacy will be.

Finally, at the end of the story, Abraham (and Sarah) offer a kind of sacrifice to seal their covenant. The Hebrew word for sacrifice (*l'hakriv*) comes from a root that means both "coming close" and "letting go." Therefore, preparing for the ritual as we enter this stage suggests that we think about what we are ready to let go of and to what we want to draw close.

What might rituals that evoke this familiar biblical story look like? Is it public, in a synagogue, like an adult bar or bat mitzvah? Is it a celebration with family and friends, like a wedding or a ceremony where we consciously declare that we have become an elder? Or is it a private family gathering, where we explain the process that led us to this moment, introduce the new names we are adding to ours, and read our ethical will out loud? Perhaps it is even more private, with us working through these questions in our own journal or with a spiritual director and marked, for example, by a visit to a mikveh.

However we choose to mark the transition, the important steps are to become clearer about the new "names" we are acquiring, the

---

2. Maimonides, *Mishneh Torah, Hilchot T'shuvah* 2:4.

promises to we want to make, and what we want to let go of and to what we want to draw close. Framing these questions within the Jewish narrative can bring us closer to Judaism and direct us to do the spiritual work we need to do to become the very old people we would like someday to become—openhearted, grateful, and connected to other people both young and old.

Using these questions as the basis for creating new Jewish ritual, as individuals and as communities, can unlock the potential of this new stage to teach us to look forward and give back. Through this work, we hope not only to leave a legacy but also to live our legacy. Maybe that is what it means to acquire wisdom.

RABBI RICHARD F. ADDRESS, DMin

Choosing Life

Making Sacred Choices as Life Ebbs

THE TIME to make a decision is at hand. The family has spoken to the doctor. Choices are at hand. You gather the advance directive, the health care proxy in case that is needed. You make sure that everyone who may need these documents has them. You may be dealing with a hospital or a hospice or caring for someone at home; no matter, the choices that now emerge are challenging, spiritual, and, in many ways, frightening. Who would have ever thought it would come to this? Emotions surge and are often conflicted. The time for decisions is at hand.

Our tradition is rich in guidance as this stage of the life cycle approaches. An overview of centuries of tradition and commentary can produce what I refer to as a fundamental ethic. That ethic, based on our texts, is the "dignity and sanctity of human life and the preservation of human life in dignity and sanctity." Advances in medical technology, as well as our own personal views on our choices at life's end, has made this fundamental ethic very contextual and subjective. Traditional Jewish guidelines are quite relevant to these discussions and thus can be instructive and helpful across the denominational lines. One of our key values, drawn from Talmud, is that of *pikuach nefesh*, the fact that one may abrogate just about all Jewish law in order to save a life. Thus, in illness, we are supposed to do everything in our power to restore health to someone who is sick. But what of those moments when the restoration to health may not be possible? What about those moments when the physician comes to us and asks what we wish to be done, because the arsenal of medical treatment has been exhausted?

Judaism is a religious system that allows for and encourages the continuing interpretation of texts in order to make the system relevant to life situations. In liberal Judaism, the authority for our actions is often based in the context of society. Indeed, the ability to adapt and, at times, innovate has been a key in Jewish survival. So too in the case before us. Jewish tradition identified a legal category of life called *goseis*. The tradition defined that status as a patient who is moribund and whose death is imminent. Of course, medical technology has rendered this definition to be challenging. The key to this category is, however, that once a person passes this boundary, we are under no obligation to preserve a life that may be ending. In fact, the higher mitzvah may well be to allow the flame of life to flicker out, in dignity and in sanctity. Can we continue to push the doctors to "do everything"? Yes, we can; however, the context of the case may allow us to say that to continue this treatment or to involve our loved one in more invasive treatments may not be compassionate care; rather it may be futile care. In such a context, the higher value may be to make the person as comfortable as possible so that the life ends in dignity and sanctity.

In our world, *goseis* is usually associated with those last weeks, months, or moments of life when further treatment really is futile and only serves to delay an inevitable death, rather than prolong a life. The treatment of such cases is very contextual. The category of Jewish literature known as responsa is filled with questions and answers that relate to these contexts and are drawn from tradition and reflect the cross-section of denominational belief. Several Reform responsa deal with the issue of the use of palliative care and the use of drugs to make sure that no one suffers undue pain.[1]

---

1. For example: "Relieving Pain of a Dying Patient," in *American Reform Responsa*, ed. Walter Jacob (New York: CCAR Press, 1983), 253–257; "Drugs to Relieve Pain," in *Questions and Reform Jewish Answers: New American Reform Responsa*, ed. Walter Jacob (New York: CCAR Press, 1992), #151; and *Death and Euthanasia in Jewish Law*, ed. Walter Jacob and Moshe Zemer (Pittsburgh: Freehof Institute of Progressive Halakhah, Rodef Shalom Press, 1995).

A question that is often raised is whether "quality of life" should be considered as a factor in making these decisions. Quality of life, much like dignity and sanctity, can be quite subjective. That is why Judaism believes that every case, every person, must be treated on its own. Our Reform Movement understood the contextual nature of this issue when it wrote in the responsum "Quality of Life and Euthanasia":

> We should do our best to enhance the quality of life and to use whatever means modern science has placed at our disposal for this purpose. We need not invoke heroic measures to prolong life, nor should we hesitate to alleviate pain, but we cannot also utilize a "low quality of life" as an excuse for hastening death. We cannot generalize about the "quality of life" but must treat each case that we face individually. All life is wonderful and mysterious. The human situation, the family setting, and other factors must be carefully analyzed before a sympathetic decision can be reached.[2]

In a similar vein, Rabbi Moshe Tendler and Dr. Fred Rosner, in *Tradition*, the journal of the Modern Orthodox Movement, wrote, "Judaism is concerned about the quality of life, about the mitigation of pain, and the cure of illness wherever possible. If no cure or remission can be achieved, nature may be allowed to take its course. To prolong life is a *mitsva*, to prolong dying is not."[3]

Scholars and commentators from across the denominational lines have concluded that once an individual becomes a *goseis*, it is permitted in these specific contexts to remove treatment that stands in the way of the dying process. Indeed, many of these scholars point to a traditional midrash (BT Ketubot 104a) as a foundation for this. It is told that as Rabbi Judah HaNasi lay dying, his disciples gathered at his house and prayed that he be spared. The rabbi's maidservant climbed to the roof of the house and threw down a clay pot. The sharp sound of the pot shattering on the ground caused the prayers

---

2. "Quality of Life and Euthanasia," in *Contemporary American Reform Responsa*, ed. Walter Jacob (New York: CCAR Press, 1987), #83.
3. Moshe D. Tendler and Fred Rosner, "Quality and the Sanctity of Life in the Talmud and Mishnah," *Tradition* 28, no. 1 (Fall 1993), page 26.

to stop. At that moment, Rabbi Judah's soul departed. From this, tradition has based the idea that there may come a time to allow that flame of life to flicker out.

As you contemplate these most personal and challenging of decisions, keep in mind that the Reform Movement has been on record for decades favoring hospice care and comfort care at the end of life. A 1995 UAHC (now URJ) Biennial resolution, "Compassion and Comfort Care at the End of Life," reads in part:

> Guided by the mitzvah of *pikuach nefesh*, we must strive toward an achievable goal: to provide a quality of life that is at least tolerable for each one whose journey ends in pain and suffering. Our effort must ensure that only rarely will that choice be beyond human strength. We assert that most of the tragic choices to end life can be avoided through the combined efforts of caring doctors, clergy, providers, family and community.

Included in the factors that go into making these sacred decisions is how a person's own spirituality influences the decisions. This is an important aspect of how one wishes to approach the end of life. This issue leads to the emerging necessity of making sure that each of us has an advance medical directive as well as a health care proxy. The writing of an advance directive, which puts forth your wishes, as well as a health care proxy, which empowers a designated person to make medical decisions for you if you are not able, has become a necessity. These documents need to be discussed within a total family system and need also to be reviewed on a regular basis, as medical technology and one's personal preferences often change as time moves on. It is also important that these documents be given to *all* interested parties—children, physicians, clergy, lawyers—so that in case of emergency they are readily available. To aid in this, we also recommend that your congregation create an annual educational forum on how to make an informed Jewish decision as life ends. The more education and information we acquire on this issue, the easier, less stressful, and less guilt inducing will things be when and if the time comes to proceed on this journey.

As you consider the challenges and choices that are contained in these discussions, also keep in mind that the moments we are alluding to can be ones of great personal and spiritual transition and transformation. These are moments of meaning, in many cases. Your presence with a loved one as life ebbs is one of the great mitzvot that we have. If you are given the gift of being able to say goodbye to a loved one, you can be comforted in the knowledge that your presence and your love helped make this journey one of dignity and sanctity. These decisions are not easy, for we know they raise so many issues and emotions on so many levels. Yet, this too is part of our cycle of life, included in the mystery that we call life and death.

RABBI LAWRENCE W. RAPHAEL

Ethical Wills

T HE CUSTOM of writing directions for the religious and secular
guidance of children, known as ethical wills, can be traced back
to the twelfth century.[1] The habit of addressing *verbal* counsel is, of
course, much more ancient. There are numerous biblical examples
of such counsel. The first is in Genesis 18:19, with God speaking to
Abraham: "For I have selected him [Abraham], so that he may teach
his children and those who come after him to keep the way of the
Eternal, doing what is right and just, so that the Eternal may fulfill
for Abraham all that has been promised him." The Bible records several other instances, most prominently the blessing of Jacob (Genesis 27:27), the dying request of Jacob to Joseph and his brothers
(Genesis 49:1–27), the address of Moses and Joshua to the people
of Israel (Deuteronomy 33), and the advice of David to his son Solomon (I Kings 2:1–9). We also find in Proverbs 1:8 the admonition
"My child, heed the discipline of your father, and do not forsake the
instruction of your mother." The Apocrypha, the Talmud, and medieval and modern Hebrew literature all contain examples of ethical
wills parents have left their children.

A classic medieval source is "The Letter of Ramban" (Rabbi
Moshe ben Nachman, 1195–1270), written to his son. In this document, Ramban admonishes him to pursue self-control, the perfection of his character, and the purification of motives.

> When your actions display genuine humility—when you stand
> meekly before man, and fearfully before God; when you stand
> wary of sin—then the spirit of God's presence will rest upon you,

---

1. Israel Abrahams, *Hebrew Ethical Wills* (Philadelphia: Jewish Publication Society, 1926).

as will the splendor of God's Glory; you will live the life of the world-to-come.

Let your words be spoken gently; let your head be bowed. Cast your eyes downward, and your heart heavenward; and when speaking, do not stare at your listener. Let all men seem greater than you in your eyes.

Speak with reverence and awe, like a servant who stands in the presence of his master.

Read this letter once a week and neglect none of it. Fulfill it, and in so doing, walk with it forever in the ways of God, and God be Blessed, so that you may succeed in your ways. And merit the world-to-come that lies hidden for the righteous. Every day that you shall read this letter, heaven shall answer your heart's desires. Amen.

The publication in 1983 of *Ethical Wills: A Modern Jewish Treasury* by Jack Reimer and Nathaniel Stampfer has given us many wonderful contemporary examples and instructions on how to think about writing an ethical will. They provide the following writing prompts to help you get started:

- These were the formative events of my life . . .
- This is the world from which I came . . .
- These are some of the important lessons that I have learned in my life . . .
- These are the people who influenced me the most . . .
- These are some of the favorite possessions that I want you to have and these are the stories that explain what makes these things so precious to me . . .
- These are causes for which members of our family have felt a sense of responsibility, and I hope you will too . . .
- Some of the Scriptural passages that have meant the most to me . . .
- These are the mistakes that I regret having made the most in my life that I hope you will not repeat . . .
- This is my definition of true success . . .
- This is how I feel as I look back over my life . . .
- I would like to ask your forgiveness for and I forgive you for . . .

› I want you to know how much I love you and how grateful
I am to you for . . .[2]

Included in the Riemer and Stampfer book is an ethical will from teacher, TV host, and comedian Sam Levenson. He addressed this to his children and grandchildren:

I leave you my unpaid debts. They are my greatest assets. Everything I own—I owe:

1. To America I owe a debt for the opportunity it gave me to be free and to be me.
2. To my parents I owe America. They gave it to me and I leave it to you. Take good care of it.
3. To the biblical tradition I owe the belief that man does not live by bread alone, nor does he live alone at all. This is also the democratic tradition. Preserve it.
4. To the six million of my people and to the thirty million other humans who died because of man's inhumanity to man, I owe a vow that it must never happen again.
5. I leave you not everything I never had, but everything I had in my lifetime: a good family, respect for learning, compassion for my fellowman, and some four-letter words for all occasions: words like "help," "give," "care," "feel," and "love."

Love, my dear grandchildren, is easier to recommend than to define. I can tell you only that like those who came before you, you will surely know when love ain't; you will also know when mercy ain't and brotherhood ain't.

The millennium will come when all the "ain'ts" shall have become "ises" and all the "ises" shall be for all, even for those you don't like.

Finally, I leave you the years I should like to have lived so that I might possibly see whether *your* generation will bring more love and peace to the world than ours did. I not only hope you will. I pray that you will.[3]

Perhaps the most famous modern ethical will comes from writer Sholom Aleichem's will (1859–1916). His will was read into the Congressional Record and published in the *New York Times*. Here is part of what he wrote:

---

2. Jack Reimer and Nathaniel Stampfer, *Ethical Wills: A Modern Jewish Treasury* (New York: Schocken Books, 1983), page 215.
3. Ibid., page 162.

Let there be no arguments or debates among my colleagues who may wish to memorialize me by erecting a monument in New York. I shall not be able to rest peacefully in my grave if my friends engage in such nonsense.

At my grave, and throughout the whole year, and then every year on the anniversary of my death, my remaining son and my sons-in-law, if they are so inclined, should say Kaddish for me. And if they do not wish to do this, or if it against their religious convictions, they may fulfill their obligation to me by assembling together with my daughters and grandchildren and good friends to read this testament, and also to select one of my stories, one of the really merry ones, and read it aloud in whatever language they understand best, and let my name rather be remembered by them with laughter than not at all.

He appended his wish for how his tombstone should be engraved:

Here lies a plain and simple Jew
Who wrote in plain and simple prose;
Wrote humor for the common folk
To help them to forget their woes.

He scoffed at life and mocked the world,
At all its foibles he poked fun,
The world went on its merry way,
And left him stricken and undone.

And while his grateful readers laughed,
Forgetting troubles of their own,
Midst their applause—God only knows—
He wept in secret and alone.

What follows are two contemporary examples of ethical wills written by participants in workshops that I led on writing ethical wills. The authors first studied some of the classical ethical wills that are mentioned earlier in this chapter and the next day returned with their own efforts.

In the excerpts that follow (presented with their permission) I have changed the names and any other personal references that were made, to protect the identity of the people who wrote these documents.

The writer of the following ethical will is a young father of two girls whose own parents died some years ago. Though deceased, his parents are a vital presence in his writing. He wants to articulate a legacy that a neighbor of his parents had the opportunity to spell out. His emphasis on family and community is central to his ethical will.

Ma, I've learned, over the years, that the choices I make, small and great, are my opportunity to live out my values. I have learned to set my table with the things I know to be of utmost importance. I am free to miss you, and can enjoy what you would have said if you were still here to say it yourself. Your life, Mother, is a constant blessing to our family. Is—not was—is a blessing to our family. And our family means *your* family—for you are still very much in it.

Pop, I think when I wrote Mom last time, your death was still too big for me to grasp. It felt good to know that you were both together, but it felt real bad to miss you all over again, and to feel that terrible hopeless confusion that overcame me when you died a few months before my sixteenth birthday.

Twenty-five years later, I can still feel the places where you were part of me. In fact, I can see them much better now. I'm proud of who I have become: a happy, successful Jewish father, because I've "turned out" like you. As I take my place in the circle of the Jewish community, drawn, as you were, to Jewish education, I've become—chosen to become—the "best of" you an Mom. What greater tribute can a son pay to his parents?

You both have all my love and my respect and my deepest gratitude for the values and the life and the blessings—for the full and abundant table you set for our family. May it come to pass that I might receive such a letter as this from my kids, while I am still living—so I can share it with you. Shalom.

This writer is a mother of two girls who sought to emphasize the centrality of family relationships in her life. She intended to share it with her daughters very soon after the workshop.

Over the past twenty-six years Dad and I have built a life together. First based on love, our home is secured by trust, respect, an ability to be both dependent and independent at the same time, and a specific knowledge that our intertwined lives support each other with unconditional love.

When you girls were born, a whole new world opened—our small family circle grew, but remained firmly connected. Our love for you each is boundless . . . lion-like in its devotion. I believe that you are God's most special gifts to us, borrowed treasures we have nurtured and set on life paths. Our role as parents will never cease (too bad that you will always have to call and say, "I got here safely, Mom!").

Even as little girls, you both sensed how important developing a close relationship with each other was to me. Because of the eventual lack of an adult relationship with my brother, it has become an almost irrational imperative that you two build a nurturing dependence based on love, respect, and an unconditional support system.

I often repeat the same petitionary prayers for you. They ask for good health. You have both experienced way too much illness for your young years. On the other hand, perhaps you grew stronger with each nasty experience. I would have the audacity, however, to tell God, enough is enough!

Finally girls, I ask each of you to think of two life approaches, ways to enable your days to expand to their fullest: (1) Never lose your sense of humor. Life can be very serious! Always sing, tell jokes, and bask in laughter when something tickles your fancy! (2) Since we get only one chance at this thing called life, live every day to its fullest. Take chances with calculated risks. You'll continue to challenge yourself and becoming fascinating women.

Remember who you are and from whom you have descended; always listen to your "gut" and be true to yourself; appreciate that life is a gift from God; and allow your Jewish soul to pervade how you live every single day. Be happy and healthy all the days of your lives. And, always know how much I love you.

Many who prepare ethical wills find it a great spiritual exercise that then informs the rest of their life. In some cases the writers follow a Jewish tradition of revisiting and sometimes rewriting their ethical will around the time of the High Holy Days. This exercise can provide an important way to think about one's legacy and to be sure that family or heirs have clarity on how one thinks about one's life. As with making an estate plan, people are tempted to put it off because no likes to contemplate their own death. It is important to make an estate plan and write an ethical will while one is in good health; otherwise one may not have the strength or time to do it. Sometimes death comes after a long illness, but sometimes it is the result of a catastrophic event.

There is a separate question of whether to share the document with the family while the writer is still alive. This largely depends on different circumstances, having to do with the age of children and/ or grandchildren, relationships that exist, and what can be perceived as the value of sharing such a personal statement with loved ones. While no one answer can suffice in all circumstances, I would lean in the direction of finding an opportunity to share if at all possible.

RABBI SIMEON J. MASLIN

The Mourner's *Kaddish*

T HE *KADDISH* is like a time machine linking the generations. For many, the *Kaddish* has the power to transcend time and space. It can renew the connection between the mourner and the deceased. Through the aegis of memory, the life of the deceased can be celebrated, and old wounds can often be healed. Primarily, the power of the *Kaddish* derives from its language. That too is a kind of a paradox, in that the *Kaddish* ultimately expresses the concept that God is beyond verbal description. Indeed, its core idea is precisely that language is inadequate for providing a vocabulary that conveys the praise of God in a manner befitting God's grandeur and magnificence. As part of their regular daily worship, myriads of Jews all over the world recite the *Kaddish*. The emotional appeal of the *Kaddish* is so compelling that even Jews who do not generally attend worship often commit to this mitzvah as an act of reverence for their departed loved ones. Some will recite it three times daily at synagogue services during the year following the death of a parent, and thirty days for other relatives; some will recite it at Shabbat services; and many will recite it on the *yahrzeit* (anniversary) of their loved ones' death and at *Yizkor* services throughout the Jewish calendar year.

What is the origin of this beloved prayer? And what is its meaning? Why does it respond so obviously to the deep needs of the bereaved? Scholars believe it is probably one the earliest prayers. Originally the *Kaddish* had nothing to do with death. It was a brief doxology, a formulaic praise of God recited by preachers and teachers at the conclusion of their lectures during the Talmudic period. It was written in Aramaic, the vernacular language at that time. The wording was inspired by a passage in Prophets that foretells the ultimate victory of God and concludes with the following words: "Thus will I make

Myself great and holy, and I will make Myself known in the eyes of many nations, and they shall know that I am the Eternal" (Ezekiel 38:23).

The essential phrase of the *Kaddish*, based on this messianic passage in Ezekiel, comes at the very beginning: "Exalted and hallowed be God's great name in the world which God created, according to plan. May God's majestic be revealed in the days of our lifetime and the life of all Israel—speedily, imminently, to which we say: Amen." Those present at the lecture or study session would then respond, "Amen! Blessed be God's great name to all eternity." This, then, is the basic *Kaddish* prayer; it was not until post-Talmudic time that the remaining three paragraphs that we find in the prayer book today were added (see *Mishkan T'filah: A Reform Siddur*, page 598).

Sometime in the medieval period, the idea developed that reciting *Kaddish* would help rescue the souls of the dead. There is a legend about Rabbi Akiva (second century CE) and a condemned soul who was allowed to enter aradise only after Rabbi Akiva found the man's son and taught him to pray on behalf of his father (*Tanna D'Vei Eliyahu Zuta* 10:7; *Kallah Rabbati* 2:9; *Or Zarua, Hilchot Shabbat* 50). In some versions of this tale Akiva teaches him to pray "*Baruch Adonai ham'vorach*," from the *Bar'chu* prayer, and in other versions he teaches "*Yitgadal v'yitkadash*," from the *Kaddish*. It is possible that both of these doxologies were, at various points in Jewish history, considered helpful for redeeming the dead. By the eighth century, though, it had become customary to recite *Kaddish* after a funeral, and by the twelfth century, a *Kaddish* in the prayer service was designated for mourners.

The Mishnah teaches that "the wicked are punished in Gehenna for twelve months" (*Mishnah Eduyot* 2:10). Elsewhere in the Talmud we learn that "the dead are not forgotten until after twelve months" (BT *B'rachot* 58b). And so people began reciting the *Kaddish*, particularly in memory of parents, for twelve months. In the Middle Ages the folk custom developed to recite the *Kaddish* for eleven months only so that it should not appear that one considered one's parent so wicked as to merit punishment for the full twelve months (*Shulchan*

Aruch, Yoreh Dei-ah 376). Since Reform Judaism does not recognize the *Kaddish* to be an intercessionary prayer but rather a mitzvah rooted in tradition and respect for the deceased, mourners who have lost a parent will most often recite it for the full twelve months. Thus, Reform Jews generally recite *Kaddish* during the post-interment periods of shivah (seven days), *sh'loshim* (thirty days), in the ensuing twelve months (for a parent only), and then annually at *yahrzeit*, and during *Yizkor* services on Yom Kippur, Sh'mini Atzeret–Simchat Torah, the seventh day of Pesach, and Shavuot.

The power of the *Kaddish* plays a critical role in the mourning process. It helps mourners to process their loss by showing their ongoing connection to their deceased loved one. There are many moving accounts by mourners about the effect of reciting the *Kaddish*. One of the most extensive is in Leon Wieseltier's magisterial book *The Kaddish*.[1]

The words of the *Kaddish* express hope amid despair and yearn for unity at a time of brokenness. It imagines a world in which God's presence is manifest and goodness and peace prevail. The *Kaddish* also honors the memory of the departed by framing ritual remembrance in the trappings of the sacred. Mourners often recite *Kaddish* accompanied by family and other loved ones. Customarily a minyan (prayer quorum of ten adults) must be present as well. Although many Reform Jews will recite the *Kaddish* without a minyan, when recited with a minyan the *Kaddish* can help strengthen the ties of family and community. "The loved and pleasant in life are not wholly divided even in death. . . . The *Kaddish* also enables one to express hope for the time when grief, suffering, and pain will cease."[2] Since the Shoah and still today in the wake of communal tragedies, Jewish communities will often gather to recite the *Kaddish* to mourn the communal loss, to express solidarity with the deceased, and to lend strength to one another.

---

1. *Kaddish*, by Leon Wieseltier (New York: Vintage Books, a division of Knopf Doubleday, 2000).

2. *Maagalei Tzedek: Rabbi's Manual* (New York: CCAR, 1988), pages 255.

The Mourner's Kaddish

Yitgadal v'yitkadash sh'mei raba,　　　　　　　יִתְגַּדַּל וְיִתְקַדַּשׁ שְׁמֵהּ רַבָּא,

b'alma di v'ra chiruteih,　　　　　　　　　　　בְּעָלְמָא דִּי בְרָא כִרְעוּתֵהּ,

v'yamlich malchuteih,　　　　　　　　　　　וְיַמְלִיךְ מַלְכוּתֵהּ,

b'chayeichon uv'yomeichon　　　　　　　　　בְּחַיֵּיכוֹן וּבְיוֹמֵיכוֹן

uv'chayei d'chol beit Yisrael,　　　　　　　וּבְחַיֵּי דְכָל בֵּית יִשְׂרָאֵל,

baagala uviz'man kariv.　　　　　　　　　　בַּעֲגָלָא וּבִזְמַן קָרִיב.

V'imru: Amen.　　　　　　　　　　　　　וְאִמְרוּ: אָמֵן.

Y'hei sh'mei raba m'varach　　　　　　　יְהֵא שְׁמֵהּ רַבָּא מְבָרַךְ

l'alam ul'almei almaya.　　　　　　　　לְעָלַם וּלְעָלְמֵי עָלְמַיָּא.

Yitbarach v'yishtabach, v'yitpaar　　　　יִתְבָּרַךְ וְיִשְׁתַּבַּח, וְיִתְפָּאַר

v'yitromam v'yitnasei,　　　　　　　　וְיִתְרוֹמַם וְיִתְנַשֵּׂא,

v'yit'hadar v'yitaleh v'yit'halal　　　　וְיִתְהַדָּר וְיִתְעַלֶּה וְיִתְהַלָּל

sh'mei d'Kudsha B'rich Hu,　　　　　　שְׁמֵהּ דְּקֻדְשָׁא בְּרִיךְ הוּא,

l'eila min kol birchata　　　　　　　　לְעֵלָּא מִן כָּל בִּרְכָתָא

v'shirata, tushb'chata v'nechamata,　　וְשִׁירָתָא, תֻּשְׁבְּחָתָא וְנֶחֱמָתָא

daamiran b'alma. V'imru: Amen.　　　דַּאֲמִירָן בְּעָלְמָא. וְאִמְרוּ: אָמֵן.

Y'hei sh'lama raba min sh'maya,　　　יְהֵא שְׁלָמָא רַבָּא מִן שְׁמַיָּא,

v'chayim aleinu v'al kol Yisrael.　　　וְחַיִּים עָלֵינוּ וְעַל כָּל יִשְׂרָאֵל.

V'imru: Amen.　　　　　　　　　　　וְאִמְרוּ: אָמֵן.

Oseh shalom bimromav,　　　　　　עֹשֶׂה שָׁלוֹם בִּמְרוֹמָיו,

hu yaaseh shalom aleinu,　　　　　הוּא יַעֲשֶׂה שָׁלוֹם עָלֵינוּ,

v'al kol Yisrael.　　　　　　　　　וְעַל כָּל יִשְׂרָאֵל.

V'imru: Amen.　　　　　　　　　וְאִמְרוּ: אָמֵן.

A Basic Library for the Jewish Home

Prayer

Mishkan T'filah: A Reform Siddur. Edited by Elyse Frishman.
New York: CCAR Press, 2007.
The standard contemporary Shabbat and weekday prayer book for the
Reform Movement. Available for adults and children.

Mishkan T'filah for the House of Mourning. Edited by Hara E.
Person and Elaine Zecher. New York: CCAR Press, 2010.
An innovative approach to services in a house of mourning.

Mishkan HaNefesh: Machzor for the Days of Awe. Edited by Edwin
Goldberg, Evan Kent, Janet Marder, Sheldon Marder, Leon Morris,
et al. New York: CCAR Press, 2015.
The contemporary High Holy Day prayer book for the Reform Movement.

Divrei Mishkan HaNefesh. Edited by Edwin Goldberg.
New York: CCAR Press, 2015.
A resource for opening up and giving context to the meaning of the many pieces
of *Mishkan HaNefesh.*

Mishkan R'fuah: Where Healing Resides. Edited by Eric Weiss.
New York: CCAR Press, 2013.
This beautiful compilation contains contemplative readings and prayers for
many different moments of spiritual need, including illness, surgery, treatment,
chronic illness, hearing good news, transitions, addiction, infertility, end-of-life,
and more.

Birkon Mikdash M'at: NFTY's Bencher. Edited by Jeremy Gimbel.
New York: Reform Judaism Publishing, 2005.
This groundbreaking publication fills a need for a handy source for Shabbat,
weekday, and holiday blessings and songs.

Birkon Artzi: Blessings and Meditations for Travelers to Israel.
Edited by Serge Lippe. New York: CCAR Press, 2012.

This book provides spiritual opportunities and responses for the thousands of Jews who journey each and every year to visit, study in, and get to know the State of Israel.

Gates of Shabbat, Revised Edtion. Edited by Mark Dov Shapiro.
New York: CCAR Press, 2016.

A how-to guide about Shabbat observance and practices.

Exploring Torah—Reference Works

The Torah: A Modern Commentary. Edited by W. Gunther Plaut.
Rev. ed. New York: Reform Judaism Publishing, 2005.

A contemporary Torah commentary, combining modern scholarship with traditional Jewish thought.

The Torah: A Women's Commentary. Edited by Tamara Cohn Eskenazi and Andrea L. Weiss. New York: Reform Judaism Publishing, 2008.

A groundbreaking Torah commentary written by women scholars, rabbis, and poets from throughout the Jewish world.

Tanakh: The Holy Scriptures; The New JPS Translation according to the Traditional Hebrew Text. Edited by Jewish Publication Society.
Philadelphia: Jewish Publication Society, 1985.

The authoritative English translation of the Hebrew Bible based in a Jewish perspective.

Exploring Torah—Other Works

Cohen, Norman J. *Hineini in Our Lives: Learning How to Respond to Others through 14 Biblical Texts and Personal Stories.*
Woodstock, VT: Jewish Lights, 2005.

Reading great Torah texts with an eye toward our own personal lives.

———. *Self, Struggle & Change: Family Conflict Stories in Genesis and Their Healing Insights for Our Lives.* Woodstock, VT: Jewish Lights, 1996.

Reading the family stories in Genesis with applications to our own family life.

———. *The Way Into Torah*. Woodstock, VT: Jewish Lights, 2004.
How to understand and find meaning in the Torah.

Fields, Harvey J. *A Torah Commentary for Our Times*. Vols. 1–3. New York: Reform Judaism Publishing, 1993.
A helpful approach to the weekly *parashah*, juxtaposing the insights of ancient, medieval, and modern commentators (including the author). Perfect for both beginning Torah students of all ages and scholars seeking new angles on the text.

Goldstein, Elyse, ed. *The Women's Haftarah Commentary: New Insights from Women Rabbis on the 54 Weekly Haftarah Portions, the 5 Megillot & Special Shabbatot*. Woodstock, VT: Jewish Lights, 2004.
Fresh perspectives on the weekly prophetic readings from a feminist point of view.

Person, Hara, ed. *Voices of Torah*. New York: CCAR Press, 2012.
A wonderful Torah study resource. Discover multiple perspectives on every *parashah* in this rich collection of commentary. Includes holiday portions as well.

Holidays, Home, and Life Cycle

Kedar, Rabbi Karyn D. *Omer: A Counting*. New York: CCAR Press, 2014.
This volume, beginning with its informative contextual introduction, provides a spiritual guide for a personal journey through the Omer toward meaningful and purposeful living.

Knobel, Peter S., ed. *Mishkan Moeid: A Guide to the Jewish Seasons*. New York: CCAR Press, 2013.
This new volume presents a survey of the sacred days of the Jewish yearly cycle.

Stern, Chaim, ed. *On the Doorposts of Your House*. New York: CCAR Press, 2010.
This revised edition of this beloved volume includes a wealth of innovation and traditional readings for personal meditations and family home-based rituals.

Wiener, Rabbi Nancy H. *Beyond Breaking the Glass.*
New York: CCAR Press, 2012.

Explores the rich history of Jewish wedding customs and rituals throughout the centuries while providing contemporary interpretations and creative options.

Yoffie, Alan S. *Sharing the Journey: A Haggadah for the Contemporary Family.* New York: CCAR Press, 2012.

The inclusive text, commentary, and magnificent original artwork in this Haggadah will make all family members and friends feel welcome at your seder. Young and old, beginners and experienced seder participants will experience the joy of celebrating Passover together with clear step-by-step explanations, inspiring readings on the themes of justice and freedom for all, and opportunities for discussion.

General Jewish Interest

Borowitz, Eugene B. *Liberal Judaism.*
New York: Behrman House, 1984.

This book probes the varieties of Jewish thought and ritual practice from the perspective of liberal Judaism.

Citrin, Paul. *Lights in the Forest: Rabbi Respond to Twelve Essential Jewish Questions.* New York: CCAR Press, 2014.

A cross-section of rabbis respond to essential questions about God, humanity, and Jewish peoplehood.

David, Benjamin. *Seven Days, Many Voices: Insights into the Biblical Story of Creation.* New York: CCAR Press, 2017.

A collection of essays on the Creation story through the lenses of literature, theology, climate justice, science, midrash, human rights, and more.

Grushcow, Lisa J. *The Sacred Encounter: Jewish Perspectives on Sexuality.* New York: CCAR Press, 2014.

A wide-ranging anthology that takes a close look at the breadth of human sexuality from a Jewish perspective.

Maslin, Simeon J. ... *and Turn It Again: Theme and Sacred Variation*. Xlibris, 2008.

This volume continues the time-honored rabbinic process of turning the sacred verses of Torah over and over, and finding in them inspiring, poignant, and often humorous lessons for our day.

Sonsino, Rifat, and Daniel B. Syme. *Finding God: Selected Responses*. New York: Behrman House, 2002.

This book contains essays on significant Jewish thinkers attempting to answer the question looming above us all: Is there more than one way to perceive of God? How can we know God? What does God "want" from us?

Washofsky, Mark. *Jewish Living: A Guide to Contemporary Reform Practice*. New York: Behrman House, 2010.

This definitive guide for Reform Jewish practice leads the reader to an understanding of the whole of Jewish life.

Zamore, Mary L. *The Sacred Table: Creating a Jewish Food Ethic*. New York: CCAR Press, 2011.

An anthology of essays that explores the intersection of Judaism and food.

Author Biographies

Rabbi Richard F. Address, DMin, is Founder and Director of Jewish Sacred Aging, LLC, and the web site www.jewishsacredaging. com, which features resources, texts, programs, and podcasts dealing with the impact of longevity on the Jewish community. Rabbi Address served congregations in California and New Jersey and served on staff of Union for Reform Judaism for three plus decades as Regional Director and then Director of Department of Jewish Family Concerns. He is author of *Seekers of Meaning: Baby Boomers, Judaism and the Pursuit of Healthy Aging.*

Rabbi Barry H. D. Block serves Congregation B'nai Israel in Little Rock, Arkansas. After graduating from Amherst College Phi Beta Kappa and Magna Cum Laude, Rabbi Block was ordained at Hebrew Union College-Jewish Institute of Religion in 1991. He is an active CCAR volunteer who has led the faculties of two URJ camps in addition to having served as board chair of Planned Parenthood of South Texas. Rabbi Block's article, "Unplanned Fatherhood," appears in the CCAR anthology, *The Sacred Encounter: Jewish Perspectives on Sexuality.*

Rabbi Herbert Bronstein is Senior Scholar and Rabbi Emeritus of North Shore Congregation Israel, Glencoe, Illinois, where he served twenty-five years following his rabbinate at Brith Kodesh, Rochester, New York. He is editor of the Reform Haggadah, *A Passover Haggadah.* Beginning in 1997, he taught History of Religion courses at Lake Forest College, combining a successful congregational vocation with teaching, community roles, and publishing in learned and popular journals.

Rabbi Laura Geller, Rabbi Emerita of Temple Emanuel of Beverly Hills, was the first woman to be selected through a national search to lead a major metropolitan synagogue as Senior Rabbi. Ordained in 1976, the third woman in the Reform Movement to become a rabbi, she was twice named one of Newsweek's 50 Most Influential Rabbis in America, and featured in the PBS documentary "Jewish Americans." She is a Fellow of the Corporation of Brown University from where she graduated in 1971. She is a founder of the first synagogue-based village, ChaiVillageLA, which is part of the national Village Movement and is working with her husband, Richard Siegel, on a book entitled *Getting Good at Getting Older: A Practical Guide Grounded in Jewish Wisdom* to be published by Behrman House in 2018.

Rabbi Neal Gold has served as Director of Content and Programming for ARZA, the Association of Reform Zionists of America. He received *s'michah* from Hebrew Union College-Jewish Institute of Religion in 1997 and is currently pursuing graduate work in Near Eastern and Judaic Studies at Brandeis University. A committed teacher, counselor, social activist, and prolific writer, for over eighteen years, he served congregations in New Jersey and Massachusetts. He was a delegate for ARZENU, the international Reform Jewish movement, at the 37th World Zionist Congress in Jerusalem in October 2016.

Rabbi Elyse Goldstein is the visionary spiritual leader of City Shul. She is known throughout Canada as an outstanding educator. She founded Kolel: The Adult Centre for Liberal Jewish Learning in 1991; she was its director and principal teacher for twenty years. Kolel was recognized worldwide as a leading institution in the field of Jewish adult education. In 2005, she was awarded North America's highest honor for Jewish Education, The Covenant Award for Outstanding Educators.

Rabbi Lisa S. Greene has served North Shore Congregation Israel, Glencoe, Illinois since 1999. She seeks to create meaning, sacred time, and community through experiential Jewish learning and ritual, traditional and new. Lisa has written on ritual, divorce and the intersection of the ordinary and the sacred for the Huffington Post and in her blog, Intersections (www.ordinaryandsacred.com).

Rabbi Lisa J. Grushcow, DPhil, has served as the Senior Rabbi of Temple Emanu-El-Beth Sholom, Montreal's Reform synagogue, since 2012. She received her BA from McGill University in 1996. She was then named a Rhodes Scholar and spent three years at Oxford University, where she earned a master's degree in Judaism and Christianity in the Greco-Roman World, and then a doctorate. She was ordained a rabbi in 2003 at the Hebrew Union College-Jewish Institute of Religion in New York City, where she studied as a Wexner Graduate Fellow. She is the author of *Writing the Wayward Wife: Rabbinic Interpretations of Sotah*, the editor of *The Sacred Encounter: Jewish Perspectives on Sexuality*, and a contributor to *The Torah: A Women's Commentary*.

Rabbi Joui M. Hessel, RJE, was ordained and received a Masters of Arts in Jewish Education from the Hebrew Union College-Jewish Institute of Religion. Rabbi Hessel co-authored *The Hanukkah Family Treasury,* published by Running Hill Press and has also been published in CCAR publications: *The Sacred Encounter: Jewish Perspectives on Sexuality* (2014) and *Mishkan T'filah for Youth* (2014); *Moment Magazine* (June 2007); as well as in a book on parenting young adult children, *Mom, Can I Move Back in with You: A Survival Guide for Parents of Twentysomethings*, published by Mid-Atlantic Equity Consortium. Rabbi Hessel lives in Old Greenwich, Connecticut with her husband, Jimmy Hexter, and their daughter.

Rabbi Howard L. Jaffe has led Temple Isaiah of Lexington, Massachusetts, since 2000, and previously served congregations in Warren, New Jersey, and Minneapolis, Minnesota. His years as co-chair of the Reform Movement Commission on Outreach and Synagogue Community offered him some of the most meaningful opportunities and engagements of his rabbinic career.

Rabbi Peter S. Knobel is Rabbi Emeritus of Beth Emet The Free Synagogue, Evanston, Illinois. He is a past-president of the Central Conference of American Rabbis and served as the chair of the Ad Hoc New Siddur Committee, which produced *Mishkan T'filah: A Reform Siddur*. He is the editor of *Mishkan Moeid: A Guide to the Jewish Year*. He is a faculty member of the Spertus Institute in Chicago, Illinois.

Rabbi Sari Laufer was ordained by Hebrew Union College-Jewish Institute of Religion, Los Angeles, in May 2006. On the way to HUC-JIR, Rabbi Laufer graduated Cum Laude from Northwestern University, and served as an Eisendrath Legislative Assistant at the Religious Action Center of Reform Judaism. A Wexner Graduate Fellow, Rabbi Laufer was later selected for the PEER program through Synagogue Transformation and Renewal, for the inaugural year of the Rabbinic Fellowship for Visionary Leadership through UJA-Federation of New York, and was a member of the second cohort of CLAL's Rabbis Without Borders Fellowship. Rabbi Laufer served for eleven years as the assistant/associate rabbi of Congregation Rodeph Sholom in New York City. In 2017, she started as the Director of Congregational Engagement for Stephen Wise Temple and Schools in Los Angeles.

Rabbi Simeon J. Maslin has served congregations in Curacao, Chicago, and Philadelphia. He is a past-president of the Central Conference of American Rabbis, has lectured in many World Union congregations, and is the author of *And Turn It Again: Theme and Sacred Variation*, numerous articles, and the novel *Uncle Sol's Women*.

Rabbi Dr. Rachel S. Mikva serves as the Herman Schaalman Chair in Jewish Studies and the Director of the Center for Jewish, Christian and Islamic Studies at Chicago Theological Seminary. The Center and the Seminary work at the cutting-edge of theological education, training religious leaders who build bridges across cultural and religious difference for the critical work of social transformation. Dr. Mikva is author of *Broken Tablets: Restoring the Ten Commandments and Ourselves* (2000), *Midrash vaYosha: A Medieval Midrash on the Song of the Sea* (2012) and *Dangerous Religious Ideas* (forthcoming).

Rabbi Aaron Panken, PhD, serves as president of the Hebrew Union College-Jewish Institute of Religion, Reform Judaism's global seminary with campuses in Cincinnati, Jerusalem, Los Angeles and New York. He has taught Second Temple and Rabbinic Literature at HUC-JIR in New York since 1996, also serving as dean and vice president. The author of *The Rhetoric of Innovation* and a number of scholarly articles, his work explores the relationship between ancient texts and modern ideas of halachic flexibility, innovation, and change in Judaism. A graduate of Johns Hopkins University's Electrical Engineering program, he remains connected to technology and enjoying the natural world as a commercial rated airplane and glider pilot, a sailor, and a hiker.

Rabbi Lawrence W. Raphael, PhD, recently retired Senior Rabbi at Congregation Sherith Israel, San Francisco, California. Before serving Sherith Israel, he was Director of Adult Jewish Growth at the Union for Reform Judaism, and for 30 years was a dean and faculty member of HUC-JIR, New York. His long interest in Ethical Wills includes other publications on this topic and teaching workshops on how to create your own will.

Rabbi Amy Scheinerman is a teacher, writer, and hospice chaplain. She travels widely as a scholar-in-residence, teaching Talmud. Rabbi Scheinerman is a member of the CCAR Responsa Committee, and serves as editor of the "Voices of Torah" column of the CCAR Newsletter. She maintains a Torah commentary blog at http://taste-of-torah.blogspot.com and a Talmud blog at http://tenminutesoftalmud.blogspot.com. Rabbi Scheinerman was ordained in 1984 at HUC-JIR in New York, where she also received a Doctor of Divinity in 2009. She has held pulpits in Conservative, Reform, and unaffiliated congregations. She lives in Columbia, Maryland.

Rabbi Ariana Silverman graduated from Harvard University and was ordained by HUC-JIR. She has served Temple Kol Ami in West Bloomfield, Michigan, and Temple Beth Israel in Jackson, Michigan, and as the Interim Manager of Lifelong Learning for the CCAR. She is the rabbi of the Isaac Agree Downtown Synagogue, the last free-standing synagogue in the City of Detroit. She lives in Detroit with her family.

Rabbi A. Brian Stoller is the Senior Rabbi of Temple Israel in Omaha, Nebraska. A dedicated student of Torah and Jewish thought, Rabbi Stoller has published articles on Reform Judaism and Jewish law, and is currently pursuing a doctorate in halachah. Before entering the rabbinate, Rabbi Stoller had a career in politics and served as press secretary to then-U.S. Senator Peter Fitzgerald of Illinois.

Rabbi Nancy H. Wiener, DMin, is the Founding Director of the Jacob and Hilda Blaustein Center for Pastoral Counseling at Hebrew Union College-Jewish Institute of Religion in New York, where she holds the Paul and Trudy Steinberg Chair in Human Relations. She holds a Doctor of Ministry in Pastoral Counseling and a Master of Hebrew Letters from HUC-JIR, as well as a Masters Degree in Jewish History from Columbia University. She is a certified member of the National Association of Jewish Chaplains.

Rabbi Mary L. Zamore currently serves as the Executive Director of the Women's Rabbinic Network. She is also the editor of and a contributing author to *The Sacred Table: Creating a Jewish Food Ethic* (CCAR Press, 2011) which was designated a finalist by the National Jewish Book Awards. Ordained by Hebrew Union College-Jewish Institute of Religion in New York in 1997, she graduated from Columbia College and also studied at Yad Vashem and Machon Pardes. Rabbi Zamore is a frequent contributor to the Huffington Post.

Rabbi Elizabeth S. Zeller is NFTY's Director of Learning and Innovation at the Union for Reform Judaism. She previously served congregations in Tacoma, Washington and Forest Hills, New York. She is also the co-President of the Women's Rabbinic Network. While she took great pride in being single, she is now exploring a table for MORE than one, with her husband and her son.

CPSIA information can be obtained
at www.ICGtesting.com
Printed in the USA
BVHW042116251020
591776BV00024B/813